Latin America Facing China

Volume 98. Latin America Facing China: South-South Relations beyond the
Washington Consensus
Edited by Alex E. Fernández Jilberto & Barbara Hogenboom

Volume 99. Foodscapes, Foodfields, and Identities in the Yucatán
Written by Steffan Igor Ayora-Diaz

LATIN AMERICA FACING CHINA

South-South Relations beyond the

Washington Consensus

Edited by

Alex E. Fernández Jilberto
& Barbara Hogenboom

Berghahn Books
NEW YORK · OXFORD

Published in 2010 by
Berghahn Books
www.berghahnbooks.com

English language edition
© 2010, 2012 Alex E. Fernández Jilberto and Barbara Hogenboom

First paperback edition published in 2012.

Library of Congress Cataloging-in-Publication Data
Latin America Facing China: South-South Relations Beyond the Washington
Consensus / Edited by Alex E. Fernández Jilberto and Barbara Hogenboom.
    p. cm.—(CEDLA Latin America studies (CLAS); v. 98)
Includes bibliographical references and index.
ISBN 978-1-84545-739-6 (hbk.)—ISBN 978-0-85745-623-6 (pbk.)
1. Latin America—Relations—China. 2. China—Relations—Latin America.
3. Latin America—Foreign economic relations—China. 4. China—Foreign economic relations—Latin America. I. Fernández Jilberto, A. E. (Alex E.) II. Hogenboom, Barbara.
JZ1519.A57C6 2010
337.8051—dc22

                                                                    2010013475

British Library Cataloguing in Publication Data
A catalogue record for this book is available from the British Library.

Printed in the United States on acid-free paper

ISBN: 978-0-85745-623-6 (paperback) ISBN: 978-0-85745-624-3 (ebook)

Contents

Tables and Figures

Tables

Figures

Abbreviations

ALADI	Latin American Integration Association
ALCA	*Área de Libre Comercio de las Américas* (Spanish for FTAA)
APEC	Asia-Pacific Economic Cooperation forum
ASEAN	Association of Southeast Asian Nations
BCIE	Central American Bank of Economic Integration
CAN	Andean Community
CBERS	China-Brazil Earth Resources Satellites Projects
CHINALCO	Aluminium Corporation of China
CNPC	China National Petroleum Corporation
COMIBOL	*Corporación Minera de Bolivia*
CVRD	*Companhia Vale do Rio Doce*
DIRECON	*Dirección General de Relaciones Económicas Internacionales* (Chile)
DR-CAFTA	Dominican Republic-Central America-United States Free Trade Agreement
ECLAC	Economic Commission for Latin America and the Caribbean (CEPAL, in Spanish)
FDI	Foreign direct investment
FEALAC	Forum for East Asia-Latin America Cooperation
FIESP	*Federação das Indústrias de Sao Paulo*
FTA	Free trade agreement
FTAA	Free Trade Area of the Americas
GATT	General Agreement on Trade and Tariffs
IDB	Inter-American Development Bank
IMF	International Monetary Fund
LAC	Latin America and the Caribbean
LPG	Liquefied petroleum gas
MDIC	Brazil's Ministry of Development, Industry, and Commerce
MERCOSUR	Mercado Común del Sur (Southern Common Market)
NAFTA	North American Free Trade Agreement
NME	Non-market economy
OAS	Organisation of American States

OECD	Organisation for Economic Cooperation and Development
OPEC	Organisation of Petroleum Exporting Countries
PBEC	Pacific Business Economic Council
PECC	Pacific Economic Cooperation Council
PDVSA	*Petróleos de Venezuela, S.A.*
PRC	People's Republic of China
R&D	Research & Development
SICA	System of Central American Integration
SIECA	Secretariat for Central American Economic Integration
SPPNA	Security and Prosperity Partnership of North America
TNCs	Transnational companies
UNCTAD	United Nations Conference on Trade and Development
UNSC	United Nations Security Council
WEF	World Economic Forum
WTO	World Trade Organisation
YPFB	*Yacimientos Petrolíferos Fiscales Bolivianos*

Preface to the Paperback Edition

Latin America's relations with China continue to rapidly broaden and deepen. While trade flows continue to grow, Chinese companies have now become a substantial source of investment in the region. In addition, Chinese banks have started to provide several Latin American (state) companies and governments with major loans, the value of which, for 2010, even surpassed that of the credits offered by the World Bank and the IDB together. Although unforeseen at the time of writing, this new development coincides fully with this volume's subtitle.

The expanding Sino-Latin American relations are part of a process of new South-South relations. In Africa, Chinese companies, banks and government agencies are of great economic and political influence. Simultaneously, a few Brazilian companies have become big investors in that region, whereas several Indian multinationals are setting up production in Latin America and Africa. Next to the large emerging countries gaining economic weight, they also create their own platforms for policy debate and coordination, such as the BRICS of Brazil, Russia, India, China and South Africa.

Moreover, we are living in a time of global transformation. Like China, most Latin American countries soon recovered from the crisis of 2008, but Europe and the US continue to be trapped in consecutive crises. Under these two opposite tendencies, the US and Europe suddenly seem to have lost a substantial part of their financial, political and ideological capacity to dominate international institutions and developments. This has been visible in the IMF and the World Bank, and in the replacement of the exclusive G7/G8 forum of industrialized countries by the newly created G20, with among its twenty members also emerging economies like China, Brazil, Mexico and Argentina. It is a somewhat ironic coincidence that this new forum for global economic coordination bears the same name as the coalition of developing countries – lead by Brazil and China – that, in 2003, for the first time successfully contested the US-EU domination of international trade negotiations within the WTO.

Sino-Latin American relations will continue to change rapidly, yet the aim of this volume is to give the reader a better understanding of the causes and meanings of these new relations within their wider context.

Amsterdam, February 2012
Barbara Hogenboom

Preface to the First Edition

One of the major difficulties when studying the relations of Latin America with China is the high degree of ideologisation that characterises the debate about China's economic globalisation process. Next to genuine concerns, part of the criticism from Europe and the United States seems to be expressed in an attempt to influence China's globalisation. Some argue that China's political regime of a single party contradicts its market economy, and that a social and political crisis can therefore occur at any moment, whereas others stress China's environmental crisis and human rights problems. The only thing that has not been criticised is the direct participation of European and US transnational companies in the economic globalisation of China. Such opportunistic angles do not help us to comprehend the real nature of the economic relations between China and developing countries, which are often presented as a new form of economic imperialism or a 'reprimarisation' of the African and Latin American economies, given the fact that China mainly imports their raw materials in order to export industrial goods.

For Latin America, China was not a *terra incognita*. From the sixteenth to the early nineteenth century, there was already regular cross-Pacific trade by the Manila-Acapulco Galleon, controlled by the Spanish Crown. Much later, at the time of the Cold War and the China-Soviet conflict, the People's Republic of China (PRC) became politically influential in the region. The Chinese critique against the USSR and 'Soviet social imperialism' was not only expressed in its distancing itself from the Cuban revolution, but also in the expansion of Latin American Maoist parties aiming at a people's war against imperialism and capitalism. This Maoist ultra-left, of which Sendero Luminoso (Shining Path) in Peru is probably the most dramatic example, wanted to eradicate the influence of communist parties with an affinity with the USSR. Nevertheless, in the 1970s, China ended the 'export of Maoism' and changed its foreign policy, which favoured a diplomatic offensive policy to obtain international support for the expulsion of Taiwan from the United Nations and the exclusive recognition of the People's Republic of China. This shift enabled the start of political and (some) economic relations with many of the dictatorships of Latin America. China's economic liberalization and political reforms initiated by Deng Xiaoping at the end of the 1970s, and Latin America's neoliberal restructuring following the debt crisis at the start of the 1980s, created favourable conditions for extensive reciprocal economic relations based on liberalised markets.

In recent years, China's economic policy, known for short as the Beijing Consensus, and Latin America's leftist political regimes have been taking a lead in the increasing global rejection of the 'neoliberal rescue' known as the Washington Consensus. Both the Beijing Consensus and Latin America's new Left consider that the participation of the state is crucial in making the globalisation and liberalisation of the economy a sustained success. This intriguing convergence was one of the issues that urged us to undertake this research project. It also allowed us to apply a political perspective to the debate on the new South-South relations. In the context of the current international financial crisis, Latin American countries in which the state has been increasingly participating in (neo-)liberal economic policies, such as Brazil, Argentina, Bolivia, Chile and Venezuela, may be considered as precursors of the policies of economic reactivation that are now extensively applied in the United States and the rest of the developed economies. It should be reminded that during Latin America's previous crises – caused by the external indebtedness (1980s), by the Asian crisis (1997–1998) and by the Russian Moratorium (1998) – the United States and Europe made the IMF demand further economic deregulation and deepened neoliberalisation in the region. The current global crisis profoundly affects the Latin American economies as well, but the current South-South relations and the political regimes in the region allow for different policies that are not dictated elsewhere.

This volume on the relations of Latin America with China is part of a larger research project on how the rise of China is affecting the Global South. Some results have been published in two special issues of the *Journal of Developing Societies*: 'The "China Effect" on South-South Relations: A New Dimension of Globalization for Developing Regions, Africa and Indonesia' and 'The "China Effect" on South-South Relations: A New Dimension of Globalization for the Middle East, Russia and Latin America' (vol. 23, no. 3&4, 2007). As in previous publications, for the current book we have counted on the intellectual participation and collaboration of a group of scholars who are experts in the field of their case study. With their valuable contributions, we have been able to provide a critical analysis of the various ways in which Latin America is facing China, and the development of their economic and political South-South relations in a context of global markets.

Amsterdam, June 2009
Alex E. Fernández Jilberto and Barbara Hogenboom

In Memoriam

A few days after the proofs of this volume arrived, my dear friend and co-author Alex E. Fernández Jilberto passed away. Although he had been ill for quite some time, in the period this book was being prepared he continued working and travelling, and was as involved in this joint project as ever. Only after the manuscript was handed in did it become clear that his health was deteriorating rapidly.

Alex E. Fernández Jilberto was dedicated to advancing critical analyses and contemporary studies on international relations, international political economy and political science, especially those focussing on the Global South and on Latin America. Over the past two decades he initiated a range of topical books and special issues with different co-editors, and he wrote numerous articles, chapters and columns. In addition, Alex was a very active and committed thesis supervisor, educating and nourishing new generations of critical and independent scholars.

While I am sad that I can no longer share ideas, projects, jokes, worries and long coffee meetings with Alex, I am most grateful for all the things we have done together and that I have learned from him.

Amsterdam, July 2010
Barbara Hogenboom

1 Latin America and China

South-South Relations in a New Era

Alex E. Fernández Jilberto and Barbara Hogenboom

The rise of China might be the most important single event in the world's recent economic developments. To most developing countries, the last quarter of the twentieth century was 'dominated' by economic crises, increasing indebtedness and financial crises, political instability and a profound shift of development model that did not produce the 'expected' results, but to China this period stood for quite something different: an amazingly high and continuous economic growth, an increasing budget and trade surplus, political stability, and all of this based on a profound shift of development model that produced more results than anyone had imagined. In effect, although still being a developing country, China has steadily climbed up the ladder of the world's largest economies and now comes immediately after the 'top three' – the United States, Japan and Germany. This growth is based on a globalisation strategy that has rendered China a central position in global production, global trade and global finance.

Over the past few years, Latin America's experience with China's rapid insertion into the global economy has become an issue of great attention. With China being transformed into the so-called factory to the world, it exports numerous products that previously formed an important part of the industrial production in other developing countries, either for the local market or for export. The abundance of cheap labour in China implies strong competition for trade and foreign direct investment (FDI) to other countries. Simultaneously, Chinese demand for commodities has boomed as well, and Chinese companies have started to become a new source of FDI. Countries in South America tend to profit from these new possibilities, whereas Central America and Mexico are hit hardest by Chinese competition in their main export market: the United States. Due to these rapid and two-sided economic changes, the debate on 'China effects' on Latin America has often focused on the macro-economic perspective and on 'threats versus challenges'.[1]

In this volume, Latin America's dealings with the People's Republic of China (PRC) are studied from a South-South angle, applying an international political economy approach that includes economic as well as political and social change in Latin America. Economic developments, relations and interests are evidently central to bilateral diplomatic relations and multilateral political positions of Latin America and China. In international politics, China has come to present itself more prominently, stressing its position as a developing country and seeking new South-South alliances. For instance, China has strengthened its strategic relations with Latin America, Africa and the Middle East by establishing cooperation forums and business councils. More important than that was China's move, soon after its entry into the World Trade Organization (WTO) in December of 2001, to line up with countries such as Brazil, India and Russia in the G20. This G20 group of more than twenty developing countries and transition economies were very critical about the proposals of the European Union and the United States for the new round of international negotiations on a broad agenda for global trade, investments, services and (intellectual) property rights (the so-called the Doha Development Round). In 2003, their joint resistance against the US and EU agenda, which in the G20's eyes were posing too many conditions upon developing countries while insufficiently opening up their markets for agro-imports from developing countries, caused the failure of the WTO summit in Cancun. Since then, global trade negotiations have been stalled.

Apart from assessing the economic changes brought about in Latin American countries by China's rise, the authors of this volume examine the nature of the new relations between Latin American countries and China. In addition, they discuss what the economic and political South-South shifts are doing to Latin America's development plans and models. The aim of this book, in short, is to assess critically the important effects of China's global economic expansion and its new political role in Latin America's development. In our view, political economy is central to this understanding as politics and policies are as important as economic and social factors. More generally, such a joint effort by experts on (and from) Latin America can make a valuable contribution to contemporary scholarly and political debates on the actual effects of neoliberal globalisation.

In this chapter, we introduce the theme of the nature and meaning of the new relations between Latin America and China. After a short overview of the global and South-South dimensions of the rise of China, we look into some of the relations between Latin America and China. Examples from Brazil, Chile, Mexico and some other countries illustrate how the mix of economic and political interests has transformed South-South relations. Next, we review how the context of neoliberal globalisation has affected these new relations, resulting in both South-South trade and South-South competition. We then compare the economic liberalisation strategies of Latin America with those of China, which leads us to the debate on the role of the state in development. The question as to what extent Latin America has been moving out of the reach of the Washington Consensus and whether the Beijing Consensus may be coming to replace it will be left for the concluding chapter of this book. At the end of this introduction, we will present the order of the rest of the book.

China: The Number One in Globalisation

China's rapid economic expansion has impressed the world. At the beginning of the twenty-first century, China has become the third largest importing as well as exporting country, the third largest economy in the world (after the United States and Japan), and one of the top three destinations of foreign direct investment. In the period of 1985 to 2000, the figures of its increasing world export market share show that China has profited more from globalisation than any other country. China achieved an average annual export growth of 4.5 per cent, while the second and third country on this list achieved no more than 1.8 per cent (the United States) and 1.1 per cent (Korea). From 1980 to 2000, its annual growth of real GDP was even more spectacular, with an average of 10 per cent. Over this period, developing countries on average only grew 3 per cent (UNCTAD 2005b, 2004, 2003, 2002).

China has become a central place for production, investment, import and export, which are all heavily tied up in China's role as 'the factory to the world'. Between 1980 and 2003, China's share in world trade increased more than fivefold: its exports rose from 0.9 to 5.8 per cent and its imports rose from 1.0 to 5.4 per cent (UNCTAD 2005b: 133). And this trend is ongoing. The effects on the global system can be compared to those of the English industrial revolution in the second half of the nineteenth century, the development of the western part of the United States at the end of that century and Japan's industrialisation after WWII (Morrison and Brown-Humes 2005).

With its rapid economic growth and expanding export production, China has become a major consumer of natural resources and commodities, many of which originate from other developing countries. China has become the world's largest importer of several important commodities, such as iron ore. In 2004, China consumed 40 per cent of the world's coal, 25 per cent of nickel and 14 per cent of aluminium. This massive Chinese demand has contributed to rising metal prices since 2004. In 2005, the IMF metal price index rose by 26 per cent (another 7 per cent increase was expected for 2006). With energy prices rising 39 per cent, this contributed to an overall 29 per cent increase (in dollar terms) of the IMF commodities and energy prices index in 2005. This process is evidently beneficial to the exporting developing countries, as they had suffered from years of low world prices and related worsening terms of trade. The metal price level in 2006, for instance, was about twice as high as the average price level of the 1980s and 1990s (IMF 2006: 54–63).

The Chinese contribution to rising world demand and prices of oil and other hydrocarbons deserves special attention. Internationally, it is the second largest consumer of energy, after the United States. This is partly because of its enormous economic activity, but is also a result of the notorious lack of energy efficiency in the production processes taking place in China. Only two decades ago, China was the largest oil exporter of East Asia, but now China is instead importing massive amounts of oil. Since 2003, China is the world's second country in the importation of oil and is responsible for 31 per cent of the global growth of oil demand. The Middle East accounts for 45 per cent of the oil imported by China, and 29 per cent comes from Africa (Zweig and Bi 2005). Due to the economic and political importance of energy, this development is of major concern in industrialised countries. To developing countries with large reserves of hydrocarbons, on the contrary, Chinese demand and investment, and rising world market energy prices have been an economic blessing.

Next to its imports of fuels, minerals and metals, China imports large quantities of manufactures and agricultural products from developing countries. Much of this South-South trade seems to be concentrated in East Asia, but the figures are somewhat misleading since they include the large trade flows between China and Hong Kong (China), which functions as China's transhipment port. In reality, large quantities of agricultural raw materials and food for the Chinese market arrive from other parts of the world, such as, for example, soy from Latin America. Similarly, as part of East Asian production sharing, manufactures from these countries arrive in Hong Kong for further assembling or manufacturing in China. The so-called triangular trade involves China importing intermediate products from more advances economies, such as Japan and South Korea. With the cheaper labour of Chinese workers, these inputs are then further assembled into products that are exported to the United States and Europe. As a result, in 2004, China replaced the United States as Japan's main trade partner (UNCTAD 2005b: 130–41).

China's massive imports are closely related to the remarkable growth of export production in China, as well as to the attraction of enormous flows of foreign direct investment. A large share of these imports serves as input for its exports (e.g., from 1985 to 2000, the value of Chinese exports increased from $26 billion to $249 billion). Together with high levels of public investment, foreign direct investment (implying the entry and expansion of transnational companies) in China has been crucial for the growth and modernisation of exports. From 1985 to 2000, FDI inflows rose from $2 billion to $41 billion, and in 2006, foreign direct investment to China was $69.5

billion (UNCTAD 2005b; FDI Stat 2008). Thus, China is not only the biggest developing country recipient of FDI, but also globally, it comes third place, after the United States and the United Kingdom.

Transnational companies (TNCs) have played a key role in the expanding Chinese production for the world market, and even more so in the changing composition of Chinese exports. In the period from 1985 to 2000, the share of primary products and resource-based manufactures decreased from 49 to 12 per cent, whereas the share of high technology products rose from 3 to 22 per cent. Between 1989 and 2001, the share of TNCs in Chinese exports rose from 9 to 50 per cent. The exports by these companies are predominantly made up of manufactured goods (90 per cent), such as machinery and equipment. There is also a large FDI component in technology intensive products: 91 per cent in electronic circuits; 85 per cent in automatic data processing machines; and 96 per cent in mobile phones (all in 2000). Apart from US and European companies, in China there is a large number of TNCs originating from Asia, mainly South Korea, Japan, Hong Kong, Taiwan and Singapore (UNCTAD 2002: 161–66; 2005a: 2–3). To other developing countries, China thus is a competitor in export manufacturing, which includes competition in foreign direct investment as well as export markets. In Latin America, as elsewhere, the issue of China's expansion is also about 'the future "spaces" open for the development of industrial exports in a liberalised world in which PRC is pre-empting many markets for products that developing countries can export' (Lall and Weiss 2004: 23).

While China is a big shark in the sea of foreign capital, many developing countries are profiting from the fact that Chinese investments abroad have grown substantially, reaching $21 billion in 2006. China has become the world's sixth largest foreign investor in developing countries; this growing Chinese FDI is primarily driven by its growing demand for natural resources. Of the top 50 non-financial TNCs from developing countries in 2004, seven were Chinese: CITIC Group (no. 5), China Ocean Shipping Co. (no. 8), China State Construction Engineering Corporation (no. 19), China National Petroleum Corporation (no. 24), Sinochem Corporation (no. 28), TCL Corporation (no. 44) and China National Offshore Oil Corporation (CNOOC, no. 47). Compared to the list for 1993, which does not contain one single Chinese company, this is a noticeable change. CITIC and CNOOC are majority-owned by the Chinese state, and most of the other Chinese TNCs are also controlled by the state. Their rise is the result of the government's determination to create China's own 'global champions', which are internationally competitive while operating under state control (Jiang 2007; *The Economist* 3 September 2005: 53–54; UNCTAD 2006: 283, 1995: 30–31).

Taken together, to developing countries, China's success in the globalised markets has several faces. With regard to merchandise trade, China has definitely won the race of other parts of the South: between 1980 and 2003, while China increased its share of world exports from 0.9 to 5.8 per cent, Latin America's share decreased from 5.5 to 5.0 per cent. China's imports, however, have equally risen and China has become the leading importing country in South-South trade (UNCTAD 2005b: 133, 141). To developing countries that depend upon the export of a small number of commodities, this diversification of export markets, the rising world market prices and Chinese investments have all been economically beneficial. Conversely, developing countries that compete with China in export manufacturing have seen trade and investment being negatively affected by China's success. In addition, cheap Chinese imports have been hurting local manufacturing companies that produce for the internal market, especially small and medium-sized companies.

Latin America's New Relations with China

As of 1978, with the liberalisation reforms implemented by Deng Xiaoping, China started to strengthen its relations with Latin America and the Caribbean. In the beginning, due to the political situation of the region, relations were established with several neoliberal military dictatorships. China abandoned its political strategy of expanding Maoism to Latin America, which was previously done by creating Red Flag or Revolutionary Communist Parties, the most tragic and infamous expression of which was the Sendero Luminoso (Shining Path) in Peru. The Latin American version of Maoism had clearly expressed the ideological influence of the 'cultural revolution' and China's critique on 'social imperialism', Soviet communism and communist parties, thereby contributing to the ideological and political division of Latin America during the Cold War.

China's economic liberalisation, however, brought a definite end to its international ideological agenda. Central to China's modern foreign policies is the strategy of the 'Four No's'. Light years away from its international Maoist policies, China's doctrine is nowadays based on: no hegemonism, no power politics, no arms races and no military alliances. This strategic doctrine proclaimed by the Chinese President Hu Jintao (since 2003) forms part of China's global policy to favour its economic development and integration in global neoliberalism. In Latin America, this doctrine is seen as positive for improving international cooperation, strengthening mutual confidence, preventing international confrontations and thereby being positive for multilateralism as well. The strategy of the Four No's has also been at the basis of China's so-called asymmetric diplomacy, which gives privileges to certain bilateral relations while China is simultaneously participating actively in processes of economic regionalisation and globalisation. This approach has some parallels with Latin American strategies of open regionalism, involving a broad economic opening and new bilateral free trade agreements together with forms of economic regionalisation, such as NAFTA or MERCOSUR. The fact that Brazil deepened its relations with China without waiting for a joint MERCOSUR agenda toward China illustrates that the new South-South relations may come at a cost for regionalisation processes.

As part of the new South-South relations in a (post-Cold War) multipolar world, Brazil and China, together with India and Russia, have become strategic allies. This was enabled by the changes that President Lula da Silva made in Brazil's foreign policies. Both Brazil and China aim to improve their economies' added value and the international prices for primary and manufactured products, by prioritising investments involving technology transfers. As already mentioned, their new G20 collaboration in WTO negotiations has had a major impact on the Doha Round. Brazil, India and China played key roles in the group's effective resistance against industrialised countries, especially on agricultural issues. They rejected the joint EU and US proposal and instead proposed to eliminate US and EU agro-subsidies. In the WTO negotiations on services, intellectual property and investments, Brazil and China also have, by and large, coinciding agendas.

Since the 1990s, China has rapidly become important to the Latin American economies. China imports Latin American products such as sugar and fruits, soya oil (e.g., from Argentina), minerals (Brazil) and copper (Chile). Generally, China's expansion has been economically positive for the region. Trade figures show steep rises and resource-rich Latin American countries have greatly benefited from China's enormous demand for energy, minerals and other primary commodities, including benefiting from its effects on world market prices. Although to China, trade with Latin America is relatively modest, its imports from the region substantially have grown. As shown in Figure 1.1 below, in 2007, China's import from Latin America equalled $51 billion, which is more than six times as much as in 2002! The increase of Latin American exports to China, from $5.4 billion in 2000 to $21.7 billion in 2004, implies an average annual growth of 42 per cent. These exports consist mainly of primary products and manufactures based on natural resources, which represent respectively 46 and 30 per cent of the exports in 2004 (CEPAL 2005b).

The effects of the rise of China on national economies in Latin America widely differ. Most of China's imports from the region come from Brazil, which with $6.8 billion, represented 35.2 per cent of the region's total in 2005. The other main countries are Chile (22.6 per cent), Argentina (17.0 per cent) and Peru (9.4 per cent). Yet, more important for our understanding of the importance of China for Latin America are the trade figures of China's relevance to these economies. In 2005, exports to China were valued at 5.3 per cent of the total exports of Brazil and 8.3 per cent of Argentina, while China represented more than one tenth of the exports of Chile (11.1 per cent), Peru (10.7 per cent) and Cuba (10.2 per cent). In some cases, the 'China effect' can vary greatly from one country to its neighbour. For instance, Peru has one of the region's highest percentages of exports to China (10.7 per cent in 2005), selling large amounts of fish flour, copper and iron, but to Bolivia, the Chinese market is marginal (0.7 per cent in 2005) (CEPAL 2005b; see also chapters seven and eight in this volume).

Figure 1.1. China's Imports from Latin America, 2002–2007 (in US$ millions)

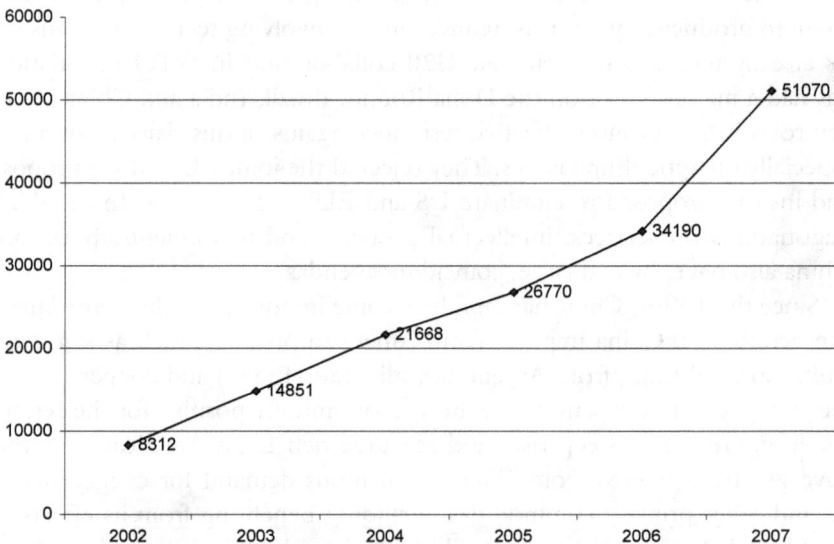

Source: CEPAL (2005b) and MofCom (2008).

Next to rising exports, China's growing demand for natural resources has given way to growing Chinese FDI in Latin America. As shown in Table 1.1, among these substantial Chinese investments are several alliances and mergers and acquisitions (M&A) in the sectors of copper, steel and oil. These investments by Chinese TNCs are part of China's global investment strategy in developing countries, especially in the exploitation of raw materials. In addition, investments sometimes have a political purpose. Important Chinese investments (mainly joint ventures) were agreed on in the context of the bilateral negotiations on China's entry into the WTO, which will be reviewed further along (CEPAL 2005b).

Table 1.1. Chinese FDI in (Seeking) Latin American Raw Materials: Some Examples
of Alliances and Cooperation, 2004–2006 (in US$ millions)

Chinese firm	Foreign companies	Type	Sector	Country	Stake/project description	Amount
China Minmetals Nonferrous Metals Co. (2004)	Noranda (Doña Inés de Collahuasi and Loma Bayas)	M&A	Copper	Canada and Chile		5,000
China Minmetals Nonferrous Metals Co. (2005)	CODELCO	Alliance	Copper	Chile	Investment and supply agreement	2,000
China National Petroleum (2005)	EnCana	M&A	Petroleum	Ecuador	Oil reserves and pipelines	1,420
Baoshan Iron and Steel (2004)	Compañia Vale do Rio Doce	Alliance	Steel	Brazil	New plant construction	1,400
Government of China (2004) (CNOOC)		Credit	Petroleum and natural gas	Venezuela	Exploration of natural gas and crude oil reserves	400
Sinopec (2004)	Petrobras	Alliance	Petroleum	Brazil, China and others	Oil drilling in several countries	
Government of China (2004-2006)		Loans	Infrastructure	Brazil	Natural gas pipe-line and export corridor	
Yanguang Group (2005)	Vale do Rio Doce / Itochu Corporation	Alliance	Coal	Brazil	New Company	

Source: CEPAL (2005b, 2006)

Yet, Latin America also faces another side of China's success. Despite Latin America's export successes, it faces competition from several Asian economies, especially those of the ASEAN (Association of Southeast Asian Nations). About one-third of ASEAN's exports to China compete with Latin American exports; most of the remaining involve high technology products in which Latin America is not competing. Moreover, while Latin America is providing mostly raw materials to China, China's exports to Latin America are strong in low technology products (e.g., clothing and footwear), which has various effects. These cheap products please Latin American consumers, but threaten local producers. In addition, low Chinese production costs in these sectors are harming Latin America's chances for export production for the US and European markets (Carrillo and Gomis 2003; CEPAL 2005b; Cornejo 2005a, 2005b; Cruz Zamorano 2005; Dussel Peters 2003, 2004).

As recipients of foreign direct investment, Latin America and China partly compete for these investments. China has become the developing countries' major recipient of FDI, accounting for 10 per cent of global investments and 31 per cent of the FDI to developing countries in 2004. As Figure 1.2 demonstrates, as a result of the steady rise of FDI inflow and the rather volatile investment trends in Latin America and the Caribbean, the gap between the FDI received by China and that received by the entire Latin American and Caribbean region is becoming smaller. And in 2003, due to a sudden decrease of investment inflows in Latin America, the net FDI inflow in China was even $8.8 billion above that of the region. For TNCs, China's rapidly growing economy and regional and international integration play a crucial role in their global investment strategies. As part of their activities within regional industrial production in Asia, TNCs have made important technology transfers a part of their operations in China. This Chinese success neutralises much of the Latin American efforts to increase the added value of its exports, especially in the manufacturing sector segments in which they compete with China. Moreover, the practice of TNCs moving production facilities to China is harmful to other (newly) industrialising economies, such as Mexico (CEPAL 2005b; Gaulier, Lemoine and Ünal-Kesenci 2005; Lemoine and Ünal-Kesenci 2002).

Figure 1.2. Net FDI Inflows in Latin America and the Caribbean (LAC) and China, 2000–2006 (in US$ millions)

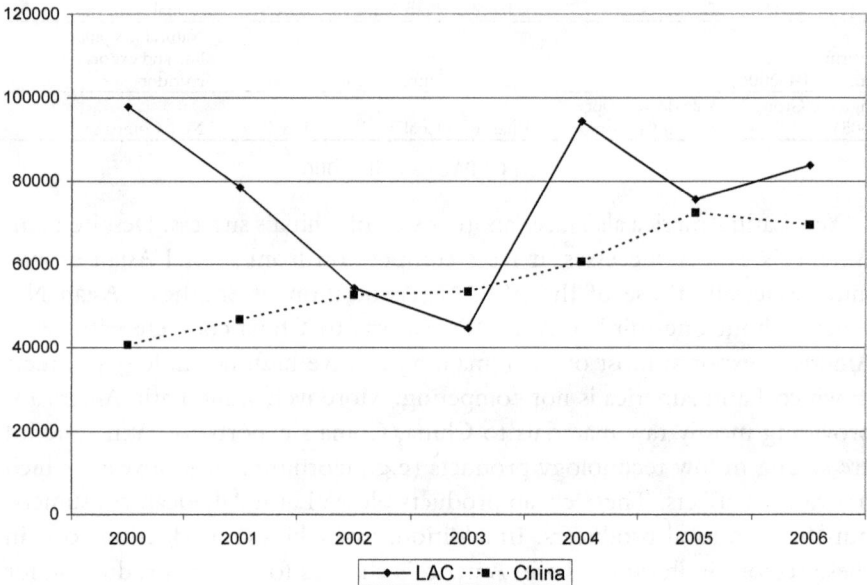

Source: FDI STAT (2008)

Despite serious competition issues, the expanding economic relations between Latin America, China and the rest of East Asia have stimulated cross-Pacific cooperation and exchange. In 1989, the Asia-Pacific Economic Cooperation (APEC) was created to integrate the economies of 21 countries with a joint population of 2.5 billion inhabitants, representing almost 60 per cent of the world's GDP and 50 per cent of international trade. Among APEC's members are several Asian countries including China, Hong Kong, Japan, Singapore, South Korea and Taiwan; from Latin America (only) Chile, Mexico and Peru; and the United States and Russia. In 1994, APEC even announced that it aimed to achieve a free trade area by 2020, but few steps toward this goal seem to have been taken. Because most Latin American and a number of Asian countries are not in APEC, in 1998, Singapore initiated the Forum for East Asia-Latin America Cooperation (FEALAC), involving 17 Latin American and 15 East Asian countries. FEALAC holds regular meetings of government officials, politicians, business leaders and academics, and various economic, cultural, educational, political and scientific projects have been undertaken.[2]

Many of China's diplomatic initiatives toward Latin America were intimately linked to its global economic objective of entering into the WTO, while also serving China's strategy of modernising its role in the global political arena. In 1986, the People's Republic of China solicited admission to GATT, beginning a fifteen year process of multilateral and bilateral negotiations that ended in 2001 with the entry of China into GATT's successor: the WTO. In contrast with its previous international isolation, since the early 1990s, China actively intensified its diplomatic relations with Latin America in the context of the GATT/WTO negotiations. While these trade negotiations formed a crucial motivation for China rapidly to improve its diplomatic relations with Latin American countries, the formalisation of relations with numerous regional organisations and institutions has also enabled and improved long-term diplomatic relations. Since 1990, China has attended the annual meetings of Foreign Affairs ministers from the countries of the Group of Rio (a permanent regional consultation mechanism), mainly to find joint positions in international institutions. In 1991, China became a permanent observer of the Inter-American Development Bank and, in 1994, of the Latin American Integration Association (ALADI). In 1998, the People's Bank of China became a member of the Caribbean Development Bank. Moreover, China has established mechanisms for permanent dialogue with MERCO-SUR and with the Caribbean Community and Common Market (CARI-COM), and, in 2004, it became a permanent observer of the Organization of American States (OAS) and of the Latin American Parliament. In addition, China signed more than one hundred agreements with Latin American countries on scientific and technological cooperation, ranging from the satellites industry to agriculture (Cornejo 2005b; Gutiérrez 2003: 23).

China's numerous bilateral initiatives to Latin American countries, which were begun under the negotiations for China's entry into WTO, show a similar link between diplomatic and economic objectives. To Latin American countries in general, the Chinese entry into WTO (as well as its rise in the global economy) meant a confrontation with three inevitable trade issues: the possibility to benefit from new export opportunities to the Chinese market; the necessity to deal with the competition with more Chinese imports; and Chinese competition in segments of the international market to which they are exporting similar products. As a result, the bilateral WTO negotiations with China were heterogeneous, contradictory and polemic, reflecting the mix of positive and negative potential economic effects on Latin America of China's membership of WTO. As a way of softening some of these negative effects, China rewarded cooperative countries with special projects and investments, which have created possibilities for further cooperation. While the country case studies in this volume give a profound account of the new relations with China, let us here briefly review the relations with some of the larger countries in Latin America to show the wide variety that is occurring. Apart from the centrality of economic interests, this overview reveals that the importance of China-Latin America relations is not confined to economic reasons.

Brazil

China's most privileged Latin American associate is Brazil, as shown by their mutually advantageous diplomatic, economic and scientific relations. During the visit of Li Ruihuan (chairman of the National Committee of the Chinese People's Political Consultative Conference) to Brazil in 1995, the Chinese government defined its relations with Brazil as a 'strategic alliance'. According to China's classification of diplomatic relations, this implies that the two countries can form the basis of an international alliance to achieve more just global trade rules, in particular to improve developing economies' access to the US and EU markets. Of all Latin America countries, Brazil has also put the most efforts in intensifying its economic relations with China (see chapter two) and the two countries have been cooperating in several high technology projects. Already in 1988, the countries started preparations that resulted in the creation of the China-Brazil company Earth Resources Satellites Projects (CBERS), which in 1999 and 2003 constructed two satellites that provide information on (new sources of) natural resources and the environment. Also, an alliance between Brazil's AVIBRAS and China's Great Wall Industrial Corporation materialised in the International Satellite Communication (INSCOM) company. In 2002, the Brazilian aeronautic company Embraer and the Chinese Air Company (aviation) established a joint programme. In addition, there is extensive cooperation in the fields of biotechnology, information technology, pharmaceuticals and new materials, and Brazil has promised to export uranium to China in return for Chinese funding for its nuclear programme, including the enrichment of uranium (CEPAL 2004b; Gutiérrez 2003; Lei 2004; Mesquita Machado and Tinoco Ferraz 2005).

Brazil supported China's entry into WTO from early on, because it was convinced that the economic benefits would not only involve Chinese investments, but even more so it would involve the opening of an important alternative market that could compensate for the negative effects of US and European protectionism. Under President Lula da Silva (since January 2003) and as part of its international political agenda, Brazil further strengthened its diplomatic relations with China and countries such as India, South Africa and Russia. In September of 2003, this resulted in the 'Cancun surprise', and the upset of the US and EU plan for the Doha Development Round of the WTO. In 2004, Lula visited China in order to consolidate their 'strategic alliance' on trade, technological development and defence, which has substantially benefited Brazil. As a result of this visit, the National Development Bank of Brazil reached an accord with the Chinese investment agency CITIC on easing the finance of Chinese-Brazilian companies. The large mining company Vale do Rio Doce signed association agreements with Baosteel (Baoshan Iron and Steel) and other Chinese companies to produce iron and aluminium in the northeast of Brazil (see Table 1.1). With the Chinese firm Yanguang, this Brazilian company also agreed to invest in oil products for export to third markets. And the state companies Petrobras and Sinopec started jointly to explore and produce oil in Africa and the Middle East (Cornejo 2005a; Mesquita Machado and Tinoco Ferraz 2005).

The rapid increase of Sino-Brazilian trade is the result of a quick yet rather balanced ('two-way') expansion of commercial flows (see Table 1.2, below). Raw materials dominate in Brazil's rapidly growing exports to China, which in 2007 was valued at $10.7 billion. Although to Brazil, China matters considerably less as an export market than the United States (which accounts for more than twenty cent), China is a major market for several products. In 2002, Brazil exported more soy (31 per cent) and iron (22 per cent) to China than to any other country. For some years after 2000, Brazil had a trade surplus with China, but this trend was reversed in 2007 when Brazil's imports from China reached $12.6 billion. These are mainly electronic (media and high technology) and chemical products, partly related to the global production strategies of TNCs. Companies such as Philips have some of their production processes in China, then send parts for assembly to their Brazilian factories, and either sell the end products in Brazil, or re-export them to other markets in the region (León 2005; Mesquita Machado and Tinoco Ferraz 2005; Pimentel Puga et al. 2004; UN Comtrade 2008).

Chile

Chile has also had good relations with China and has basically a complementary economy to China. It accepted China's accession to WTO in 1999, with an early 'yes' that stemmed from Chile's neoliberal strategy of a dynamic 'open regionalism'. Interestingly, Chile was also the first South American country to establish diplomatic relations with the People's Republic of

China, shortly after the start of Salvador Allende's presidency in 1970. While importing Chinese manufactures such as textiles, cloths, footwear, toys and electronic products, Chile exports primary commodities such as agro products, cellulose, marine products, chemicals, but most of all, copper to China. Due to this complementarity, the Chile-China economic and political relations are friendly and the two countries have cooperated in international institutions such as the UN, APEC and FEALAC.

Since the 1990s, trade between Chile and China has increased at an enormous speed from $699 million in 1995 to $8,425 million in 2006 (see Table 1.2). After the United States, China has become Chile's second largest trade partner, above traditionally important trade partners such as Argentina, Japan and Brazil. In 2006, with Chile's exports to China of $4.9 billion and China's exports to Chile of $3.5 billion, Chile had a trade surplus of almost $1.5 billion with China, which is rather substantial relative to the size of Chile's economy. This trade surplus has much to do with China being the world's largest copper importer, consuming 20 per cent of this mineral's global trade, and Chile being the world's main producer and exporter. The National Corporation of Copper (CODELCO) and the National Mining Company (EN-AMI) are responsible for one-third of the Chilean exports to China. With 80 per cent of the Chilean exports to China being minerals, Chile has benefited greatly from China's growing demand as well as from the related rise of world prices (León 2005; UN Comtrade 2008).

Chile is the first Latin American country that has a free trade agreement with China. Because of the importance and complementarity of their trade, in 2002, China proposed to Chile to extend their economic relations. From then onward, the countries worked on preparing a so-called third generation agreement, including not only trade and investment but also educational, environmental and cultural accords. Chile realised that good relations and especially a trade agreement with China would increase its access to the Chinese market and provide additional benefits in the economies with which China has already established accords. Chile equally aims to achieve a privileged position in attracting Chinese FDI, in particular in its mining sector. In November of 2004, during the APEC conference in Chile, the presidents of the two countries announced the official start of the free trade negotiations. One year later, during the APEC conference in Korea, the free trade agreement between Chile and China was signed. Also in 2005, a leading Chinese metal company, Minmetals Non-ferrous Metal Co., and the world's largest producer of copper, Chile's CODELCO, established a strategic alliance to meet the growing Chinese need for this mineral and to exploit the Chilean reserves (see also Table 1.1 and chapter four).

Mexico

In contrast with Brazil and Chile, Mexico's relations with China have been difficult. Mexico was the last Latin American country to put terms on China's WTO entry. These long negotiations had to do with China's strong competition of labour intensive products in US markets as well as in Mexico's internal market. Mexican entrepreneurs feared for major problems with unfair Chinese trade competition and demanded the inclusion of a clause that for two decades would deny China the right to call for WTO mechanisms of dispute settlement in cases where Mexico was to apply compensatory and protective tariffs against Chinese products. In the final bilateral accords, their demand for such a guarantee against unfair competition was watered down to a moratorium until 2008. Indeed, Mexico has used this clause to apply compensation tariffs ranging from 800 to 1000 per cent on Chinese products in the sectors of tools, toys and textiles (CEPAL 2004a; Cornejo 2005a; Dussel Peters 2003; León 2005).

The trade relations between Mexico and China are very uneven. China became Mexico's second largest trade partner in 2003, but mainly due to massive Mexican imports of Chinese goods. These imports are partly products for Mexican consumers, but a substantial share consists of parts and semi-manufactures to be further processed in Mexico into export products, especially for the US market. In 2007, Mexico's exports to China valued only $1.896 million, whereas its imports from China valued $29.792 million, which is more than fifteen (!) times as much (see Table 1.2). Evidently, this unbalanced trade relation produces a huge Mexican trade deficit with China. In addition to the large flows of legal imports, there are many illegal imports: possibly over half the garment consumption in Mexico is of illegally imported products, mostly from China.

The negative 'China effects' on Mexico – one of the most open economies in the region – have been particularly clear in Mexico's production of manufactured (assembly) goods for export to the United States. For a long time, Mexican exports have been predominantly directed toward the United States, and this trade dependency has only increased with Mexico's entry into the NAFTA in 1994, so that almost 90 per cent of Mexican exports are to the US market. In 2002, China replaced Mexico as the second largest exporter to the US market. Intimately linked to this is Mexico's competition with China for foreign investment in export production (Cornejo 2005a). Due to Mexico's defensive strategy toward China's entry into the WTO, and due to the fact that at least from Mexico's perspective the relations with China are dominated by competition, little progress has been made in improving the economic and diplomatic ties. Bilaterally, Mexico seems hardly interested in strengthening the relations with China, and within the WTO, it has linked up to the United States in making antidumping claims against China (see chapter three).

Table 1.2. Trade of Brazil, Chile and Mexico with China, 1995–2007 (in US$ millions)

Year	Brazil		Chile		Mexico	
	Export	Import	Export	Import	Export	Import
1995	1,204	418	287	390	37	520
2000	1,085	1,222	902	949	217	2,880
2004	5,442	3,710	3,212	1,847	474	14,373
2005	6,835	5,355	4,390	2,541	1,136	17,696
2006	8,402	7,989	4,942	3,483	1,688	24,438
2007	10,749	12,618	9,980	4,881	1,899	29,792

Source: UN Comtrade (2008)

Other Latin American Experiences

The China relations of some of the other large Latin American economies are more positive than those of Mexico, but are more complex than those of Brazil and Chile. Argentina bilaterally negotiated China's entry into WTO from 1994 to 2000. China resisted Argentine tariffs on Chinese agro products, and in the end allowed Argentina to apply tariffs on sixty products (36 of which were agricultural, including meat, fish, fruit, vegetable oil, soy and grains). Argentina benefited from several worldwide quotas that China accepted in negotiations with other countries on products such as wheat, corn and wool. While expecting significant exports benefits in some manufactures and natural resources (the service sector was excluded from the Argentine-Chinese negotiations), Argentina – like Brazil and Chile – foresaw serious problems with its agricultural exports due to China's stringent (phyto-)sanitary controls, and to tariffs, quotas or non-tariff barriers related to its policy of food security. Other issues were the likely displacement of Argentine production due to Chinese competition and China's relations with MERCOSUR, which might erode the preferential tariffs for Argentine products to the Brazilian market. Like Mexico, Argentina used a defensive policy in its negotiations with China as shown by its rigorous antidumping policy to Chinese imports, particularly in machineries, metal industry and transport. Between 1995 and the 2004, Argentina made 31 antidumping investigations against China, of which 24 concluded that sanctions should be applied, although not all were necessarily materialised (CARI 2004; Girado 2003; Gutiérrez 2001; IDB 2005; see also chapter five in this volume).

In the economic relations between the Bolivarian Republic of Venezuela and the People's Republic of China, oil is the main commodity. To President

Hugo Chávez (since 1999) China forms an alternative to its dependency on the United States for sales and investments in the energy sector, and he has visited China several times. In 2005, China provided Venezuela with a credit of $4 billion for the development of energy projects; agreements on energy, agriculture, railroads, telecom, mining and financial and technical assistance were also ratified. Venezuela's promise to daily export 600,000 barrels of fuel oil and 1.8 metric tons of orimulsion for the production of electricity (CE-PAL 2005a), however, is way above the 2005 level of 68,800 barrels per day. For economic, technical and economic reasons, it seems unlikely that China will bring about considerable changes to Venezuela's dependency on exports to the United States (see chapter six in this volume). Nevertheless, Chinese investments in hydrocarbons seem to make a difference in Venezuela as well as in Colombia. Chinese investments in the future exploitation of untouched oil reserves in Colombia by the Chinese company PETROCHEM have even enhanced the decision to construct an oil pipeline between Colombia and Venezuela and a gas pipeline from the north of Colombia to the Pacific, which are essential for exporting Venezuelan and Colombian combustibles to China. And in 2005, Hugo Chávez and his Colombian colleague Álvaro Uribe signed accords to construct the gas pipeline Transguajiro between Venezuelan refineries and the gas fields of Puerto Ballenas in the Colombian Caribbean.

Despite many positive trends in the Latin America-China relations, the first years of China's WTO membership have not been without disputes. Most problems have surged from the competition of Chinese products in the internal Latin American markets and competition for third markets, while the protection of China's internal market has also been an issue. Many Latin American countries presented antidumping claims against China; even China's 'strategic ally' Brazil presented several claims against Chinese products. These claims essentially concern China's failure to comply with its promise to eliminate the different treatment and dual pricing of goods produced for the internal market compared to the treatment of goods destined for exportation. This policy is considered as the major source of Chinese dumping, which harms the competitiveness of Latin American economies. To protect their economy from this unfair competition from China, until 2016, members of the WTO are entitled to use the so-called non-market economy (NME) methodology toward Chinese products. In the agricultural sector, for instance, China's 'market socialism' still allows for many state companies, subsidies and import tariffs. In the WTO accords that China signed, China agreed to limit the subsidies on agricultural exports to 8.5 per cent, while the import tariffs would be lowered to 15.6 per cent in 2004. Latin America's agro exports to China more than quintupled between 1999 and 2003 (increasing from $495 million to almost $2.8 billion), but countries such as

Argentina and Chile have experienced difficulties in exporting agricultural products to China, due to non-tariffs barriers such as dubious sanitary and phytosanitary rules (CEPAL 2005b; OMC 2004).

As soon as possible, China wants to be officially recognised as a market economy (instead of NME) by as many countries as possible, and several Latin American countries have already done so. To China, this recognition should help to reduce the number of antidumping claims, but it could also be in the best interests of Latin America, as it would probably raise the prices of Chinese products, thus improving the competitiveness of Latin American products.[3] Contrary to the resistance of the United States, the European Union and Japan, in Latin America and the Caribbean a more pragmatic approach seems to prevail. In 2004, Brazil, Chile, Argentina, Venezuela, Peru and several Caribbean countries decided to grant market economy status to China. Most importantly for this decision was that such recognition does not impede the application of a flexible mechanism of antidumping claims. Another reason was the ASEAN countries' recognition of China as a market economy, which was improving the trade possibilities of the member Asian countries with China.

China awarded this recognition as a 'market economy' by its main Latin American trading partners – Brazil, Chile, Argentina and Peru – with additional deals. With Brazil, agreements were signed on Chinese investments in information technology, the financial sector, infrastructure, energy, natural gas, biotechnology and minerals, including an agreement on the joint fabrication of aeroplanes by China Southern Airlines. For Chile, recognising China as a market economy was beneficial for solving phytosanitary conflicts over Chilean exports to China, and in particular for Chile's copper exports. And to Argentina, China promised that its Argentine imports were to rise from the $2.5 billion in 2004 to as much as $6.5 billion in 2009 (Oviedo 2005).

Other Latin American countries, however, have acted with less pragmatism. For example, MERCOSUR was unable to agree on the recognition of China as a market economy because of the opposition of Paraguay. As a result of its anti-communist stand during the dictatorship of Alfredo Stroessner (1954–1989), in 1957, Paraguay recognised Taiwan, Republic of China, as its own country and this recognition was and has been unacceptable to China. One of the priorities of President Hu Jintao's visit to the region in 2004 was to achieve the recognition of China as a 'market economy' by MERCOSUR as a whole, but in the end, China only signed bilateral accords with Argentina, Brazil and Chile, whereas Uruguay postponed a decision because of its presidential elections (Oviedo 2005).

Apart from Paraguay, the diplomatic relations of some Central American and Caribbean countries with Taiwan also complicated the relations with the People's Republic of China. Since the early 1970s, when China was accepted and Taiwan was expelled as member of the United Nations, and as part of its 'One China' policy, China demands that countries end diplomatic relations with Taiwan before establishing economic relations of any sort with China. Although in the 1990s China softened this requirement in the case of developing countries (using its so-called 'economic diplomacy'), China and Taiwan continue their competition for diplomatic relations. Especially in Central America, Taiwan has good relations (see chapter nine). Between 1998 and 2004, Taiwan has supported Central America with $240 million for various development projects. In return for $100 million in Taiwanese support, in 1990, Nicaragua ended its diplomatic relations with China, and in 2006, Nicaragua even signed a free trade agreement with Taiwan. In contrast, in 2007, Costa Rica decided to swap its friendship with Taiwan for the People's Republic of China (Cornejo 2005a; 2005b; Domínguez 2006).

South-South Trade and Competition

Since the 1990s, as a share of total FDI, foreign direct investment to developing countries has increased significantly, representing as much as 30 per cent in 2004 as compared to 17 per cent in 1995. This tendency demonstrates the ongoing transnationalisation of Asia, Latin America, and other developing regions. Simultaneously, the globalisation (or 'Southernisation') of financial capital is related to the ongoing transnationalisation of large companies from the Global South, in particular economic groups and conglomerates. In Latin America, especially Mexican and Brazilian conglomerates have successfully used foreign capital to modernise and expand regionally and globally, and in 2004, the total sales of the 25 largest 'multilatinas' equalled $130 billion. Interestingly, within Latin America, the sales of these conglomerates are growing as compared to those of foreign companies. In the manufacturing sector, for instance, in 2003, the regional sales of the multilatinas even slightly exceeded those of foreign TNCs (CEPAL 2005a; Fernández Jilberto and Hogenboom 2004).

The rapid growth of the world's largest developing country – China – and some other emerging economies in the East and the South is creating a new global economic outlook for all developing countries, including Latin America. In UNCTAD (United Nations Conference on Trade and Development), this is qualified as the 'new geography of trade', shaped by three interlinked trends: the increasing share of developing countries in world trade; South-South trade (commodities and manufactures) and economic cooperation 'reaching a critical mass'; and the changing context of North-South interdependence and terms of engagement. Within this new context, as a 'new growth pole in the world economy', China has a major impact on developing regions: 'the most important reason for the rapid growth of South-South trade is that output growth in some large developing countries, particularly China, has been much faster that in the developed countries … the growth dynamics in China and other Asian economies have positive effects', but they are also posing 'new challenges for many countries' (UNCTAD 2005b: iii–v).

Indeed, next to short-term benefits, the rise of China also represents a challenging development to many Latin American countries. Even countries that so far have not been threatened by the 'China effect', in the longer term, they may well face some serious problems as future efforts for technological upgrading are likely to be met with a major competitive threat by China. Compared to China, Latin America and the Caribbean will remain a high wage region, which can only be offset by high levels of technological competence or skill. Together with the relatively weak position of Latin America's global production networks (except for Mexico and Central America), there is thus reason for concern about the region's competitive position in the world economy. Lall and Weiss (2004) stress the striking tendency in the bilateral trade between China and Latin America and the Caribbean (LAC), with the latter specialising in exporting primary products and importing manufactures. 'The patterns of the two regions are almost a classic textbook illustration of trade between developing and industrialized regions', in which Latin America strengthens its specialization in primary products and process resources while China does the reverse. 'What is surprising is that LAC is the richer region, with a longer history of modern industrialisation, higher human resources, more FDI per capita and with more liberal trade and investment regimes. The result is arguably a massive downgrading of comparative advantage in a dynamic sense, which is surprising for such a relatively industrialised region' (Lall and Weiss 2004: 23).

Between China and Latin America, there are substantial differences in the role and the impact of foreign direct investment on the economy. To accelerate its economic growth, China has greatly diversified and expanded its export markets, assigning an important role to local companies. Although recently transnational companies have gained terrain in China, in the first phase of its liberalisation policies (1978–85), local companies benefited directly from the growing foreign investment in China (UNCTAD 2005a). The Chinese state has actively used diverse instruments to profit from all of the effects of the productive development generated by foreign direct investment, such as capacitating local human resources, transfers of technology and the development of production chains. The policy of the Chinese state has been explicitly designed to favour productive foreign investments that strengthen China's industrial and technological development, in order to process exports and later on to create new industrial zones, linked to centres for research on national development (Díaz Vázquez 2003).

Contrary to China's broad policy spectrum, Latin America's privatisation policies were central to neoliberal restructuring. This gave way to a process of substantial economic concentration in economic groups and conglomerates. While temporarily attracting large sums of FDI and being profitable to both Latin American and transnational companies, privatisation together with policies of liberalisation and deregulation did not bring about the envisioned development and modernisation of the region. Aimed at helping major private companies to take over the role of state companies as the motor for economic growth, this strategy failed because little was done to deal with Latin America's weaknesses in infrastructure, human resources and technological development. Moreover, rather than stimulating entrepreneurship, the massive support of the public sector for 'big business' and the close relations between technocrats and important entrepreneurs – during privatisation as well as after it – gave way to the creation of a new oligarchy. With their globalised assets and capital, this new oligarchy has limited interest in the development of the domestic economy (Fernández Jilberto and Hogenboom 2004, 2008).

Mexico's experience since 2000 demonstrates that the reason for a negative 'China effect' is competition in similar sectors of manufacturing. Between 2000 and 2003, Mexico's *maquiladora* sector, one of its most important export manufacturing sectors, experienced a crisis resulting in a loss of almost 230,000 jobs. One-third of the production that left Mexico moved to China. Like Central America and the Caribbean have done more recently (and contrary to Argentina, Brazil and Chile), since the 1980s, Mexico has concentrated its exports in chains of global subcontracting (outsourcing) for the US market. Since the late 1990s, however, China is swiftly replacing Mexico on several points of these global production chains. For instance, in 2003, China took over Mexico's primary position in the US market of processors, equalling a loss of 21,000 jobs and $500 million in investments. As much as twelve of Mexico's main twenty export sectors to the United States compete with China, such as textiles, footwear and clothing, as well as industrial machinery, televisions and video players. China's WTO membership reduced the NAFTA-based preferential advantages of Mexico at the US market, and in 2003, China replaced Mexico as the second largest source of US imports (after Canada) – a position that Mexico had taken over two years earlier from Japan. Cheap Chinese products and aggressive Chinese policies to attract foreign investments caused a process of industrial South-South delocalisation that harmed Mexico's *maquiladora* industry, and several large TNCs moved production facilities away, including technological plants of NEC, ON Semiconductor, Sony and Kodak. Further restructuring of Mexico's participation in global production networks (according to the ideology of the Washington Consensus) and diversification of its global trade seem to be the only structural alternatives in order for Mexico to deal with the 'China effect' (CEPAL 2004a; Dussel Peters and Xue Dong 2005; *La Jornada* 9 May 2005).

In Latin America as a whole, there is a fear that China is causing a displacement of foreign investment in manufacturing. While this fear has been partly refuted by studies showing that most flows to China have different motivations than those to Latin America (Lora 2005; IDB 2005), the compatibility of China's economy with business strategies of transnational companies is evidently greater than Latin America's.[4] These strategies give priority to investments in regions that successfully combine the existence of a large internal market, low labour costs, abundant natural resources and stimulus for investments with a high technological component. Compared to Latin America, China is in a better position to satisfy the priorities of transnational investments, due to its combination of economic strategies based in the search for financial means to exploit natural resources, the formulation of the necessary policies to assure the efficiency of the size of the market, the application of a high technological development and the offer of its abundant labour at low cost (CEPAL 2004b). The latter is China's largest competitive advantage as compared to Latin America as it possesses a labour market of 712 million workers, who on average cost $0.61 hourly instead of the $2 hourly in Mexico. In the manufacturing sector labour costs in China are 3.7 times lower than in South America's poorest country, Bolivia, and 12.5 times lower than in Chile. In the clothing sector, the labour costs in Guatemala are 3 times those of China, and in Costa Rica, more than 12 times higher (Gutiérrez 2003; Shafaenddin 2002). As a result, China is favourably competing with Latin America in the labour intensive segments of the international markets.

Transnational companies investing in Latin America and in the Caribbean have implemented two different strategies. In the case of Mexico and the Caribbean, these investments have come predominantly from the United States and the US companies have established an international system of integrated production in the manufacturing sector. As a result, the international competitiveness of this region has risen, as can be deduced from its participation in global exports, but this has not stimulated the integration of the economy, technology transference, human resource capacity or local business development (CEPAL 2004a). In South America, in turn, a large part of FDI is by European TNCs in the service sector and in the exploitation of natural resources, resulting partly from the many privatisations and economic deregulation of the 1980s. The international competitiveness of this sub-region has been improved by the modernisation of the infrastructure and services used by the export sector, but its sustainability has been negatively affected by the economic crisis of Brazil and Argentina. Due to the effects of the Asian crisis that materialised in Latin America in 1998, China was able to recover more effectively, as its countercyclical policies permitted a rapid macro-economic stability (IDB 2005; CEPAL 1998).

The shifts in FDI and export production have affected the world market share of exports from China vis-à-vis those from Latin American and the Caribbean. From 1990 to 2002, China's world market shares in all products rose, increasing its total share from 2 to 6 per cent. Above all, increases were seen in the share of China in low technology (from 5 to 15 per cent) and high technology (from less than 1 to 7 per cent) manufacturing. Meanwhile, the world market share of Latin American exports increased from 4 to 6 per cent, but mainly as a catch-up from the lost decade of the 1980s. Its world market share in primary products was surprisingly stable for such a resource-rich region: 12.4 per cent in 1990 and 12.7 per cent in 2002. Most of Latin America's growing world market share in medium technology (from 1.8 to 5.2 per cent) and high technology (from 0.6 to 3.7 per cent) manufacturing was due to the expansion of Mexico, which, in 2002, was a larger exporter of manufactured products than the rest of the region's 17 countries altogether (respectively 3.0 and 1.9 per cent of world market share). Simultaneously, as we have seen, the similarities between Mexico's and China's technological trade development have a very negative 'China effect' on Mexico's *maquila* sector (Lall and Weiss 2004).

Economic Liberalisation and the State

China's high rate of economic expansion is based on a development model that combines a modernisation of state-led economic organisation and regulation with a gradual, controlled liberalisation in which (foreign) transnational companies play a central role. The government has fostered industrial export policies, including tax reforms, currency devaluations and duty free imports, resulting in high productivity gains, especially in the export-oriented regions in the southern provinces that could attract investment from Hong Kong and Taiwan. China has thus developed an economically successful model that involves public as well as private actors and investment in order to achieve growth through integration in the world market (Houweling 2004).

China's economic miracle of 'market socialism' has been the result of the structural transformations that started in 1978 under Deng Xiaoping at the time when China was economically devastated by Mao Zedong's 'cultural revolution' (1966–76). Economic development was central to Deng's pragmatic approach: 'the practice is the only criterion of the truth' and 'development represents the ultimate truth' (Falkenheim 1989). Deng initiated the process of the 'four modernisations' (education and science, industry, agriculture and defence), which opened the way for implementing 'market socialism'. Foreign investment was to play an important role in the creation of the socialist market economy. In 1980, four special economic zones were designated along the Chinese coast, involving special incentives to foreign investors such as duty exemptions, tax breaks and flexible labour regulation. After domestic companies were encouraged to link up with transnational companies and the infrastructure as well as the legal framework were improved, the investment and growth rates exceeded all expectations (the GDP of these zones grew as much as 35 per cent per year) and soon more zones were opened up (World Bank 2004: 167).

Decisive in the implementation of China's market economy was the second phase of restructuring that started in 1984. The Chinese state renounced its traditional monopolies in the industrial and commercial sector, and resources traditionally belonging to the state were transferred to the market and the private sector. State companies were reformed and became more independent while more room was created for the private sector through privatisations, mergers and bankruptcies of state companies. As a result of these and other improvements in its investment climate, between 1980 and 2000, private investment as a share of GDP almost doubled in China (World Bank 2004: 2). However, in this context of radically changed production relations and a decentralisation of economic policies, the regulation of labour relations – always a crucial component of social and political stability – was no longer completely controlled by the state. Nevertheless, Deng's aim was to achieve economic liberalisation that would contribute to the preservation of the power of the state, the party and the state-party's political regime.

Finally, in December 2001, China consolidated its policies of economic liberalisation by signing the protocols for entry into the WTO. For this purpose, in the preceding decennium, China had significantly reduced its import barriers and economic protection. The average level of import taxes was gradually reduced from 43 per cent in 1992 to 17 per cent in 2002. This deregulation was to enhance the industrial export sector (concentrated in the coastal area) that 'dinamises' China's foreign trade through international business operations based on sub-contracts with transnational enterprises (Lemoine 1999, 2002). Taken together, what started as a gradual move from socialist to capitalist economic measures turned into China's profound economic restructuring. And this development has a strong resemblance to the processes of economic restructuring in numerous other developing countries, as related to the triumph of capitalism and the hegemony of neoliberalism that came with the end of the Cold War (Demmers, Fernández Jilberto and Hogenboom 2004: 16).

Like in China, in several Latin American countries, it was an authoritarian state that started policies of economic opening while excluding civil society, or it was that of an independently operating political society. In these cases, neoliberal restructuring was either implemented by the state bureaucracy under a model of state-party authoritarianism as in Mexico by the PRI (Institutional Revolutionary Party), or under military dictatorships as in Chile (1973–89) and Argentina (1976–83). Through these bureaucracies, the authoritarian state started a 'passive revolution' in order to achieve the substitution of Keynesianism by neoliberalism, while in China, Maoist economic socialism was substituted by a capitalism called 'market socialism'.

Yet contrary to China where the policies of economic liberalisation were of an endogenous nature, in Latin America, neoliberal economic reforms were largely of exogenous origin. US government pressures related to the (pro-market) struggle against 'international communism', followed by IMF and World Bank conditionalities during the debt crisis, which eventually shaped the joint Washington Consensus. These powerful institutions actively developed an internationally hegemonic view on the economy (known as TINA: There Is No Alternative), and supported like-minded Latin American political elites and technocrats in organising sufficient strategic relations and room for manoeuvre while weakening actors from political and civil society. From the late 1980s onward, Latin America's gradual democratisation allowed for the compatibility of neoliberalism with democratic political regimes. For this shift, however, it was necessary to neoliberalise the ideologies of the traditional populist parties that, from the 1940s to the 1970s, had followed Keynesian principles for economic development in order to achieve stable and redistributive growth (Demmers, Fernández Jilberto and Hogenboom 2001).[5]

As a result of these different trajectories of economic restructuring, the Chinese state still maintains the capacity to regulate and control the process of globalisation of China's economy, whereas Latin America's neoliberalisation has basically left the state as subsidiary to economic globalisation. Several Latin American analysts claim that the larger intervention capacity of the Chinese state in its economy's globalisation is a weakness. According to this view, it expresses a lack of separation between the state and the market, of which the latter is the principal agent in economic decisions and the main source of employment. Compared to countries such as Chile, Mexico and Argentina, current policies in China hinder corporate governance and market discipline while its limited deregulation of the financial sector is negative for its access to credit. Indeed, the banking system of China is dominated by only four large banks (the Bank of China, the Bank of Construction of China, the Bank of Industry and Commerce of China and the Agricultural Bank of China), as there are major restrictions for the operations of foreign banks. Although China has tried to deal with some of the problems with its banks,[6] this situation does not in any way resemble the profound privatisation and liberalisation of the financial sector in Latin American countries. Contrary to China, (only) after several financial crises have developed were extensive supervision systems by Central Banks and regulations set up in Latin America. Simultaneously, multinational banks and insurance companies have become completely dominant: the financial sector is Latin America's most transnationalised sector (Lora 2005; Cornejo 2005b; Fernández Jilberto and Hogenboom 2008).

Although the trends of rising China and new South-South relations have come about in the context of neoliberal globalisation and involve developing economies that have been profoundly liberalised, these trends implicate important criticism of the dominant neoliberal development model. In contrast to the situation of the third quarter of the twentieth century, when China's economic and political development was very different from most of the rest of the Third World, starting in the late 1970s, China went through several phases of economic restructuring that in many ways resembled the liberalisation that was generally taking place in developing countries. Yet despite this policy convergence, China never aimed at a free market and a small state, and economic liberalisation has been as central to China's miraculous growth as has been the strong state and its active economic role. This difference has been crucial as shown by the wide gap between the GDP growth of China and any developing country or transition economy that reformed its state and economy according to the lines of the Washington Consensus.

Apart from setting an example for alternative development strategies, China's recent global economic influence may be seen to encourage such alternatives for developing countries in several ways. By joining the G20 in the WTO negotiations, China has been of great support in advancing the interests of developing regions in global politics and the world market. Meanwhile, as a new export market and an emerging source of foreign investment, there is a 'China effect' in this area as well. Having increased growth in developing countries, which are benefiting from exports to China and rising world market prices, diminishes these countries' dependency on international financial institutions and their policies. And countries that receive Chinese investments or development assistance find that there are no economic policy conditions attached. On the other hand, China's global agenda has a clear and purely economic goal, and it has been its economic – and not political – liberalisation within a neoliberalising global system that paved the way for China's remarkable economic development. As a result, while China can be expected to further enhance the South-South agenda and support international demands of developing countries, it may also further enhance a globalisation that seriously neglects human rights and environmental degradation, while also making it very hard for Latin American manufacturing to survive and modernise.

China's success story is consistent with other findings on capital accumulation regimes and economic growth of developing countries that 'raise serious questions about the strategies adopted in a number of developing countries for activating a dynamic process of capital accumulation and growth through a combination of increased FDI and reduced public investment and policy intervention' (UNCTAD 2003: 84). In this respect, and irrespective of many differences, China's successful strategy of insertion into the world economy is bearing some resemblance to the development models of other East Asian countries with an economically (pro-) active state. While by the end of the 1990s, the remarkable development of several emerging economies in Southeast Asia became (for some part unjustly) blurred by the Asian financial crisis, China's rise shows developing countries that there are viable alternatives to the Washington Consensus.

About this Book

China's rapid insertion into the global economy and its new political role have affected all Latin American countries, yet in different ways. In order to further our understanding of the various important new relations between these countries and China, this volume presents studies of Brazil, Mexico, Chile, Argentina, Venezuela, Peru, Bolivia and Central America. These case studies represent an interesting mix of countries from all parts of Latin America: large and small economies; with global insertion based on raw materials or instead on manufacturing; and countries with close ties with China as well as countries with very distant relations with the PRC. The aim of critically analysing their experiences with the rise of China from a political economy perspective implicates that, next to economic changes, also politics, policies and social dimensions are addressed. The contributions to this volume thus also provide insight into the changing nature of globalisation, the emergence of new economic and political South-South relations, and their effects on development in Latin America.

The book starts with Latin America's two largest countries and economies, Brazil and Mexico, which have experienced the rise of China in completely opposite ways. Brazil holds major and complementary trade relations with China, Chinese companies have been making several large investments in Brazil, and China defines their relation as a strategic partnership. As Henrique Altimani de Oliveira explains in chapter two, this partnership is focused on scientific and technological cooperation, and on joint political-strategic efforts in international forums. Altimani analyses the intensive relations between Brazil and China based on mutual interests, but also points out some Brazilian concerns that this South-South cooperation will become outstripped by competition. In contrast, Mexico's relations with China have been dominated by economic competition; only recently has the distant and even hostile attitude of the Mexican government been changing in a somewhat more positive direction. Indeed, the effects of China's competition in global manufactures markets have been dramatic for Mexico, and bilaterally China's trade and investment relations are troubling Mexico as well. In chapter three, in addition to analysing the Sino-Mexican political and economic relations, Barbara Hogenboom looks into Mexico's problem with competitiveness in international markets by comparing its development and globalisation strategies with those of China.

The following two chapters deal with China's relations with the Southern Cone's main countries: Chile and Argentina. Chile has gained extensively from the Chinese demand for copper, which made export volumes and international prices rise, and triggered major Chinese investment in the Chilean copper sector. Moreover, Chile was the first country in Latin America and the world to establish a free trade agreement with China, which went into effect in 2006. In chapter four, Alex E. Fernández Jilberto describes the phenomenal relations that Chile holds with China, including its exceptional position in the region: Chile has been the first and most loyal follower of the neoliberal model, the most reliable ally of the United States, and it has used a globalisation strategy based on extreme economic pragmatism. In the case of Argentina, China's need of natural resources has also formed an important impetus for intensified relations, as chapter five shows. Carla V. Oliva studies their economic as well as political and cultural relations and activities, and the relevance of the intensified bilateral relations in multilateral forums. Interestingly, she notes that whereas Argentina's foreign policy has been generally characterised by interruptions, its policies toward China have been exceptional for their continuity.

The chapters on Venezuela and Peru could be summarised as Andean attempts for rapprochement with China, yet with different intentions and outcomes. President Hugo Chávez has been most eager to deepen Venezuela's ties with China, which he has unilaterally called a strategic alliance. However, Javier Corrales analyses in chapter six why, despite China needing energy, Venezuela having energy, and both wanting to diversify their energy markets, so far their bilateral energy trade has not really been booming. Apart from the technical obstacles to export Venezuelan oil to China, he explains that unequal economic needs and incompatible foreign policy objectives have posed limits to realising President Chávez's China dreams. In comparison, the relations between Peru and China have been more straightforward and mutually satisfactory, as chapter seven by Rubén Berríos reveals. Their bilateral trade has increased rapidly over the past few years and has overall been balanced and complementary, with Peru exporting several primary products. In addition, Peru and China negotiated a free trade agreement that in 2009 was implemented. But although Chinese trade and investment have improved

Peru's competitiveness, there is also unease in Peru over Chinese competition in manufacturing.

Chapters eight and nine study countries that have had relatively limited relations with China. To Bolivia, Asia has become economically very relevant, but so far, Japan and South Korea have been more important trade and investment partners than China. Still, since Bolivia exports raw materials that China requires, this may change in the near future. On the other hand, the Development Plan of Bolivia's President Evo Morales was announced as a break with the country's long history of economic dependence and raw material exports. In chapter eight, Pablo Poveda discusses the prospects of this plan and Bolivia's future relations with China. The limitations of Central America's ties with the PRC result from the diplomatic relations of these countries with Taiwan. Gabriel Aguilera Peralta explains in chapter nine how and why this 'historical brotherhood from the Cold War' is still important to the Isthmus today. Nevertheless, weak economic relations with Taiwan and the evident economic attractiveness of China put serious pressure on this brotherhood and caused a first rupture in 2007, when Costa Rica announced that it was going to establish diplomatic relations with the PRC instead of Taiwan.

Finally, chapter ten draws conclusions about the new economic and political relations between Latin America and China, the nature of these South-South relations and their relevance for the region's development. These issues are linked to the debate about the rise of the Left in Latin America and the end of the Washington Consensus. Together with the current international crisis, these profound regional and global changes tempt us to consider whether the 'Beijing Consensus' may be playing a role in Latin America in the near future.

References

CARI. 2004. *República Popular China: Un Desafío y una Oportunidad para el Sector Agroalimentario de la República Argentina*. Buenos Aires: CARI (Consejo Argentino para las Relaciones Internacionales) & CEPAL.

Carrillo, Jorge and Redi Gomis. 2003. 'Los Retos de las Maquilladoras ente la pérdida de Competitividad'. *Comercio Exterior* 53(4): 318–37.

CEPAL. 1998. *Impacto de la Crisis Asiática en América Latina*. Santiago: Naciones Unidas.

———. 2004a. *La Inversión Extranjera Directa en América Latina y el Caribe 2003*. Santiago: Naciones Unidas.

———. 2004b. *Panorama de la Inserción Internacional de América Latina y el Caribe 2002– 2003*. Santiago: Naciones Unidas.

———. 2005a. *La Inversión Extranjera Directa en América Latina y el Caribe 2004*. Santiago: Naciones Unidas.

———. 2005b. *Latin America and the Caribbean in the World Economy, 2004—2005 Trends*. Santiago: United Nations.

————. 2006. *Foreign Investment in Latin America and the Caribbean, 2005*. Santiago: United Nations.

Cornejo, Romer. 2005a. 'América Latina ante el Crecimiento Económico de China'. VI Reunión de la Red de Estudios de América Latina y el Caribe sobre Asia-Pacífico. Buenos Aires: Redealap / Banco Interamericano de Desarrollo.

————. 2005b. 'América Latina en la perspectiva de China'. In *Política exterior de China. La diplomacia de una potencia emergente*, ed. Xulio Rios. Barcelona: Ediciones Bellaterra.

Cruz, Zamorano and Alma Rosa. 2005. 'China: Competencia Comercial con México y Centroamérica'. *Comercio Exterior* 55(3): 281–89.

Demmers, Jolle, Alex E. Fernández Jilberto and Barbara Hogenboom, eds. 2001. *Miraculous Metamorphoses. The Neoliberalisation of Latin American Populism*. London: Zeds Books.

————. 2004. 'Good governance and democracy in a world of neoliberal regimes'. In *Good Governance in the Era of Neoliberal Globalisation. Conflict and Depolitization in Latin America, Eastern Europe, Asia and Africa*, eds. Jolle Demmers, Alex E. Fernández Jilberto and Barbara Hogenboom, 1–37. London: Routledge.

Díaz Vázquez, Julio. 2003. 'China en la OMC: Repercusión en los Países en Desarrollo'. Centro de Investigaciones de Economía Internacional, Universidad de la Habana (February).

Domínguez, Jorge I. 2006. 'China's Relations with Latin America: Shared Gains, Asymmetric Hopes'. Working paper, Inter-American Dialogue (June).

Dussel Peters, Enrique. 2003. 'Ser maquila o no ser maquila, ¿es esa la pregunta?' *Comercio exterior* 53(4): 328–36.

————. 2004. *La Competitividad de la Industria Maquiladora de Exportación en Honduras. Condiciones y retos ante el CAFTA*. México DF: CEPAL.

Dussel Peters, Enrique y Liu Xue Dong. 2005. *Oportunidades y Retos Económicos de China para México y Centroamérica*. México: CEPAL.

Falkenheim, V.C. 1989. *Chinese Politics from Mao to Deng*. New York: Paragon House.

FDI STAT. 2008. UNCTAD trade statistics, http://stats.unctad.org/FDI/ (accessed 1 September 2008).

Fernández Jilberto, Alex E. and Barbara Hogenboom, eds. 2004. *Latin American Conglomerates and Economic Groups under Globalisation*. Special Issue of *Journal of Developing Societies*, 20(3–4).

————. 2008. 'Latin American Conglomerates in the Neoliberal Era: The Politics of Economic Concentration in Chile and Mexico'. In *Big Business and Economic Development: Conglomerates and Economic Groups in Developing Countries and Transition Economies under Globalisation*, eds. Alex E. Fernández Jilberto and Barbara Hogenboom, 1–28. London: Routledge.

García-Herrero, Alicia and Daniel Santabárbara. 2005. 'Does China have an impact on Foreign Direct Investment to Latin America?' Documentos de Trabajo no. 0517, Banco de España.

Gaulier, Guillaume, Françoise Lemoine and Deniz Ünal-Kesenci. 2005. 'China's Integration in East Asia: Production Sharing, FDI and High-Tech Trade'. Paris: CEPII.

Girado, Gustavo. 2003. *Comercio Argentina/Asia Pacífico. Una Carrera de Obstáculos*. Buenos Aires: Corregidor.

Gutiérrez, Hernán. 2001. 'Las relaciones de China y América Latina: Perspectivas desde Argentina, Brasil y Chile'. *Integración y Comercio* 5(14): 75–116.

————. 2003. 'Oportunidades y desafíos de los vínculos económicos de China y América Latina el Caribes'. Serie Comercio Internacional 42. Santiago: CEPAL.

Houweling, Henk. 2004. 'China's transition to industrial capitalism: tracing institutional reform'. In *Good Governance in the Era of Neoliberal Globalisation. Conflict and Depolitization in Latin America, Eastern Europe, Asia and Africa*, eds. Jolle Demmers, Alex E. Fernández Jilberto and Barbara Hogenboom, 265–86. London: Routledge.

IDB. 2005. *The Emergence of China: Opportunities and Challenges for Latin America and the Caribbean*. Washington, DC: Inter-American Development Bank.

IMF. 2006. *World Economic Outlook: Globalisation and Inflation*. Washington, DC: International Monetary Fund.

Jiang, Wei. 2007. 'Outward FDI hits $21.16b for 2006'. *China Daily*, 15 September, http://www.chinadaily.com.cn/china/2007-09/15/content_6109739.htm (accessed 25 August 2008).

Lall, Sanjaya and John Weiss. 2004. 'People's Republic of China's Competitive Threat to Latin America: An Analysis for 1990–2002'. ADB Institute Discussion Paper no. 14. Tokyo: Asian Development Bank Institute.

Lei, W. 2004. *China: un mercado estratégico para as exportações brasileiras*. Rio de Janiero: BNDES.

Lemoine, Françoise. 1999. 'Les Délocalisations au cœur de l'expansion du commerce extérieur chinois'. *Economie et Statistiques*, juin-juillet: 326–27.

———. 2002. 'Gagnants et perdants de l'ouverture chinoise'. *Le Monde Diplomatique*, avril: 22.

Lemoine, Françoise and Deniz Ünal-Kesenci. 2002. 'Chine: Spécialisation Internationale et Rattrapage Technologique'. *Économie Internationale* 92: 11–40.

León, José Luis. 2005. 'La Relación Económica China-América Latina. Expresiones y Causas de dos Trayectorias Distintas'. VI Reunión de la Red de Estudios de América Latina y el Caribe sobre Asia- Pacífico. Buenos Aires: Redealap / Banco Interamericano de Desarrollo.

Lora, Eduardo. 2005. '¿Debe América Latina Temerle a La China?' Departamento de Investigación, Documento de Trabajo 536, Banco Interamericano de Desarrollo, Washington, DC.

Mesquita, Machado, João Bosco and Galeno Tinoco Ferraz. 2005. *Comércio Externo da China e Efeitos sobre as Exportações Brasileiras*. Brasil: CEPAL/IPEA.

MofCom. 2008. Ministry of Commerce of People's Republic of China, various trade statistics, http://english.mofcom.gov.cn (accessed 1 September 2008).

Morrison, Kevin and Christopher Brown-Humes. 2005. 'On the clime: a natural resources boom is unearthing both profits and perils'. *Financial Times*, 11 april: 13.

OMC. 2004. 'Informe al Consejo del Comercio de Mercancías sobre el Examen de Transición de China'. Comité de Agricultura, Organización Mundial de Comercio (3 de noviembre).

Oviedo, Eduardo. 2005. 'Crisis del Multilateralismo y Auge de la Diplomacia Bilateral en la Relación MERCOSUR-China'. VI Reunión de la Red de Estudios de América Latina y el Caribe sobre Asia-Pacífico. Buenos Aires: Redealap / Banco Interamericano de Desarrollo.

Pimentel Puga, Fernando, Lavína Barros de Castro, Francisco Rocha Ferreira and Marcelo Machado Nascimento. 2004. 'O Comércio Brasil-China: Situação Atual e Potencialidades de Crescimento'. Textos para Discussão 104. Rio de Janeiro: Banco Nacional de Desenvolvimento Econômico e Social.

Santiso, Javier, ed. 2007. *The Visible Hand of China in Latin America*. Paris: OECD Development Centre.

Shafaeddin, S. 2002. 'The Impact of China's Accession to WTO on the Exports of Developing Countries'. Discussion Papers No. 160, United Nations Conference on Trade and Development.

UN Comtrade. 2008. http://comtrade.un.org/db (accessed 10 September 2008).

UNCTAD. 1995. *World Investment Report 1995: Transnational Corporations and Competitiveness*. New York and Geneva: United Nations.

———. 2002. World Investment *Report 2002: Transnational Corporations and Export Competitiveness*. New York and Geneva: United Nations.

———. 2003. *Trade and Development Report 2003*. New York and Geneva: United Nations.

———. 2004. *Handbook of Statistics*. New York and Geneva: United Nations.

———. 2005a. *World Investment Report 2005: Transnational Corporations and the Internationalization of R&D*. New York and Geneva: United Nations.

———. 2005b. *Trade and Development Report 2004*. New York and Geneva: United Nations.

———. 2006. *World Investment Report 2005: FDI from Developing and Transition Economies: Implications for Development*. New York and Geneva: United Nations.

World Bank. 2004. *World Development Report. A Better Investment Climate For Everyone*. Oxford: Oxford University Press.

Yeo, George. 2005. 'Re-encounter of Latin America and Asia'. Speech by Singapore Minister for Foreign Affairs at the annual conference of the Council of the Americas, Washington, DC (3 May).

Zweig, David and Bi Jianhai. 'China's Global Hunt for Energy'. *Foreign Affairs* 84(5): 25–38.

Notes

1. This tendency is, among other things, visible in some reports by international institutions such as the IDB's *The Emergence of China: Opportunities and Challenges for Latin America and the Caribbean* (2005), and the OECD's *The Visible Hand of China in Latin America* (Santiso 2007).

2. From East Asia, apart from China, it is primarily Japan that is actively pursuing relations with Latin America. Japan and Latin America have a long history of trade relations, investment and migration, but the Latin American crisis of the 1980s and Japan's crisis in the 1990s harmed the economic relations (Yeo 2005). In the 1990s, China replaced Japan as the leading Asian trade partner of Latin America and the Caribbean. Recent initiatives show that Latin America is becoming more of a priority to Japan, perhaps to keep up with China's closer ties to the region. In September 2004, for instance, Japan's Prime Minister Koizumi visited Brazil and Mexico and signed the Japan-Mexico free trade agreement.

3. The advantages have to do with international antidumping rules: Article VI authorizes WTO members to use prices in so-called surrogate markets in order to determine the normal value of the goods and service of economies such as China that do not follow market rules (usually Mexico, Turkey and India are used as referee countries). To the United States and the European Union, this article provides a means (of power) to diminish the competitiveness of the Chinese economy. The United States has established a series of criteria to determine the market condition of an economy, including the convertibility of one's currency, rights of association between local and foreign capital, state control on companies, and freedom of the market. The European Union decided to apply the condition of 'transition economy' to China, stating that China has not yet sufficiently limited the influence of the government in the functioning of state companies, while it still lacks an effective legal framework for corporate activities, such as on bankruptcies, the protection of private property, and the convertibility of capital (CEPAL 2005b).

4. Colombia and Mexico, however, clearly suffered from a negative 'China effect' from 1995 to 2001, when global FDI flows were booming and China's WTO membership was near. The two countries would have attracted more investment if it were not for China 'suck(ing) away' global capital: a $100 million increase of Chinese inward FDI reduced Colombian and Mexican inward FDI by $84 and $29 million, respectively (García-Herrero and Santabárbara 2005).

5. In China, since 1992 (after the Tiananmen events of 1989), the centrally planned economy has become subordinated to market mechanisms as an instrument for assigning productive resources in the economic process. With these last reforms, the political class of the Chinese state has hoped to maintain its position, thus using the economic successes of China's capitalism to legitimize its monopolised control over the state and political processes.

6. For instance, in 1998, the Chinese governments gave the banks a capital injection of $33 billion, in 2003 it created the Banking Regulation Commission, and in 2004 it gave the Bank of China and the Bank of Construction of China a new injection of $45 billion.

2 Brazil and China
From South-South Cooperation to Competition?
Henrique Altemani de Oliveira

At the beginning of the 1990s, two specific factors influenced Brazil to adjust its international insertion strategy. The first factor was the end of the Cold War and the subsequent international restructuring process aimed at redefining the International System, including the emergence of new rules that reconfigured patterns in international relations. The second factor was Brazil's adhesion to the liberal trade system, which involved a process of opening up its internal market and reforming the state.

As a result of these developments, East Asia began to represent a strategic area in Brazil's international insertion process, with important economic and political dimensions. Asia emerged from the Cold War as an international actor of undisputed relevance. Japan was the second largest economy in the world, and as a result of the development and integration of Southeast Asian countries, South Korea and China, the regional economy of East Asia had become very dynamic. Brazil thus began to see the Asian region as special, considering its great demand for investments and access to high technology, as well as its potential consumer market. And importantly, Brazil became of interest to Asia as an important supplier of raw materials, especially food products and basic commodities. Since then, with Asia further specialising in manufactured products, the Asian interest in importing raw materials from Brazil has only increased.

Politically, Brazil began to act strategically in this new international context. Its two central objectives were to strengthen the South American region as a base for international insertion, and intensify relations with other regional poles. This approach was based on the premises that the process of redefinition of the international order, in all of its aspects, would be long and require intense negotiation; that the difficulty of attaining new global arrangements made the case for more local solutions and regionalism; and that South America would tend to remain in the United States' sphere of influence. In this context, to Brazil it became a priority to use its relations with Asia as a negotiation instrument with the two major poles of the United States and Europe.

This political and economic Brazilian interest in Asia has also generated positive expectations as to the role that might be played by China. As President Lula expressed in 2003, 'I have said again and again that South America will be a priority in my administration, as I am convinced that the full development of Brazil is only possible as part of the integration of the continent as a whole.... If, on the one hand, we have a regional calling, on the other we are also a global country. Just as national integration must be a part of regional integration, I am convinced that the strengthening of ties with Asia, and, particularly, China, will be decisive for Brazil to realise its grand destiny' (da Silva 2003).

While until the 1970s Brazilian relations with Asia were basically limited to Japan, in the 1990s, they were broadened and acquired new vigour with the presence not only of South Korea, but also of other Southeast Asian countries as well as China. As a consequence of its accelerated development, China was no longer just a political actor, but represented a strong consumer and supplier market as well. Broad initiatives such as the *Special Partnership between Brazil and South Korea for the XXI Century,* the *Strategic Partnership* with China and the *Alliance for the XXI Century* with Japan reflect the perception, on both sides, of the potential of this relationship.

While Japan presented itself as an essentially economic partner, the relations between Brazil and the People's Republic of China have always (since the start of official diplomatic relations in 1974) been defined from the perspective of South-South cooperation. Thus, during the Cold War, Brazil and China, conscious of their status as developing countries, cooperated in the political-strategic field, with the aim of exerting pressure on the reform process of multilateral institutions, especially economic and financial ones. This cooperative process was extended in 1988 to technological cooperation in the fields of aerospace and missiles. Additionally, during the initial post-Cold War period, relations appeared to be thriving as a *Strategic Partnership* was formed between the two countries and as Brazil officially recognised China's status as a market economy.

Considering the extraordinary economic growth experienced by China in recent years, especially after its entry into the World Trade Organisation, this chapter on the Sino-Brazilian relations will analyse the historical process in its different dimensions. The aim is to determine whether current relations can still be understood from the perspective of South-South cooperation, and whether the Chinese economic boom may be defining a new, much more competitive than cooperative relationship.

Development of Brazil's Relations with Asia and China

Up until the end of the nineteenth century, there existed no relations whatsoever between Brazil and Asia, despite the signing of a Treaty of Friendship,

Trade and Navigation with China in 1881, and the opening of a Consulate in Shanghai, as well as the signing, in November 1895, of a Treaty of Friendship, Trade and Navigation with Japan. These ties with Asia were basically the consequence of Brazilian interests in establishing a migratory flow of Asian workers for coffee plantations in the state of Sao Paulo. Initially, the option was for a Chinese workforce, which motivated a Brazilian Mission to China in 1879. However, China officially prohibited migration to Brazil (due to the problems experienced by Chinese people in other parts of the Americas, especially Cuba, Peru and the United States). The arrival of the ship *Kosato Maru*, in 1908, marked the beginning of Japanese migration to Brazil, which grew steadily until 1934 (when a new Brazilian Constitution limited migration into the country) and resumed only after 1955. As for China, bilateral contacts were scarce due to the succession of internal and external conflicts that affected that country during the end of the nineteenth century and the first half of the twentieth century. After Mao Zedong's victory in 1949, Brazil continued to maintain diplomatic relations with the Republic of China, which was then established in Taiwan.

From the 1950s to the 1970s, there were no substantial Brazil-Asia relations. Despite Asia being mentioned in Brazilian foreign policy speeches, especially after the launching of the *Independent Foreign Policy*[1] during the Jânio Quadros administration, there was only limited interaction in the multilateral sphere. This involved the construction of a common political agenda of developing countries against the rise of a bipolar world economic order. In 1959, Sukarno was the first Asian president to visit Brazil, and, in 1961, a bilateral economic agreement was signed between Brazil and Indonesia, but no further concrete relations were established with this or other Southeast Asian countries. The Bandung Conference (Indonesia) formed the centre of Brazil's political imaginary concerning the strengthening of ties with the Afro-Asian world under the premises of an independent foreign policy. In Brazil, as in Africa and Asia, the intensification of South-South relations with the Afro-Asian world was related to the need for self-determination and the common fight to overcome poverty and underdevelopment. Brazil became more involved with the African Continent and developed what was called its *African Policy*. This policy symbolically represented Brazil's *Third World Policy* and its involvement in the struggle for a new international economic order (Oliveira 1987).

China was the only country in Asia with which Brazil managed to successfully establish significant ties in the context of South-South cooperation. After the re-establishment of diplomatic relations with mainland China on 15 August 1974, the Sino-Brazilian partnership aimed at joint action on topics of common developmental interests in the international agenda. In spite of different political systems, Brazil and China discovered similarities in some of their principles of foreign policy, in particular their common search to enhance their international autonomy, national sovereignty and territorial integrity.

China and Brazil also shared similar stances with regard to other international issues, such as their opposition to the US human rights diplomacy, and the importance of South-South cooperation in the face of protectionism by developed nations (Shang 2003). Despite its military regime, at the end of the 1960s, Brazil's foreign policy returned to the premises of an independent foreign policy. At the start of the Costa e Silva administration, Brazil refused to sign the Treaty of Nuclear Non-Proliferation, stressed the participation in multilateral forums, and regained its relative role as a leader in the United Nations Conference on Trade and Development (UNCTAD). Brazil became actively engaged with the Third World agenda and consequently began to see the People's Republic of China, which reclaimed its seat in the United Nations Security Council (UNSC) and defended the same ideals as Brazil, as a promising partner in the defence of common interests. Simultaneously, China searched for a place for itself in world politics and, from 1969 onward, it decreased its support of revolutionary movements in Latin America. Instead, China attempted to undertake a strategic state-to-state diplomacy, promising to respect the principle of non-interference with internal matters (Mann 2002).

While the re-establishment of relations with China lent credibility and legitimacy to Brazil's foreign policies, with its emphasis on multilateral forums and Third World theories, there was also some interest on the part of Brazilian businessmen in the Chinese market. In 1961, President João Goulart coordinated the first Brazilian trade mission to Beijing. A Chinese trade mission in response, however, was interrupted due to the military coup of 1964 and the arrest of its nine members. Overall, Sino-Brazilian economic relations remained limited and the potential for bilateral trade at that time was low. The first export of Brazilian sugar to China took place in the early 1970s, mediated by Minister Pratini de Morais, who convinced President Medici that the sale had nothing to do with politics. This was followed by the pioneer mission of Horácio Coimbra of Companhia Cacique de Café Solúvel in 1971 (Duqing 1999).

As the tangible results of the new Sino-Brazilian ties turned out to be very limited, Brazil's relations with Asia in this period were basically restricted to Japan. Since the 1960s, their economic relations significantly increased, as Japan gradually became the second market for Brazilian exports and the third largest investor in Brazil. However, this increase was essentially due to Japanese initiatives and based on complementarity between the two economies: supply of raw materials in return for investments and manufactured products. While Brazil presented itself as an important supplier of raw materials and agricultural commodities, Japan was able to satisfy Brazilian demand for basic industrial and capital goods. Meanwhile, Japan aimed to secure a stable supply of raw materials and to establish itself as an exporter of manufactured products.

During the 1970s, the economic complementarity of Brazil and Japan led to close political relations. Although scholars attribute this new dimension only to Japanese initiatives (Horisaka 1997; Abdenur 1994), Brazilian efforts should be noted as well. In 1976, President Geisel made the first visit to Japan by a Brazilian Head of State, demonstrating Brazil's interest in this bilateral relationship as a d*ependency reducer*. The Japanese investments made in association with Brazilian public corporations indicated a convergence of economic and political interests of the two states. A political similarity was their aim to reduce the preponderant position of the United States in their foreign affairs. Deepening the relations with Japan must thus be interpreted as part of Brazil's foreign policy strategy to turn the country's formerly passive international role into a more active insertion into the international arena. In the 1980s, however, the Japanese-Brazilian complementarities were negatively affected by Brazil's economic crisis,[2] and Japan's new economic interest in China and Southeast Asia, especially since the rise of the Yen in 1985 and the subsequent capital reallocation of Japanese firms.

New Brazilian Interest in Asia since the 1990s

Due to the end of the Cold War and the political and economic changes that took place in the world, Brazil was forced to review its strategy of international insertion and began to prioritise better relations with East Asia. In 1993, during the Itamar Franco administration, Asia was defined as one of the priorities of Brazilian diplomacy, due to its cooperative potential in the fields of science and technology, as well as its significant import and export markets. This new positioning on the part of Brazil reflected a double interest. Firstly, it was motivated by the perspective of an association with a region of the world that presented itself as a model for economic as well as scientific and technological development, with plenty of potential for complementarity and partnership. Secondly, Asia was a region that politically answered to Brazilian needs in terms of bilateral relations and similar positions in multilateral forums, thereby furthering Brazil's agenda of autonomy and partnership diversification. In his inauguration speech on 1 January 1995, President Fernando Henrique Cardoso defined Asia as one of the priorities of his administration's foreign policy. He made official visits to China, Malaysia and Japan during his first administration. During his second term in office, in the early twenty-first century, Cardoso made historic visits to Seoul, Dili and Jakarta, as the first Brazilian Head of State to visit these capitals. Similarly, President Luiz Inácio Lula da Silva, in his inaugural speech on 1 January 2003, stressed the need to strengthen ties with Japan, China and India.

The rebirth of Brazil's relations with Asia since the 1990s had some marked differences to those in previous periods. Firstly, Japan initially remained Brazil's most important partner in the commercial and investment fields, but gradually lost this preponderance to other competitors. Relations with China, South Korea and the Association of Southeast Asian Nations (ASEAN) were improved considerably. These improvements were, however, affected by the Asian crisis, which provoked a drastic reduction in Brazilian exports to Asia. Conversely, Brazilian imports from Asia were not affected and remained at pre-crisis levels. In the case of ASEAN, there was a broadening of trade relations and an attempt to create a direct association with MERCOSUR. Brazil's interest in an ASEAN-MERCOSUR link flowed from its strategy to use regional blocks as instruments in the negotiation process of new international arrangements, and from its attempts at insertion in Asia-Pacific multilateral organisations, especially APEC.[3] When ASEAN's Secretary-General visited Brazil and Argentina in 1997, alternatives were discussed for greater approximation between MERCOSUR and ASEAN. It was concluded that mechanisms should be developed to address the political priorities between the two regions as well as to overcome the mutual lack of information. Based on the perception of a certain distance in the relationship, it was also agreed that the moment was not yet right for the establishment of a Free Trade Area between the two regions.[4]

The Asian crisis and the Brazilian crisis of 1999 have had some contrasting effects on Brazilian-Asian relations. While, on the one hand, theses crises caused a reduction of trade and investment flows, on the other hand, they did give way to some political rapprochement by pointing at the need for multilateral cooperation to deal with the challenges of economic globalisation. Nevertheless, in most analyses the Brazilian-Asian relations tend not to be seen as a priority when compared to Brazil's other international relations and commitments. Although there are real and significant Brazilian interests in the strengthening of political ties and commercial partnerships with Asia, it seems that the means to do so have not yet been defined. And, the relations Brazil initiates are rather reactive to conjunctural factors or to the Asian initiatives.

In 1999, an interesting new interregional mechanism was institutionalised under the name of Forum for East Asia-Latin America Cooperation (FE-ALAC).[5] The Forum is based on an initial proposal from Singapore, and it includes from Asia the ASEAN members as well as Japan, China and South Korea. This initiative aimed at institutionalising a high-level communication channel for political approximation and to implement plans and programs that strengthen economic, political and cultural ties between the two regions. At the first meeting of Ministers of Foreign Affairs, in March 2001, it was decided that FEALAC would 'be defined within the context of globalisation and of the strengthening of relations between different regions of the world and would have the objective of filling a gap in the relationship between Asia and Latin America. The main purpose of this multidimensional inter-regional dialog and cooperation mechanism is to stimulate political dialog, understanding and cooperation' (Fujita 2001: 3). FEALAC has a strong symbolic meaning as it seeks to broaden and deepen relations between Asia and Latin America without the presence of the United States. It shows not only a growing Asian interest in Latin America, but also the willingness of states such as Japan, China and South Korea to participate in this process. One of the incentives for this Asian initiative was the assumption that the proposal for the creation of the Free Trade Area of the Americas (FTAA) would eventually be realised and that this might negatively affect Asian possibilities for insertion in Latin America.

Asian interests increased when Brazil regained its international attractiveness for investment, due to the opening up of its markets and its financial stability, and to the regionally integrated market of MERCOSUR. Related to the struggle for markets and power taking place in the World Trade Organisation (WTO) and other multilateral forums, this interest has been economic as well as politically strategic. Within FEALAC, the new mutual interests have gone beyond the obvious search for trade and political alliances. There was again political will to establish partnerships, not only in the process of the distribution of international power, but also in the struggle for access to markets. As Olivet (2005: 17) points out, the creation of three Working Groups (Economy and Society, Politics and Culture, and Education, Science and Technology) proves that trade and investment are not the only goals of FEALAC. However, FEALAC has so far been of quite limited political and economic relevance when compared to other regional arrangements. Toledo (2005: 23) argues that both regions prioritise their relations with developed countries (Europe and the United States), and they are not willing to face possible hostility from the United States as a reaction to a real strengthening of regional ties. According to Wilhelmy (2007), since its creation FEALAC has not yet taken off and constitutes only a secondary, low profile diplomatic channel, with scarce influence on decisions made by its member states.

The Sino-Brazilian Relations since the 1990s

When Brazil re-established diplomatic relations with the People's Republic of China in 1974, it was diversifying its international partnerships and looking for a more competitive insertion in global markets. However, as mentioned above, at that time Sino-Brazilian relations remained largely limited to the political-diplomatic field, based on similar positions in the international arena. Only during the 1990s, after the opening up of the Brazilian market and China's greater economic insertion, did the two countries start to complement these political relations with initiatives to stimulate bilateral trade.

Considering the potential for the strengthening of their relations in the long-term, the expression *strategic partnership,* coined in 1993 by Chinese Prime Minister Zhu Rongji, has been widely used in both countries. Although its meaning has not clearly been defined (nor any mechanisms for its development), relations between China and Brazil have clearly changed since then. When visiting Brazil in 1995, the high Chinese official Li Ruihuan (Chairman of the National Committee of the Chinese People's Political Consultative Conference) attempted to define the idea of a *strategic partnership:*

> Latin America represents one of the most dynamic regions of the planet in terms of economic development. In the political sphere, the region, particularly Brazil, occupies an important strategic position in the world. Brazil is the largest developing nation in Latin America, and China is the largest developing nation in the world. There are many similarities between the two countries: they both intend to reach economic development and improve the living conditions of their population. Thus, cooperation carries a very significant meaning for both countries, as there is no fundamental conflict of interests. In fact, the two countries are complementary. Therefore, I see a very promising horizon for relations between our two countries, especially in the economic field. (FSP 1995)

In the political sphere, one central issue of both countries' international agenda are their intentions concerning the WTO and the UN. China used its permanent seat in the Security Council to get closer to developing countries, and considered supporting Brazil in its efforts to obtain a permanent seat in the Council.[6] In line with its striving for more adequate rules in international trade and defending the multilateral trade system, Brazil supported China's entry into the WTO, which was realised in 2001. And Brazil and China have been important in redirecting WTO negotiations since 2003 as members of the G20.[7]

Brazil has taken the position that, in spite of its great economic development, China's characteristics and problems are still very similar to those of developing nations, and that in international negotiation processes, China should therefore participate on the side of developing countries. However, in the debate about China's international role, the question has been raised whether China is not, in fact, already an economic world power with international interests that are more similar to those of the developed nations that are represented in the G7. Oviedo (2005b: 48) argues that China's participation in the G20 stems from the need to show leadership over emerging countries without having to participate in the G7 structure, which is lead by the United States.[8] According to Gutiérrez (2003: 43), 'most Brazilian scholars estimate that Brazil and China are both important influence poles in the developing world and deserve to be taken into account in the consideration of the most important issues that affect humanity. For the construction of a new order and a new global architecture in the new millennium, the balanced participation of all important actors is required.' Brazil's official position holds that China remains fragile and vulnerable due to the strong asymmetries in the country and the concentration of its development in coastal areas, and due to the fact that it is still dependent on technology and services. For example, approximately 60 per cent of its exports are produced by foreign companies, which base their research, development, marketing, sales, logistic and distribution departments outside of China. In addition, China is the last stage in the Asian productive chain, which causes it to have an elevated and constant deficit in its commercial relations with Asia.

The strategic partnership between Brazil and China has become more well-defined in the area of technical, scientific and technological cooperation since their joint efforts for the development of remote sensing satellites (China-Brazil Earth Resources Satellite, CBERS). Signed in 1988 and extended in 1995, the CBERS agreement aimed at enabling both countries to become independent in the field of satellite imagery, making it even possible for them to become exporters of such services. The first satellite was launched in 1999 and the second in 2003. Cunha (2004: 79) stresses that this space cooperation project is of special significance for the Chinese government as it represented an instance of South-South cooperation – one of the priorities of Chinese diplomatic action. There is no other such project in the world, neither between developing nations, nor between North and South. A third satellite was launched in 2007 to initiate a new monitoring program of the Amazon rainforest to detect and prevent selective logging (i.e., only the more commercially valuable trees are removed, using the rest of the canopy for cover against satellite detection). The Selective Logging Detection System (DETEX, in Portuguese) is one of the monitoring tools in the Federal Public Forest Concession Program. Sino-Brazilian cooperation is also being extended to other sectors, such as biotechnology, information technology, and development of new materials. In the field of health, joint initiatives are in progress in the struggle against HIV/Aids, the production and sale of generic drugs, Chinese traditional medicine, and in the research for new drugs.

While maintaining the *universal* tendency of Brazil's foreign policy, the administrations of Fernando Henrique Cardoso and Lula have given much attention to the so-called emerging nations, such as China, India, South Africa and Russia. The partnerships with emerging markets involve ample possibilities for the absorption of Brazilian products as well as access to products or investments required by Brazil. In addition, they involve regions with strong political expression, generating expectations for joint action in international organisations. The latter is quite significant considering that, since the end of the Cold War, a process of redefinition and reorganisation of the International System has been in progress, which is marked by a continuous stalemate in the definition of rules that will discipline international trade. In this sense, what is sought is *South-South Cooperation* in order to establish a united front to discuss and defend the relatively common interests of these countries vis-à-vis developed nations. The objective is by no means to form a movement in opposition or in resistance of relations with developed nations. What is desired is a positioning strategy in face of the current state of negotiations in different multilateral forums. The creation of the G20 in 2003 reflected the will to design a new model for South-South cooperation without it being an alternative proposal to relations with the North (the dimension in which countries such as Brazil and even China materialise most of their interests) (Lessa 2004).

China, with its impressive economic growth, represents a great opportunity for the intensification of relations with Brazil in countless areas, from agriculture to manufactured products, from technological cooperation to engineering services, from strategic areas such as steel production and fossil fuels to pharmaceutical patents, among many others that are open to fruitful cooperation. The earlier process of building an atmosphere of mutual trust through joint action in the international sphere, which came to be known as a *strategic partnership*, has also been a favourable factor in recent years toward the greater Brazilian presence in the Chinese market, and it is likely to be so in the near future as well.[9] In the economic field, however, it is clear that Brazil needs China more than China needs Brazil. Brazil's main export to China is soy and Brazil faces great competition in this market, especially from the United States. The US government pressures China to increase its purchases of US soy as a way to reduce the high trade deficit of the United States with China. In this context, the creation of the Brazil-China Business Council,[10] which is gathering important Brazilian and Chinese companies together, is a very positive development. It enables a more coordinated and professional treatment of issues not only in the commercial sphere, but also in the political sphere, by representing the mutual satisfaction of respective national interests.

The strategic partnership between Brazil and China is thus concentrated in two clearly defined fields of action: firstly, scientific and technological cooperation in order to break the monopoly held by developed nations,[11] and secondly, cooperation in the political-strategic field in order to develop joint strategies in international forums. It should be noted that the perspective of a strategic partnership does not apply to commercial relations. On the contrary, China is further inserting itself in the East Asian economic process and has reproduced the region's typical trade pattern with Brazil and South America: manufactured products in exchange for ores and agricultural commodities. In his visit to China in May 2004, President Lula reaffirmed the continuity of joint projects for the construction of satellites and small-sized airplanes (Embraer), and signed fifteen cooperation agreements in the areas of steel, coal, oil and automobile production. Among other things, he signed agreements on the cooperation of Companhia Vale do Rio Doce (CVRD) with the Baosteel Corporation for the production of aluminium; with Baosteel and Yongcheng for coal production; and with the Aluminium Corporation of China for bauxite production. It was agreed to set up a Petrobras office in Beijing (China has shown great interest in the technology developed by Petrobras for deep-sea oil drilling) and to establish a joint venture by Petrobras and Sinopec in other countries, including Africa and the Middle East. In addition, the two countries agreed to negotiate a nuclear cooperation agreement by means of which Brazil would export enriched uranium to China in exchange for the financing of the Brazilian nuclear project (Cornejo 2005: 24–25).

Brazil's official recognition of China as a market economy was a very important step in their relations, but it was more controversial than their strategic partnership. Instead of a transition economy or non-market economy, Brazil as well as Latin American countries, such as Argentina, Chile, Cuba and Venezuela, have recognised China as a market economy in the WTO (see also chapter one). Considered as an inhibiting factor for establishing commercial safeguards in the case of dumping and subsidies, the recognition has generated and is still generating extensive discussion and discord among productive sectors that consider themselves harmed by Chinese competition. The recognition took place during Hu Jintao's visit to South America in November 2004. The first stop on the trip was Brazil, where Hu Jintao stayed for five days. Next were two days in Buenos Aires and Santiago de Chile. Oviedo (2005a) states that China viewed Brazil as the pivotal actor in the process, figuring that the other countries in the region would follow it in the recognition process. Independently of economic or academic considerations, there is no doubt that this decision was essentially political and tied to the concept of *strategic partnership*, through which the possibility of joint action with China in the process of redefinition of the international order is materialised.

Trade Relations since the 1990s

Since the beginning of the 1960s, Brazilian foreign policy has constantly been directed at maintaining diversified trade relations so as to avoid excessive dependence on any single country or region. The objective has been to preserve and enhance the multilateral nature of Brazilian economic insertion. Brazil's recent trade figures show a balanced situation of the country's main partners: the United States, European Union, ALADI (Latin American Integration Association) and Asia. In 2006, 18 per cent of Brazilian exports went to the United States and 22.1 per cent to the European Union. ALADI accounted for 22.8 per cent, Asia for 15.1 per cent, while the rest of the world accounted for 22 per cent. Therefore, all of the main regions of the world are important markets for Brazil (see Tables 2.1 and 2.2).

Table 2.1. Brazilian Exports to Economic Blocs, 1970–2006 (%)

	1970	1980	1985	1990	1995	2000	2001	2002	2003	2004	2005	2006
United States	24.7	17.4	27.1	24.2	18.7	23.9	24.7	25.7	23.1	21.1	19.2	17.8
European Union	34.9	26.6	26.9	32.4	27.8	26.8	25.5	25.0	24.8	25.0	22.4	22.1
ALADI	11.1	17.2	8.7	10.4	21.5	23.4	21.0	16.4	17.7	20.4	21.5	22.8
Mercosul	-	-	-	4.2	13.2	14.0	10.9	5.5	7.8	9.2	9.9	10.2
Africa	2.2	6.5	7.9	3.2	3,4	2.4	3.4	3.9	3.9	4.4	5.1	5.4
Asia	8.3	9.9	12.4	16.9	17.6	11.5	11.9	14.6	16.0	15.1	15.7	15.1
Total in $ billion	2.739	20.132	25.639	31.213	46.506	55.086	58.223	60.362	73.084	94.475	118.308	137.470

Source: Cacex, Secex, MDIC.
Note: The data presented in the Tables and the Figure of this chapter have been gathered by the author from various statistics and reports from Cacex (the Foreign Trade Desk that is part of Brazil's Central Bank), from Secex (Secretariat of Foreign Trade), and from MDIC (Brazil's Ministry of Development, Industry and Commerce).

Table 2.2. Brazilian Imports from Economic Blocs, 1970–2006 (%)

	1970	1980	1985	1990	1995	2000	2001	2002	2003	2004	2005	2006
United States	32.9	17.8	19.8.	21.3	21.1	23.1	23.5	22.1	20.2	18.3	17.5	16.1
European Union	29.5	15.2	14.7	22.3	27.7	25.2	26.7	27.8	28.3	25.4	24.7	22.0
ALADI	10.5	11.7	12.3	17.7	20.0	20.9	18.0	17.4	17.0	16.0	15.7	17.9
Mercosul				11.2	13.7	14.0	12.6	11.9	11.8	10.2	9.6	9.8
Africa	3.1	4.9	13.2	2.8	2.4	5.2	6.9	5.7	6.7	9.8	9.1	8.9
Asia	6.9	6.9	8.6	8.6	16.5	15.4	16.1	16.9	18.5	19.6	22.9	25.0
Total in $ billion	2.849	22.955	13.153	20.650	40.858	55.835	55.581	47.240	48.260	62.782	73.551	91.396

Source: See Table 2.1

Compared to its trade relations with the rest of Asia, Brazil's trade with China has seen a surprisingly high growth rate. While in 2000 Japan received 4.5 per cent and China 2 per cent of Brazilian exports, in 2006, China accounted for 6.1 per cent of Brazilian exports and Japan for 2.8 per cent. As for Brazil's imports, Japan was responsible for 5.5 per cent in 2000 and 4.2 per cent in 2006, while China increased its exports to Brazil from 2.2 per cent to 8.7 per cent during the same period (see Tables 2.3, 2.4, 2.5 and 2.6). In 2005, China became the third main destination of Brazilian exports, while Japan occupied the eighth position and South Korea the seventeenth position. Brazilian imports from these countries are among its top ten: China is number four, Japan number five, and South Korea number nine.

Table 2.3. Share of Asian Economies in Total of Brazilian Exports, 1970–2006 (%)

Year	Japan	China	Great China	ASEAN 5	India	South Korea
1970	5.3		2.0	0.4		0.1
1980	6.1	0.4	0.7	1.0	1.2	0.2
1990	7.5	1.2	3.5	3.3	0.5	1.7
1995	6.7	2.6	4.3	3.4	0.7	1.8
2000	4.5	2.0	3.5	1.7	0.4	1.1
2001	3.4	3.3	4.6	1.5	0.5	1.3
2002	3.5	4.2	5.8	2.5	1.1	1.4
2003	3.2	6.2	8.1	1.9	0.8	1.7
2004	2.9	5.6	7.3	2.2	0.7	1.5
2005	2.9	5.8	7.2	2.4	1.0	1.6
2006	2.8	6.1	7.4	2.2	0.7	1.4

Source: See Table 2.1

Table 2.4. Share of Asian Economies in Total of Brazilian Imports, 1970–2006 (%)

Year	Japan	China	Great China	ASEAN 5	India	South Korea
1970	6.2		0.3	0.2		
1980	4.7	1.1	1.2	0.8		
1990	6.0	0.6	1.4	0.7		0.3
1995	6.6	2.1	4.4	2.2	0.3	2.7
2000	5.3	2.2	4.3	2.4	0.5	2.6
2001	5.5	2.4	4.3	2.2	1.0	2.8
2002	5.0	3.3	5.4	2.9	1.2	2.3
2003	5.2	4.5	6.3	3.5	1.0	2.2
2004	4.6	5.9	8.0	3.1	0.9	2.8
2005	4.6	7.3	9.6	3.7	1.6	3.2
2006	4.2	8.7	11.4	4.2	1.6	3.4

Source: See Table 2.1

Table 2.5 Brazilian Exports to Asia as Share of its Total Exports, 1970–2006 (%)

Year	Japan	China	Great China	ASEAN 5	India	South Korea
1970	64.1	0.6	24.6	5.3	0.3	0.8
1980	62.0	3.6	6.9	10.6	12.4	1.9
1990	44.6	7.3	20.6	19.7	3.2	10.3
1995	37.9	14.7	24.6	19.5	3.9	10.1
2000	39.1	17.2	30.3	14.4	3.4	9.2
2001	28.6	27.4	38.6	12.7	4.1	10.6
2002	23.9	28.7	39.6	16.9	7.4	9.7
2003	19.8	38.8	50.7	12.2	4.7	10.5
2004	19.0	37.4	48.3	14.6	4.5	9.8
2005	18.7	36.8	46.1	15.5	6.1	10.2
2006	18.7	40.4	49.0	14.8	4.5	9.4

Source: See Table 2.1

Table 2.6 Brazilian Imports from Asia as Share of its Total Imports, 1970–2006 (%)

Year	Japan	China	Great China	ASEAN 5	India	South Korea
1970	90.8		3.9	3.6	0.2	
1980	68.1	15.6	17.3	11.8	0.1	0.2
1990	70.1	6.7	16.3	7.7	0.5	3.4
1995	40.0	12.5	26.7	13.6	2.0	16.2
2000	34.4	14.2	28.0	15.7	3.2	16.6
2001	34.4	14.9	27.1	13.7	6.1	17.7
2002	29.4	19.4	31.8	17.0	7.2	13.3
2003	28.2	24.1	34.2	18.8	5.4	12.1
2004	23.4	30.2	41.0	16.0	4.5	14.1
2005	20.2	31.7	41.9	16.1	7.1	13.8
2006	16.8	34.9	45.5	16.7	6.4	13.6

Source: See Table 2.1

Brazil has by and large a similar pattern of trade with Asian countries in which Brazil serves as a strong supplier of raw materials, especially ores and agricultural commodities, and as a consumer of manufactured products. China, Japan and South Korea are important importers of Brazilian iron ore and its concentrates, iron and steel products, as well as soy grain and soy oil. Japan is also a major destination for aluminium, and in recent years, for poultry. While in 2006 commodities made up 29.3 per cent of total Brazilian exports, 58.7 per cent of these exports went to Asia. Several Asian countries import great quantities of commodities, but China's demand is the highest of all. As for Brazil's imports from Asia, they consist mainly of electronic products, manufactured products, and heavy machinery. The recent increase in Chinese imports has provoked strong internal pressure in Brazil, especially in the textile and toy sectors. Although they represent only a small part of its total imports, they are labour intensive sectors that affect many domestic jobs, and therefore are a politically delicate issue within Brazil. The growing pressure for the imposition of safeguards or antidumping rights against China has come mainly from the Sao Paulo Industry Federation (Federação das Indústrias de Sao Paulo, FIESP). According to Barbosa and Mendes (2006: 9):

> The Lula Administration has allies in their foreign policy towards China in the form of a number of companies with commercial interests in that market, mostly basic product-exporting sectors such as meat, vegetable oil, food, wood, coffee, and pulp, as well as banks operating in international trade, transport and trading companies. For this group of companies, the demand led by FIESP and the textile industry to regulate safeguards may overburden bilateral relations, eventually hampering their Chinese market operations. This group of companies has formed the Brazil-China Business Council, which not only advocates their interests to Brazilian and Chinese authorities but has also been promoting a positive agenda that tries to enhance the profile of economic relations between both parties.

Brazil has imposed antidumping measures on China since the 1990s. As of September 2007, 18 measures were in place. Shixue (2003: 322) considers this practice to be an obstacle for the strengthening of ties between the two countries.[12] In order to satisfy the demands of domestic producers who claimed losses due to Chinese products entering the country at very low prices, in June of 2007, Brazil decided to raise import taxes on different products imported from China: speakers, hairbrushes, clothes irons and table fans, among other things. Meanwhile, in MERCOSUR, member states approved a raise in the Common External Tariff for textiles, garments and shoes, with the objective of restricting Chinese imports of such products.

Brazil has made great efforts to diversify its exports to China and even to make productive investments in the country. In 1995, Embraco, a producer of compressors who has been exporting products to China since 1986, was the first Brazilian company to form a joint venture with the Chinese government, creating the Beijing Embraco Snowflake Compressor Company. The most symbolic cases, however, are those of Companhia Vale do Rio Doce (CVRD) and Embraer. Since 2001, CVRD has been one of the main suppliers of ores to China. It has formed various partnerships for the construction of an iron ore beneficiation plant in China; for the production of steel and aluminium, together with Baosteel; for the production of coal with Baosteel and Yongcheng; and for the production of bauxite in association with the Aluminium Corporation of China (CHINALCO). These Chinese companies are all state-owned.

As for Embraer, producer of regional commercial jets, it has established a partnership with the Harbin Aircraft and Hafei Aviation Industries, both controlled by the China Aviation Industry Corporation II (AVIC II), for the production of the Embraer RJ 145 regional jet, for 50 passengers, in Harbin. The first aircraft produced by Embraer in China made its maiden flight test in December 2003. As this partnership did not generate the results initially expected by the Brazilian government, a certain malaise within the Sino-Brazilian relationship developed. However, tensions were practically overcome when the President of China's National Assembly visited Brazil, in August of 2006, with contracts for the acquisition by HNA Airlines of fifty ERJ 190s produced by Embraer in Brazil, and fifty ERJ 145s made by the joint venture Harbin Embraer Aircraft Industry (HEAI) in the city of Harbin (China). According to some analysts, the Chinese decision to order one hundred aircraft from Embraer with an estimated value of $2.7 billion was a reaction to pressures from Embraer and the Brazilian government, who expected China to honour the promise of making significant orders to Embraer in exchange for the construction of a factory in Chinese territory, in a joint-venture with a local company. However, the Chinese order could also be part of a deal in the process of Brazil's recognition of China as a market economy. In this case, the aircraft purchase from Embraer will probably be followed by renewed Chinese pressure on Brazil to actually define the parameters of its recognition of China as a market economy since Brazil has been slow to do (arguing that China has committed itself to a wider agenda including investment and the removal of trade barriers to products such as meat).

Conclusions

The Sino-Brazilian relations have always been seen as highly promising due to various complementarities in the economic sphere, and the long-term existence in both countries of a genuine political will to establish cooperation, not only bilaterally, but also multilaterally. Mann (2005: 132) considers that 'in the Chinese leaders' opinion, cooperation generates world peace and development and thus represents the appropriate means to achieve national and international goals. To sum up, cooperation, central to Chinese foreign policymaking, functions as a means to obtain certain benefits and to strengthen the country's position in the international system.' For Brazil, cooperation offers similar benefits. Brazil's relations with East Asia as a whole, and specifically with China, are part of its strategies of both economic and political international insertion.

There is, however, reason for concern over the complementarity and mutual interests in the Sino-Brazilian relations. As a result of its economic, political and strategic role in the present international context, China might start to consider its partnership with Brazil as less important. In this sense, the following two questions require serious attention and systematic examination. Firstly, is the Chinese economic boom giving way to new, more competitive relations rather than cooperative relations with Brazil? And secondly, if China, with its successful development plans and international insertion, is benefiting from the present international order, is there any real interest on its part in making structural changes to the current international status quo? This second question may be less important if we consider that the present concept of South-South cooperation is not the same as it was during the Cold War. Nowadays, this cooperation is selective and hierarchical, involving emerging economies that are not so much aimed at structural changes in the international order, but rather are aimed at reforming the rules of the game so as to promote their respective interests.

There is no doubt that part of the Brazilian population feels a certain disillusion and scepticism toward the Sino-Brazilian relationship. The press continually taps on this dissatisfaction, emphasising images of a 'Chinese threat', the need for safeguards, and the naiveté of Brazil's recognition of China as a market economy. The possibilities of technological cooperation are also beginning to be questioned, due to the fact that China has increasingly better means of investment than Brazil. And even the political partnership has been criticised in Brazil due to China's non-explicit support of Brazilian interests, be it in the struggle for reform of the United Nations Security Council or in the WTO's never ending Doha Round. It is clear that China's development and insertion process had, and still has, the final objective of guaranteeing the full and independent economic survival of the Chinese State and the Communist Party. To achieve this goal, China makes no compromise. It is similarly evident that the success of the Chinese economic model depends on its acceptance of the rules of the international game. However, those rules are not immutable. On the contrary, they are the result of a long negotiation process and that is why it is crucial for China to participate in the various negotiation forums and seek support for their initiatives.

With respect to the perception of political interests and the disputes with major powers, China considers its development directly to depend upon the confrontation between the United States, the European Union and Japan. This Chinese perspective points at an apparent contradiction between a strong China and a fragile and vulnerable China, and especially the contradiction between a China that wishes to maintain its autonomy and a China that is depending on the international system. This vulnerability and dependence support the idea that Sino-Brazilian relations have been and continue to be based on a mutual perception of the strategic importance of South-South cooperation. Despite the major relevance that China has taken on in recent years, especially after its entry into the WTO, the country still has many problems that prevent it from effectively being considered a consolidated world power. It faces the challenge to extend its economic growth to other regions than the coastline, provide for fairer income distribution and include the peasant population in the domestic development process. In addition, there are also huge problems with the supply of electricity and water, the lack of a social security policy, environmental degradation, real estate speculation, counterfeiting, smuggling and corruption. And in the international sphere, China struggles with the problems that arise from maintaining a socialist state ruled by a communist party, and from human rights issues and child labour, among others.

The political will to develop mechanisms that will enable the formation of mutually more advantageous Sino-Brazilian partnerships still exists. China sees Brazil as a strategic partner in the process of redefining the international order, as both countries are still considered to be intermediate powers. Thus, political and technological partnerships, especially in the multilateral sphere, are crucial. This corresponds plainly to Brazil's negotiation strategy for its place in the international system and is based on the principle that despite their differences, the emerging nations of the South all suffer from a system that prioritises northern countries, and so consequently they must act together in order to increase the opportunities for the South. This explains the current Brazilian emphasis on its partnership with the People's Republic of China, be it under the name of South-South cooperation or of Strategic Partnership.

References

Abdenur, Roberto. 1994. 'O Brasil e a nova realidade asiática: uma estratégia de aproximação'. *Política Externa*, 2 (3): 43–69.

Barbosa, Alexandre de Freitas and Ricardo Mendes. 2006. 'Economic Relations between Brazil and China: A Difficult Partnership'. FES, Briefing Paper January. http://www.fes-globalization.org/dog_publications/information.htm (accessed 9 September 2007).

Cornejo, Romer. 2005. 'América Latina ante el crecimiento económico de China'. Paper presented at VI REDEALAP, Buenos Aires, BID-Intal, October. http://www.iadb.org/intal/aplicaciones/uploads/ponencias/Foro_REDEALAP_2005_16_Cornejo (accessed 14 September 2006).

Cunha, Lílian Fernandes. 2004. *Em busca de um modelo de cooperação Sul-Sul - o caso da área espacial nas relações entre o Brasil e a República Popular da China (1980–2003)*. Brasília: Universidade de Brasília (Dissertação de Mestrado).

Duqing, Chen. 1999. 'Os 25 anos das relações sino-brasileiras'. *Tempo Brasileiro*, 137: 9–29.

FSP. 1995. 'Dirigente chinês quer aproximação com Brasil'. *Folha de Sao Paulo*, 17.06.1995.

Fujita, Edmundo. 2001. 'Fórum de Cooperação América Latina-Ásia do Leste. Primeira Reunião de Chanceleres (Santiago-Março de 2001)'. *Carta Internacional*, IX (98): 3.

Gutiérrez B, Hernán. 2003. *Oportunidades y desafios de los vínculos económicos de China y América Latina y el Caribe*. CEPAL Serie Comercio Internacional, no. 42. Santiago de Chile: CEPAL.

Horisaka, Kotaro. 1997. 'A Alvorada das Relações Econômicas Nipo-Brasileiras'. In *Fragmentos sobre as Relações Nipo-Brasileiras no Pós-Guerra*, org. Paulo Yokota, 55–78. Rio de Janeiro: Topbooks.

Lessa, Antônio Carlos. 2004. *Balanço do primeiro ano do governo Lula.* Brasília: Correio Internacional, RELNET. http://www.relnet.com.br (accessed 6 August 2005).

Mann, Stefanie. 2002. *Discovery of a Terra Incognita: five decades of Chinese foreign policy towards Latin America.* Mainz: Institut für Politikwissenschaft (Dokument und Materialien nr. 31).

———. 2005. 'China and Latin America'. In *Latin America and East Asia—Attempts and Diversification*, eds. Jörg Faust, Manfred Mols, and Kim Won-Ho, 129–46. Seoul/Korea: KIEP; Münster/Deutschland: LIT Verlag.

Oliveira, Henrique Altemani. 1987. *Política Externa Brasileira e as Relações Comerciais Brasil-África.* Sao Paulo: Universidade de Sao Paulo (Tese de Doutorado).

Olivet, Maria Cecília. 2005. 'Unravelling Interregionalism Theory: A Critical Analysis of the new Interregional Relations between Latin America and East Asia'. Paper presented at the VI Reunión de la Red de Estudios de América Latina y el Caribe sobre Asia-Pacifico (REDE-ALAP), Buenos Aires, BID-Intal. http://www.iadb.org/intal/aplicaciones/uploads/ponencias/Foro_REDEALAP_2005_16_Olivet.pdf (accessed 14 September 2006).

Oviedo, Eduardo Daniel. 2005a. 'Crisis del Multilateralismo y Auge de la Diplomacia Bilateral em la Relación Mercosur-China'. Paper presented at the VI Reunión de la Red de Estudios de América Latina y el Caribe sobre Asia-Pacifico (REDEALAP), Buenos Aires, BID-Intal, October. http://www.iadb.org/intal/aplicaciones/uploads/ponencias/Foro_REDEALAP_2005_16_Oviedo.pdf (accessed 12 September 2006).

———. 2005b. *China en Expansión.* Córdoba: Universidad Católica de Córdoba.

Severino, Rodolfo. 1998. 'Forging ASEAN-Mercosur Ties'. *Carta Internacional*, 60 (2).

Shang, Deliang. 2003. 'Cooperação política entre China e Brasil versus multipolarização'. In *Brasil e China: Multipolaridade*, comp. Samuel Pinheiro Guimarã, 291–308. Brasília: IPRI-FUNAG.

Shixue, Jiang. 2003. 'China, Latin America, and the Developing World'. In Peter H. Smith, Kotaro Horisaka, and Shoji Nishijima, *East Asia and Latin America: The unlikely alliance*, 311–31. Langham: Rowman & Littlefield Publishers.

da Silva, Luiz Inácio Lula. 2003. Speech at the opening ceremony of the Brazil–China Seminar: A Necessary Leap, BNDES, Rio de Janeiro, 30 April, Palavra Internacional do Brasil. http://www.relnet.com.br (accessed 25 March 2005).

Toledo, Ana Manuela. 2005. *Seguimiento y Monitoreo de las actividades de Foros de Cooperación establecidos entre países de Asia- Pacífico, Europa y América Latina.* Informe Número III, REDEALAP, Buenos Aires.

Wilhelmy, Manfred. 2007. 'FOCALAE: Interrogantes hacia el futuro'. Academic Seminar of the FEALAC III Ministerial Meeting, 20 August, Itamaraty Palace, Brasília. http://www.funag.gov.br (accessed 10 September 2007).

Notes

1. The *Independent Foreign Policy*, implemented during the early 1960s, constituted an attempt to implement an autonomous policy aimed at the promotion of real Brazilian interests. The term 'autonomy' was an opposition to the notion of automatic alignment with the United States, which previously had been dominant. The *Independent Foreign Policy* was to broaden Brazil's economic and political partnerships and to further its ties to developing nations in order to jointly defend their common interests.

2. One important consequence of the Brazilian crisis was the *decasségui* phenomenon, a migratory flux of descendants of Japanese immigrants to Brazil who returned to Japan in search of work, creating a significant capital flow from Japan to Brazil in the 1990s.

3. At the time, Mexico, Chile and Peru were being admitted into the Asia-Pacific Economic Cooperation forum (APEC). However, Brazil and Argentina, not being located on the

Pacific Rim, were not able to demand direct association. This explains Brazil's strategy of approaching these multilateral organizations through ASEAN.

4. After his visit to Brazil and Argentina, the then Secretary-General of ASEAN, Rodolfo Severino, wrote an article on the possibilities for MERCOSUR–ASEAN associations, which was published in Brazil (Severino 1998).

5. FEALAC had its inaugural meeting in September 1999, in Singapore. The second Senior Official Meeting took place in August 2000 in Santiago de Chile, followed, in October 2000 by the first academic meeting. In March 2001, the first meeting of Ministers of Foreign Affairs was held. Even if FEALAC has not been able to motivate the various actors on both sides, it remains as an institution aimed at working for closer relations between Asia and Latin America.

6. However, the attempt made in 2005 by Germany, Brazil, India and Japan (the so-called G4) was strongly opposed by China. This Chinese opposition did not refer directly to Brazil, but to Japan and India. Additionally, there are now doubts on whether China will support any reform of the UNSC at all.

7. The G20 is a group of developing nations formed on 20 August 2003, during the final phase of preparation for the V Ministerial Conference of the WTO, held in Cancun, from 10 to 14 September 2003. The group focuses its action on agriculture, the central issue of the Doha Development Agenda. The G20 has vast and equally distributed geographical representation, being presently composed of 21 members: five in Africa (South Africa, Egypt, Nigeria, Tanzania and Zimbabwe), six in Asia (China, Philippines, India, Indonesia, Pakistan and Thailand), and ten in Latin America (Argentina, Bolivia, Brazil, Chile, Cuba, Guatemala, Mexico, Paraguay, Uruguay and Venezuela).

8. A low profile and prudent politics seem to be the strategy proposed by the theory of the Three Worlds, even if this results in an outcome that turns out to be obsolete for Chinese purposes: a supposed alliance against the major powers. However, in fact, China decides not to take part in the Group due to its low impact on the decision making process and to the fact that it is afraid to be criticized for what it now is: a new partner to the northern powers. In this way, China maintains its image of developing country and, at the same time, begins to demand greater participation in the multilateral organizations of which it is part: IMF, World Bank, WTO, and, especially, the United Nations. (Oviedo 2005b: 48)

9. After examining the history of cooperation between Brazil and China, Shang Deliang (2003: 307), in a speculative analysis, aimed at predicting the future of the strategic partnership in the twenty-first century and stated that:

    The leaders of both countries should keep up their contacts, continue frank, deep-going political dialogues, seek common ground on major issues while reserving differences on minor ones so as to increase mutual trust. Within international organizations, China and Brazil should consult more with each other over international affairs. In respect to the political and economic problems existing in the bilateral relations, China and Brazil should appropriately make the choice between the immediate interests and the long-term interests. As to the questions that have instant benefits but harm to the state-to-state relations in the long run, one must think twice before acting.

10. The Brazil-China Business Council was founded in 2004, during the visit of President Luiz Inácio Lula da Silva to China, by 45 Brazilian and Chinese companies. From 2004 to 2006, the Brazilian section of the Council expanded its action around three main axles: relations with the Brazilian and Chinese governments in favour of the interests of the members of the Council, the spreading of high level information on China and Brazil, and institutional support for the realization of business between the two countries.

11. It should be noted that the present Chinese competitiveness is concentrated on labour-intensive consumer goods (electric and electronic equipment, home utilities, clothing, textiles, and shoes), and that 'Made in China' labels hide the fact that China is the last link in

the Asian chain of production. This explains China's positive trade balance with the West and its trade deficits with East Asian countries.

12. According to Shixue (2003: 322), 'in recent years, the use of antidumping measures seems to have added another obstacle to the development of Sino-Latin American economic relations. On 15 April 1993, Mexico decided to levy antidumping tariffs on ten categories of imports from China. This was the first action ever taken in Latin America to limit Chinese exports. Since then Argentina, Brazil, Chile, Colombia, Ecuador, and Venezuela have all employed this trade practice against China.'

3 Mexico vs. China
The Troublesome Politics of Competitiveness
Barbara Hogenboom

For most developing countries, neoliberal globalisation has proven to involve a series of powerful processes that cause an ongoing flow of drastic and
swift changes. Mexico is no exception to this tendency. In the early 1990s,
when Mexico and the United States were negotiating the North American
Free Trade Agreement (NAFTA), there were serious US concerns about the
'sucking sound' from Mexico: labour unions and others feared that opening
the border with Mexico would come at the cost of extensive US job losses
due to cheap Mexican labour. Less than a decade later, however, Mexico itself
started to experience a 'sucking sound', in this case from China. Both in its
national market and in its almost singular export market (the United States),
Mexican products are facing fierce competition from Chinese products, and
Mexico is losing out in several important sectors.

While most Latin American countries have gained from its economic
rise, China's competition in trade and investment has been hitting Mexico
extremely hard, especially since China's accession into the WTO in 2001.
Mexico's foremost problem is Chinese competition in manufacturing, which
is both a problem of trade and of foreign investment. Mexico is the country
with the largest trade deficit with China, and due to massive Mexican imports
of Chinese goods, China became Mexico's second largest trade partner in
2003. The negative 'China effect' on Mexico, which is one of the most open
economies in the region, has been particularly clear in Mexico's production
of manufactured (assembly) goods for the local market and for export to the
United States. Despite Mexico's advantages as neighbouring on the United
States and being in the North American Free Trade Area, in 2002, China
replaced Mexico as the second largest exporter to the US market. Although
China has also been going through a profound process of economic liberalisation, unlike Mexico, its successes as 'champion of globalisation' are not
based on free market principles alone, but instead on a particular kind of
mixed economy in which a strong state plays an active and intervening role
in the economy (see chapter one). Next to the negative effects of China's
successes on Mexico, this new reality indicates that Mexico's neoliberal economic model, with privatisation and regional integration as central elements,
may be part of the problem. In fact, Mexico could probably learn a few things

from China with respect to stimulating specific industrial sectors and enhancing their insertion in global (rather than only North American) markets.

The substantial damage of China's success on the Mexican economy has been triggering a renewed debate on Mexico's competitiveness. Evidently, China is only part of Mexico's problems with global competition. From 1998 to 2004, Mexico went down from position 34 to position 48 in the competitiveness rankings of the World Economic Forum (WEF). How is it possible to exploit Mexico's comparative advantages in globalising production and markets? And how can its levels of productivity be raised? In this debate, a large number of issues are raised: macro-economic stability, the cost of labour and energy, infrastructure, education, problems of corruption and illegal imports and markets, rule of law, tax system, financial sector, monopolies, research and technology, and more. While these are all important issues, the analysis here will approach Mexico's 'China problem' and the debate about competitiveness from the political and economic perspective of its neoliberalisation since the 1980s. As in most of Latin America, and many other parts of the world, after more than twenty years of neoliberal policies, Mexico has experienced that the economic growth based on free market principles is lower and more volatile than anticipated, and it is unsuccessful in producing the kind of social progress Keynesian policies did before. This shows, above all, in employment: liberalisation and privatisation resulted in a wide and structural gap between formal jobs and employable persons. Almost half of Mexico's population employs one or several informal economic activities, and some forty per cent of GDP is in this informal sector. Two decades of neoliberalisation in Mexico (as in other developing countries) have shown that marginalisation and modernisation can go hand in hand, or rather, can be two sides of the same coin.

For those who do not accept this destructive form of 'development', the predominant question is how to further genuine (sustainable, equitable and pro-poor) development in a context of global competition. Since the end of the 1990s (triggered by the financial crises and contagion in Latin America and Asia), this question has fed renewed scholarly and political debates on the role of the state in economic development. This development debate can be summarised as a search for new balance: between the private sector and the public sector; within the private sector, between the large, transnationalised companies and the rest; and within society, between the social gains and costs (or winners and losers) of global competition.

This chapter starts with a discussion of Mexico's troubled development and its struggle to counter its decreasing competitiveness under global neoliberalisation. The policies as of the mid 1980s to modernise Mexico through some kind of three-stage rocket of liberalisation-regionalisation-democratisation have not reached their proclaimed goals. The negative economic effects as well as the future threats of China's rise on Mexico are a clear indication that Mexico is in trouble. What are the causes of this trouble? And why has so little been done to tackle them? To answer these questions, we will first briefly review how Mexico is affected by China's economic growth and integration in the world market. Then, we will analyse how and why regionalisation and privatisation were central to Mexico's neoliberal programme, resulting in an even larger economic dependency on the United States than before, and internally resulting in an economy of privileges. Finally, we will look into the debate on China and Mexico's competitiveness, and the lack of Mexican policies toward this troublesome South-South competition.[1]

The China Factor in Mexico's Weakening Competitiveness

While by the late 1990s, most Latin American governments had agreed to China's entry into the WTO by granting it the status of most favoured nation, Mexico had not. As the last country to put terms on its entry, Mexico bilaterally negotiated with China until three months before its WTO accession in December of 2001. These long negotiations had mostly to do with Mexican concerns about the strong Chinese competition on the US market of labour intensive products. While its exports were already mainly directed toward the United States, Mexico's trade dependency further increased with its entry into the NAFTA in 1994. Since that time, around 90 per cent of Mexican exports are for the US market. Fearing major problems with unfair Chinese trade competition, Mexican entrepreneurs strongly criticised the bilateral WTO negotiations with China and demanded a clause that for two decades would deny China the right to call for WTO mechanisms of dispute settlement in case Mexico was to apply compensatory and protective tariffs against Chinese products. In the final accords, however, their demand for a guarantee against unfair competition was watered down to a arrangement according to which Mexico was allowed to apply compensation tariffs ranging from 800 to 1000 per cent on Chinese products in the sectors of tools, toys and textiles, but only until 2008 (cf. Dussel Peters 2003).[2]

China's entry into the WTO was generally expected to give way to increased flows of foreign direct investment to China and deepened regional integration in Asia, with Mexico ending up as Latin America's main loser in GDP and exports. Mexican concerns were based on previous experiences with Chinese competition for local markets, export markets and foreign direct investment. For instance, during the global boom of foreign direct investment (FDI) in the late 1990s, Mexico would have attracted more foreign investment if it were not for China 'sucking away' global capital. It has been calculated that from 1995 to 2001, a $100 million increase of Chinese inward FDI reduced Mexican inward FDI by $29 million. Next to its cheap labour, China is very attractive for foreign investors because of the size of its internal market (Dussel Peters 2003; ECLAC 2004; García-Herrero and Santabárbara 2005).

Since 2001, Mexican concerns for negative trade effects of China's competitive force have been proven right. Bilateral trade has only become more unbalanced. While Mexico is exporting some goods such as cement, cotton, drinks (beer and tequila) and food to China, Chinese exports to Mexico are much larger. As Table 3.1 shows, in 2007 Mexican exports to China were valued at $1,895 million, while Chinese imports to Mexico totalled $29,792 million, which is almost sixteen times as much. In effect, Mexico's trade deficit with China was $28,897 million. Car parts and electronics are two important categories of goods in which massive flows of Chinese products enter Mexico. Since 2003, China is Mexico's second source of imports, accounting for 5.5 per cent of Mexico's total imports; although this is substantial, it is less than a tenth of Mexico's imports from its largest trade partner, the United States. However, these figures are without the large flows of illegal imports from China. For instance, an estimated 58 per cent of garment consumption in Mexico is of illegally imported products, mostly from China and some other Asian countries.[3] Mexico's trade deficit with China contrasts with the surpluses of resource-rich Latin American countries that have benefited from China's growing demand for energy, minerals and other primary commodities. Mexico exports some copper and other minerals to China, but predominantly exports electronics and auto parts. In 2004, China's Latin American

Table 3.1. Mexico's Export to China and Import from China, 1998–2007
(in US$ millions)

Year	Export	Import
1998	192	1,615
1999	126	1,920
2000	217	2,880
2001	385	4,027
2002	654	6,274
2003	874	9,400
2004	474	14,373
2005	1,136	17,696
2006	1,688	24,438
2007	1,895	29,792

Source: UN Comtrade (2009)

imports valued $21.7 billion – four times more than in 2000 – of which 40 per cent came from Brazil, 17 per cent from Chile, 15 per cent from Argentina, and only 10 per cent from Mexico. Chinese demand for commodities has pushed up prices at the world market and gives occasion to Chinese direct investment, but the first is not beneficial to Mexico and the latter is hardly seen there (ECLAC 2005b; Fernández Jilberto and Hogenboom 2007).

Even more worrisome for Mexico is China's strong trade competition in export manufacturing. Figure 3.1 demonstrates that until 2001, US imports from Mexico were higher than from China, and that this pattern changed structurally after China's WTO membership by the end of 2001. In 2003, China replaced Mexico as the number two source of imports of the United States (after Canada),[4] and since then the ongoing growth of Chinese imports has created an ever larger gap between China and Mexico in the US market. China is competing in twelve of Mexico's twenty main export sectors to the United States, such as textiles, footwear and clothing, as well as industrial machinery, televisions and video players. And China's WTO membership reduced the NAFTA-based preferential advantages of Mexico in the United States.

As of the late 1980s, Mexico has been concentrating its exports in chains of global subcontracting (outsourcing) for the US market, but since the late 1990s, China has swiftly been replacing Mexico on several points of these global production chains. For instance, in 2003, China took over Mexico's primary position in the US market of processors, equalling a loss of 21,000 jobs and $500 million investments. Due to the similarities between Mexico's and China's technological trade development, there is a very negative 'China effect' on Mexico's export manufacturing. Mexico is the manufacturing giant of Latin America, exporting more manufactured products than the rest of the region's 17 countries altogether (respectively 3 and 1.9 per cent of world market share in 2002). Between 1985 and 2000, Mexico's exports of medium and high technological level rose from 28 per cent to as much as 64 per cent of total exports, which is even higher than the average share in industrialised countries. Simultaneously, in China this share increased from 10 per cent to almost 40 per cent. However, since then Mexico's main non-oil exports are losing dynamism (Dussel Peters 2005; ECLAC 2004; *La Jornada* 9 May 2005; Gallagher, Moreno-Brid and Porzecanski 2008).

Figure 3.1. US Imports from Mexico and China, 1998–2007
(in US$ millions)

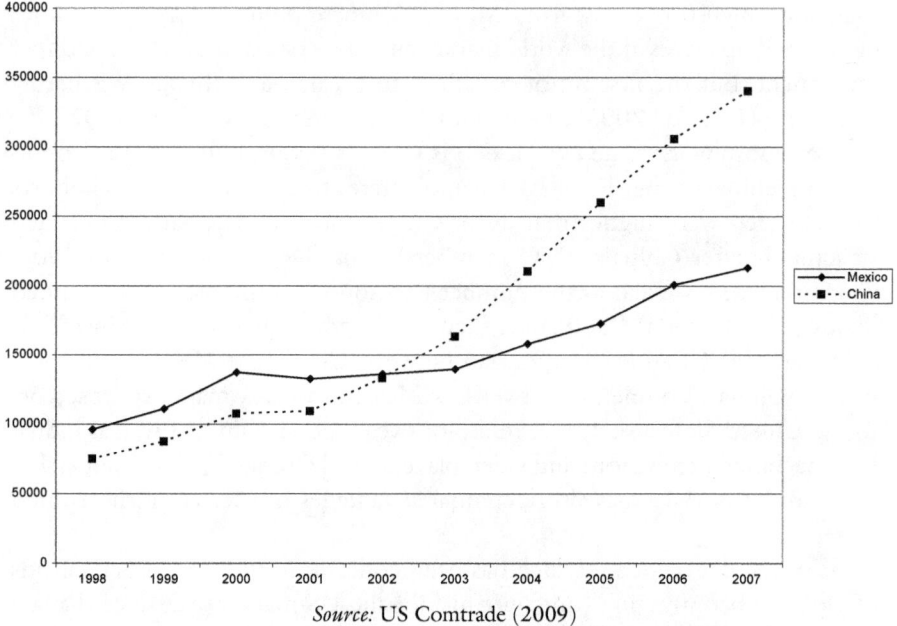

Source: US Comtrade (2009)

Cheap Chinese products (low prices) and aggressive Chinese policies to attract foreign investments have caused a process of industrial South-South delocalisation that particularly harms Mexico's *maquiladora* (assembly) industry – one of its most important export manufacturing sectors. One globalised sector in which China's successes are strongly affecting Mexican manufacturing is the production chain from yarn to textile to garment, as research by Enrique Dussel Peters (2005) shows. This sector in Mexico is concentrated in a few products that are by and large (95 per cent) made for the US market, whereas China produces everything for a large number of markets, including one-third for US consumers. In the period of 2000–2003, the growing Chinese textile and garment exports to the United States came at the cost of Mexico's *maquiladoras*. Despite US policies of limited taxation favouring imports from Mexico as well as Central America and the Caribbean, China has become the world's number one in the chain of yarn to textile to garment. Its textile capacity is ten times bigger than Mexico's, and in terms of jobs, its chain is almost forty times bigger than that of Mexico. This chain is an important motor of China's industrialisation and in 2000, it had 18,900 companies with 13 million workers producing exports valued at $52 billion. In China, the yarn to textile to garment chain has been stimulated by a mix of economic liberalisation and high state subsidies, resulting in a coordination of companies based on public-private interests (Dussel Peters 2005).

Computers are another important export product for Mexico in which China is a direct competitor. The production chain of personal computers is very globalised and capital intensive, with a high degree of innovation and diversification, and a widespread transfer of segments of production. Since the 1990s, Asia has turned into a massive regional export platform of PCs, and China has become the world's number one in PC assembly. While 90 per cent of the PCs produced in Mexico go to United States, China is increasingly replacing Mexico in this market. Since 1984, Chinese exports and the number of companies are growing as a result of government policies that promote high-tech innovation. China's five year development plan for 2001–2005 considered the high-tech sector as strategic, focussing public sector efforts on stimulating industry, higher education and high-tech industrial parks, and providing a series of funds, credits and tax advantages (Dussel Peters 2005).[5]

Transnational companies play a central role in this South-South competition for export production (as will be further discussed below). Both in Mexico and in China, US and European transnational companies (TNCs) are dominating the global production chains, and their investments are crucial for industrialisation. China's integration in the world market has generally pushed prices of manufactures down, which is a problem for Mexico if it continues to specialise in export production based on cheap labour. From 2000 to 2003, Mexico's *maquiladora* sector experienced a major crisis that caused it to shrink to about 20 per cent. Investment in the sector dropped and almost 230,000 jobs were lost. Several large transnational companies moved production facilities away, including technological plants of NEC, ON Semiconductor, Sony and Kodak. One third of the production that left Mexico moved to China (ECLAC 2004).

Recently, there has been some Chinese direct investment in Mexico, but generally Mexico has failed to take advantage of the rise of China. FDI from China comes in the (indirect) form of mergers or acquisitions of Chinese companies with TNCs having production facilities in Mexico. In 2003, the Chinese company TCL established a joint venture with the French transnational company Thomson, which was producing televisions in Mexico. Through the new company TCL-Thomson Electronics, of which two-thirds are controlled by TCL, there is Chinese investment in a Mexican assembly production for the US market. Thus, this Chinese company has opted to profit from Mexico's comparative advantages of being close to the United States and is producing within the North American Free Trade Area. Such Chinese investment in Mexico, however, is still rather exceptional.

Amazingly, instead of developing strategies to deal with these threats and opportunities, both the Mexican state and Mexico's private sector have turned a blind eye to China. Enrique Dussel Peters (2007: 17) points at the extreme weakness of the Mexico-China trade and FDI data of Mexican official sources, the overall lack of information and analysis on these bilateral economic relations within the Mexican private sector, and the non-existence of a single publication by Mexico's public sector on the issue. After a region wide comparison, José Luis León (2005) concludes that Mexico's state policies to take advantage of China's growth have been the weakest of all of Latin America.

Neoliberalism *à la Mexicana*: NAFTA and Economic Concentration

Mexico's economic liberalisation was started before its political liberalisation, and so the state-party that ruled Mexico since 1929, the Partido Revolucionario Institucional (PRI), was responsible for implementing a neoliberal programme that differed profoundly from its previous economic policies. Under President de la Madrid (1982–1988), Mexico's economy became the subject of neoliberal restructuring. In 1986, Mexico became a member of the GATT (precursor to the WTO), and in the following years, import tariffs were heavily reduced. President Salinas (1988–1994) aimed to complete the restructuring process, and privatisation and the liberalisation of trade, services and capital were widened and deepened. Salinas aimed at growth through private investment, export of manufactured goods, and public investment in infrastructure. Legislative reforms served to strengthen financial intermediaries: commercial banking was reprivatised in 1990; foreign investment in banks, production and portfolio was liberalised; a new act encouraged the integration of financial groups, predominantly by allowing the establishment of financial holding companies; and Salinas' modernisation programme included a repeal of regulations restricting private investment and the abolition of most price controls.

Of Salinas's efforts to improve Mexico's regional and global position and relations (with investors, creditors and governments), the creation of the North American Free Trade Area between Mexico, the United States and Canada was evidently the most effective result. Next to free trade of goods, NAFTA allows for the free flows of services and capital. Most particularly, the liberalisation of flows from and toward the largest economy of the world (the United States) was promising to Mexico. In addition, its membership implied the regional locking in of Mexico's neoliberal policies. Together, these implications of NAFTA added strongly to the attractiveness of investing in Mexico. For Mexican companies, it eased their access to strategic alliances with foreign capital. Besides NAFTA, Mexico has extended its economic relations through bilateral free trade agreements, agreements with MERCOSUR and the European Union, and membership of the OECD and APEC (Asia Pacific Economic Cooperation).

Privatisation was another crucial element of Mexico's neoliberal restructuring. Major transfers of parastatal companies to the private sector took place under President Salinas, valuing in total about $20 billion. The companies were not sold on the open market, but through a far from transparent state-controlled system of selection. For prices (much) below their real value, 93 per cent of them were sold to large Mexican enterprises and economic groups (Guillen 1994: 32–33). Teléfonos de México (Telmex), for instance, was sold to the powerful Grupo Carso for $443 million, whereas its official value was estimated at over $700 million (*Proceso* 4 December 1995: 19). By thus transferring a considerable share of the state's economic power to large Mexican enterprises, the privatisation process strengthened them as the new pioneers of growth and development. However, these enterprises became increasingly less 'national' through their links with foreign capital.

Regionalisation and Growing Dependency on the United States

The many negative effects on Mexico of China's economic rise point at some serious problems for Mexico's position in the global economy, and lead to some questions about its economic integration in North America as its main globalisation strategy. Efforts to achieve more balance in its international trade and investment relations gave way to increased global flows, but as the NAFTA effects were bigger, it turned out that globalisation of Mexican production became dominated by its regional integration in North America. Mexico's globalisation strategy thus turned out to draw Mexico only closer to the US market, thereby enlarging the importance of any changes of its position in that market, such as the US recession of 1999 to 2003 and its current crisis. As we have seen in the previous section, the rise of China as a strong competitor has worsened Mexico's vulnerability. From 2000 to 2004, China's share of US imports rose from 8.6 per cent to 13.8 per cent, while Mexico's share decreased from 10.9 per cent to 10.3 per cent. Only in agricultural, agro-industrial and primary resources is there no Chinese competition. Since 2002, Mexico's share of world exports has also decreased, partly due to China's successes (Dussel Peters 2005; ECLAC 2006: 25–35).

Mexico is remarkably dependent on the United States, both as a provider of FDI and as market for export production financed by FDI.[6] The preponderance of regionalisation in Mexico's globalisation strategy has important effects on its participation in global production networks, in which transnational companies play a central role. The competition between Mexico and China in computers, for instance, is mostly because of intra-firm strategies (that is within TNCs) toward production in these two countries. China's rise plays a crucial role in the global investment strategies of TNCs. Within their regional industrial production chains in Asia, TNCs have made important technology transfers to China. This in effect neutralises Latin American efforts to increase the added value of its manufacturing exports. Moreover, the practice of TNCs of moving production facilities to China is harmful to Mexico, as these two industrialising economies are clearly competing for FDI (Dussel Peters 2005; ECLAC 2006; Gaulier, Lemoine and Ünal-Kesenci 2005).

While FDI has contributed to Mexico's international competitiveness, it has not stimulated the integration of the economy, nor technology transference, human resource capacity or local business development (ECLAC 2004). In general, ECLAC studies have found that foreign direct investment has produced conflicting results in Latin America. Especially efficiency-seeking FDI has been criticised for bringing low added value and having weak links with the local economy. 'FDI of TNCs does not necessarily improve competitiveness of the domestic sector, which determines long-term economic growth ... It only works out positively with good educational levels of the workers, good institutions and infrastructure. Therefore, FDI policy has to be good and part of coherent development strategy' (ECLAC 2006: 36). As we will see further along, Mexico's levels of technology, science and research are low, and this is problematic for the immediate and mid-term future of Mexico's competitiveness, especially with respect to competition with China.

The 'China Factor' is most likely to deepen Mexico's economic dependency on the United States, and its political dependency will deepen as well. The two countries experience some similar problems with China's economic success, especially a large and growing trade deficit, fierce competition in manufacturing, and piracy. Mexico is also drawn closer to the United States because, to the latter, China represents a serious (geo-)political threat. There is a particular US concern for global foreign investments by Chinese parastatal companies in sensitive products and areas such as computers and aeronautics. Software for US banks or US mobile phones is not something the US government wants to see directly imported from China or bought from Chinese TNCs. As a result, some new advantages and niches for Mexican export production for the US market have appeared, such as placing the communication software in cell phones that are produced in China. Next to other US security concerns, the joint interests with Mexico and Canada vis-à-vis China has been an important reason for the creation in 2005 of the Security and Prosperity Partnership of North America (SPPNA), which has also become known as 'NAFTA-plus'. This declaration illustrates that, whereas the United States has been losing influence in South America, partly due to

China's growing influence, Mexico's ties to the United States have only been strengthened.

Economic Concentration and Plutocracy

The process and nature of economic concentration in Mexico is another major factor to be taken into account when we try to understand the country's profound problems with Chinese competition. In general, one may expect that a certain degree of economic concentration is necessary in order for Mexican companies to compete globally with large Chinese firms, in particular in the US market. However, we will see that the specific nature of Mexican conglomerates and economic groups as well as their relations with the government contributes to a situation that is harmful for both Mexico's international competitiveness and its prospects for pro-poor growth.

Since the mid 1980s, next to US transnational companies, large 'local' companies have gained ground in Mexico.[7] Expansion in foreign and local markets, but especially the national bias in privatisations, allowed Mexican companies to strengthen their position. Through new financial strategies, such as constructions created to obtain only the smallest number of shares necessary to dominate a firm, Mexican economic groups have started to take control over a large number of privatised companies. When banks were (re-)privatised from 1990 onward, most of them were bought by economic groups that already owned stock markets. The result is a major concentration of power into the hands of some 274 investors. Contrary to traditional family companies, the new conglomerates of economic groups involve holdings, stock market quotation, and international funding through credits, strategic alliances and joint ventures. With these new financial groups that can take the lead over various functions of capital, a powerful financial oligarchy with centralised command over economic processes has come into being. And this *nueva oligarquía* is more powerful and more associated to transnational capital than the old oligarchy (Concheiro Bórquez 1996; Garrido 1998: 403–406; Morera Camacho 1998: 50).[8]

Apart from economic policies for privatisation, the rise of this new oligarchy was a result of political processes. Since technocrats lacked popular support for their programme of market reform, they became dependent on the political and financial support of 'big business'. And these close relations between the Salinas government and the top of the corporate sector have profoundly affected the outcome of economic restructuring. Contrary to official claims that privatisations would enhance competition and efficiency, in the process, several monopolistic groups were created that have also become big transnational players, such as in telecommunication (Slim's TelMex) and copper (Grupo México of the Larrea family). Close ties also allowed for effective business pressure on policymaking processes with respect to (foreign) competition in the financial sector, telecommunications and airlines. And they enabled conglomerates to capture the regulatory boards that are officially supposed to ensure fair competition. Although the technocrats' goal was free and open markets, they had to settle for arrangements that would protect the powerful position of conglomerates. This turned their pro-market agenda into a pro-conglomerates programme (Hogenboom 2004a; Teichman 2001).

In the 1990s, there came an end to the traditional antagonism in Mexico between the government and especially the large members of the private sector: conglomerates and economic groups. With the NAFTA negotiations, for the first time a consultation process with the private sector took place; Mexican companies started lobbying for the agreement in the United States via their US counterparts; and, this experience was a breeding school for corporate lobbying and lobbyists. Large companies and the chambers of important sectors learned to operate professionally in their comments and proposals, and many of the current top corporate lobbyists (of large companies or of private sector organisations) in Mexico took part in the NAFTA negotiations and lobbying process.

However, the unprecedented political role of Mexico's private sector was clearly biased to the business elite (a relatively small group of large entrepreneurs), while leaving many small producers with even less access to government. Simultaneously, in Mexico two economies have come into being: the economy of economic groups, and the economy of the rest (Basave Kunhardt 2001: 97). This economic and political trend has a negative effect, among other things, on competitiveness. In theory, neoliberal policies produce more competitive markets in which the most productive and inventive companies are the winners (and democratisation – through less corruption and more transparency – would have similar effects). Monopolies resulting either from economic interferences by the state or from corrupt state bureaucracies would come to an end. Unfortunately so far, Mexico's reality is very different. This is illustrated by the Global Corruption Barometer of 2006, which shows that Mexico has a very high incidence of bribery, even when compared to other Latin American countries. Moreover, in its survey of 62 countries, Transparency International (2006: 19) found that the percentage of respondents stating that their government does not fight but actually encourages corruption was nowhere as high as in Mexico: 43 per cent.

The increased power of large conglomerates as a result of economic concentration and close ties with the government is one of a series of perverse developments that run counter to Mexico's formal democratisation process. The fact that economic restructuring was performed in opaque and corrupt ways – initiated by a semi-authoritarian state-party and implemented by a technocratic elite – contributed to the creation of an economy of privileges instead of an economy of chances, innovation and modernisation. In addition, what is often labelled as *pluralidad* (multi-party politics) hides the fact that there are still many political actors of the old system; that part of the traditional unions continue to be strong; that the large parastatal companies that have remained combine economic mismanagement with political privileges; that the traditional lack of accountability of politicians has continued; and, that there is great concern about the new roles of the President and the Congress, and their interaction with each other. When adding to this poor panorama the huge power of drugs cartels in Mexico, one may conclude that, rather than a market democracy, Mexico has turned into a plutocracy: a society ruled by (the interests of) the wealthy.[9]

Although the growth of Mexico's deepened economic integration with the United States has brought certain economic gains, overall liberalisation policies have not given way to sustained economic development, which has made Mexico, and in particular poor Mexicans, vulnerable for the negative effects of Chinese competition. There is growing evidence that economic openness (alone) does not lead to pro-poor growth, and Mexico supports this assessment. Mexico's economic output and employment have increased since 1980, but inequality between urban and rural areas has increased. Inflation and stabilisation in the 1980s, and the financial and economic crisis in 1995 and 1996 overshadowed positive effects of trade reforms for the poor. While poverty has in general decreased, extreme poverty and poverty in rural areas have grown as the new skill-intensive growth strategy adds to the gap of income between skilled and unskilled workers in cities, and between agriculture workers and the rest. This difference between rural and urban effects is directly related to Mexico's economic openness: due to the dominance of manufacturing in exports and (foreign) investments, capital has been moving out of agriculture, causing lower agricultural wages and output (Morley and Díaz-Bonilla 2006).

Employment is another sensitive issue. The productivity growth between 1988 and 2000 hardly generated any employment as the increased productivity was largely a result of dismissing workers, implying a loss of qualified employment that is contrary to long-term competitiveness. '(T)he formula used in the nineties evidence a concept of development that wastes resources, especially human capital formed during decades' (Ruiz Durán 2003: 8). The dramatic fall of real and minimum wages, and the failure to create sufficient new jobs have contributed to social inequality and major flows of migrant workers to the United States. In the end, (export) manufacturing is only a minor source of employment-generation, not even among the five most important branches in this respect (Dussel Peters 2000). The *maquiladora* sector is extremely import-dependent and hardly integrated in the national economy: less than 2 per cent of the assembled parts come from local providers (Alba Vega 2000). Mexico's deepening divide between a (small) modernised part of the economy and the large marginalised and underdeveloped segments forms an economically, politically and socially weak basis for confronting the many challenges linked to the rise of China.

Debating Competitiveness in Mexico

The rise of China has confronted Mexico with the limited global competitiveness of its own economy in an era of liberalised markets. China was initially seen as 'the problem' and as a threat against which Mexico had to be protected. Recently, this defensive attitude has met voices that favour an active approach, and it has become more common to see that Mexico has a problem with global competition. The so-called structural strategies for competitiveness presented under President Fox (2000–2006) proved to be little more than a list of good intentions (Arellano 2006), and the Presidential Competitiveness Board seems to have quietly dissolved. Because competitiveness is a broad concept, the debate on what actions need to be taken involves a multitude of analyses and proposals . The annual overview produced by the Mexican Institute for Competitiveness, IMCO, includes ten factors of competitiveness: rule of law, environmental sustainability, human capital, macroeconomic stability, political system, efficient markets, precursory sectors (the transport, telecom and financial sectors), efficient state institutions, international relations and high-potential economic sectors. It concludes, however, that 'so far there is no state policy that derives at a public policy in favour of economic competition' (IMCO 2007: 538, author's translation).[10]

A large part of the competitiveness debate centres around the role of the state.[11] Most contributions to the debate coincide in claiming that the Mexican state rapidly has to take initiatives to improve Mexico's competitiveness. However, on the content of these initiatives the views differ widely, depending on their analyses of the problems and causes. Is the depth of the negative 'China effect' on Mexico a result of neoliberal restructuring, or on the contrary a result of a lack of liberalisation in certain areas, thereby showing the need for second generation reforms? With respect to the energy sector, for instance, some claim that China's successes show that parastatal companies can be much better motors of development than privatised companies, while others argue that only the privatisation of Mexico's state monopolies in oil and electricity can be expected to end the situation of high energy prices and poor services that hurt the country's competitiveness. Next to these discussions there are proposals for specific public sector efforts and investments in education, infrastructure, or the rule of law. Any real policy reform, however, will have to be based on an agreement between the President and Congress. Reaching such an agreement has proven to be extremely difficult in the context of Mexico's political *pluralidad*, as the President depends on support from both chambers of Congress, where there are major divisions between and within the political parties.

Government Policies

The fact that several large Mexican companies have become regionally or globally active TNCs does not imply that the growth of 'big business' is serving Mexico's economy or society. The groups and conglomerates have restructured in order to grow in an open economy, by means of acquisitions, business integration, and capturing foreign markets through exports. A part of Mexico's economic groups have thus turned into the top of *multilatinas* (Hogenboom 2004b). Helped by Mexico's weak anti-monopoly policies, the acquisition of competing companies has been a well-known strategy among these conglomerates, which has lead to the growth of private sector monopolies. In Mexico, well-known Mexican TNCs such as Cemex and Telmex have a bad reputation because the prices of cement and telecom are higher than in other countries. Evidently this is bad for competitiveness.

In Mexico's competitiveness debate, the issue of monopolies and weak competition is tackled in different ways. As we have seen, several scholarly publications stress the economic concentration in economic groups and conglomerates in Mexico, and the negative effects of monopolies in the private sector. More recently, there have been some contributions (e.g., in conferences organised by the World Bank) that criticise public sector monopolies as much as private sector monopolies. They claim that traditional trade unions and state companies in Mexico are also very negative for competitiveness, and propose policies that tackle problems with these powerful public institutions at the same time as private monopolies (cf. Guerrero, López-Calva and Walton 2006; Mayer-Serra 2006). Meanwhile, the anti-monopoly policies of the Mexican state have become more prominent, but with very mixed results. For instance, shortly after entering office in December 2006, President Felipe Calderón decided by decree to reform the Federal Law of Economic Competitiveness. Also, the Federal Commission for Competition has started to play an active role, but in many other federal councils and state institutions, the interests of the largest companies continue to prevail. In the end, few people seem to know how Mexico's political regime can be effectively moved away from a plutocracy. This was one reason for the major disappointment to many Mexicans when Andrés Lopez Obrador did not win the presidential elections in 2006, because he was seen as someone who could bring about this move in a more democratic and productive direction.

Another reason why Mexico's economy does not seem to find a dynamic insertion in the global economy, in particular with the competition posed by China, has to do with its monetary policy and the Central Bank (Banco de México, also known as Banxico). Tensions in Mexico's monetary policy are due to expanding inflows of foreign capital (short-term financial capital, FDI and remittances of migrants). Thus, Mexico has become dependent on flows for which there is major global competition, in order to finance its trade deficit. To prevent exchange instabilities by speculative attacks against its currency, Banxico has stored a huge foreign currency reserve (more than $50 billion in 2005). Simultaneously, Mexico has a large public debt, partly due to the political handling of the peso crisis in 1995. The bailout of banks and privatised companies that were going bankrupt was not passed in parliament, and as a result of this extra-parliamentary 'solution', the extensive debts have remained outside of the regular government budgets. Collusion among businessmen, bankers and public officials gave way to good deals for private companies and an even higher public debt. Since then, parliamentary resistance against presidential initiatives to tackle the budget problem (by normalising the debt payments by bringing these debts into the public budget) has rendered the operations of Banxico on monetary policies rather complicated (Garrido 2005: 42–48). This shows again how political dominance of economic elite interests has had substantial effects, especially on public budgets.

The State as Investor

A lack of public budgets is negative for many things, but also for competitiveness because improving infrastructure, knowledge and technology, the workforce, or the local economy requires extensive public funding. Mexico's limited public investment is in sharp contrast to the massive (co-)investments of the public sector in China. The decrease of total factor productivity in Mexico is linked to the dramatic downfall of public investment over the last thirty years, both during the end of ISI and since economic opening. Potential gains of openness seem not to have materialised because of a lack of adequate policy, in particular with respect to public spending and social investment. To prevent further public decapitalisation, a great effort is needed in the development of human capital (Núñez Rodríguez 2006).

Knowledge is an important area that the Mexican state has neglected. In knowledge-based labour, Mexico is lagging behind its Latin American peers, Brazil and Argentina, as well as emerging economies in Asia and Eastern

Europe. As the world's current development phase is based on a new articulation between the scientific-educational sector and the whole of production and social services, Mexico's delayed investment in knowledge is highly problematic. Among other things, Mexico needs to strengthen the currently weak link between this scientific-educational sector and the electronic-information sector. Otherwise, the country will not be able to benefit from the potential of electronic and software industries to create knowledge, and to participate in the strong internationalisation of knowledge (Ordóñez 2006).

Linked to the problems with knowledge is Mexico's weakness with respect to innovation. It relies heavily on foreign technology, which is partly a result of TNCs hindering technology transmission to developing countries such as Mexico. This accounts for some of the disappointing results of Mexico's trade openness (Cardero, Mántey and Mendoza 2006). Another part of the explanation lies in Mexico's low levels of investment in research and development (R&D). Its innovation system performs below par compared to economies of its income level and it is one of the least effective and efficient in Latin America. In Mexico, total investment in R&D is only 0.4 per cent of GDP, compared to 0.6 per cent in Chile and 1.1 per cent in Brazil, or 1.0 per cent in China. Private investment in R&D is insufficient: Mexican firms invest 0.1 per cent of GDP compared to 0.3 per cent in Chile and 0.4 per cent in Brazil, or 0.8 per cent in China. Mexico's international participation and linkages are also weak, and NAFTA-induced initiatives for academic and research networks with the United States and Canada have been disappointing. Other limitations are inadequate linkages between public R&D and the productive sector, and insufficient innovation capacity due to the generally low science and technology skill base, particularly in science and engineering (World Bank 2005b).

In order to do something about this backwardness, in 2005 the World Bank and Mexico agreed on a loan of $250 million for the first phase of an innovation for competitiveness project.[12] The project appraisal document argues that public sector funding is crucial in Mexico's current stage because international experience suggests that the private sector does not take the lead in R&D investments in a country such as Mexico, which has such low levels of critical mass. Education (both access and quality) is seen as the weakest pillar: although Mexico's knowledge economy index (5.70) is above that of China (4.95), it is below the index of Brazil (5.82) and Korea (7.84). 'The Programme seeks to support the Government's efforts to improve competitiveness of the Mexican economy by strengthening the innovative capacity of the private sector, accelerating advanced human capital formation, and increasing the international integration of the innovation system' (World Bank 2005b: xi).

The innovation programme is said to be successful if private R&D would increase from 0.1 per cent to at least 0.2 per cent of GDP. But is this likely to happen? From a technical perspective, the project seems to be based on an accurate assessment of Mexico's problems and weaknesses regarding innovation, while the building blocks of the project seem to have a rather accurate attitude toward solving these problems. The World Bank loan is, among other things, to be used for a programme to promote business innovation, including the support of consortia and research networks, a venture capital fund, and a sectoral fund for economic development. However, the project's technical appraisal document does not explain what the underlying *causes* are of Mexico's weak innovation. As with all World Bank credits and projects, the government of the lending country is the partner to work with, which limits the room for a more critical analysis.

From what we have learned about Mexico's politics of neoliberalisation, the deeper causes of low innovation and productivity have in part to do with economic concentration and the attitude of conglomerates. A recent Central Bank working paper on productivity in Mexican manufacturing shows that less competition due to market concentration has had a negative effect on productivity (Salgado Banda and Bernal Verdugo 2007). Since large companies have had easy access to finance as well as to high state officials, one may conclude that generally they have not been very interested in innovation. In Latin America's political culture, 'know-who' is more important than 'know-how', according to Young (2003: 249); in Mexico this seems to have become only truer since the rise of a new oligarchy and a plutocracy. The new World Bank loan for innovation may compensate for some of the Mexican government's long-term neglect of small and medium-sized companies, and stimulate companies to invest in R&D, but it remains doubtful whether it will create the anticipated results. State bureaucracy, corruption, economic uncertainty and very expensive bank credits are some of the Mexican realities that are likely to hold back still the entrepreneurs who genuinely want to invest time and money in innovation.

Conclusions

The debate on Chinese competition and Mexico's decreasing competitiveness shows that it is very important that the Mexican public sector and private sector start making major and coordinated efforts to counter current trends. From a political economy perspective, the crux is in an active and responsible attitude of powerful institutions and other actors within both sectors. Unfortunately, both sides hold bad records of initiative and transparency, and are equally distrusted by the Mexican population. Government agencies and state companies as well as large Mexican companies and (US) TNCs are seen as either incompetent or mainly serving the interests of an elite.

In Mexico, the views on what would be the best balance between the public sector and the private sector differ greatly. On the one hand, there are people who are convinced that the weakened economic role of the state is central to many of Mexico's problems, and that the Mexican state should become a more pro-active actor. On the other hand, there are people who claim that the problems lie in Mexico's incomplete neoliberalisation, and that this should be continued where it was halted in the mid 1990s. The latter wants more space and opportunities for market actors and competition by means of 'second generation reforms', especially flexibilisation of labour, liberalisation of the energy sector, and tax and pension reforms. However, both approaches embody the risk of giving more power to already very powerful actors. Paradoxically, in the phase of liberalisation and democratisation, both the Mexican state and the large entities of the Mexican private sector have had great power without much accountability. The close relations between the political elite and the economic elite have had a series of adverse effects on Mexico's development. And each approach stands the risk of worsening the situation as long as this concentration of political and economic power remains.

Several important issues remain to be further studied and discussed. What does Mexico's weakness vis-à-vis China tell us about the role of the state and politics in development and economic innovation? And does Mexico's modernisation depend on a choice between economic or social progress, or are there viable ways to solve this tension democratically within a system of relatively open markets? Interestingly, in its *World Development Report 2006,* the World Bank (2005a) comes to a remarkably nuanced conclusion on the costs and benefits of liberalisation and privatisation, especially remarkable for an institution that, during two decades, was at the centre of the Washington Consensus. The report includes figures demonstrating that trade liberalisation in Latin America has generated income inequality, while this region was already infamous for its high level of socio-economic inequality. The case of Mexico is presented to show that free trade (NAFTA) may lead to regional differences in wealth increase, with the northern parts of the country having benefited substantially whereas a lack of infrastructure and other limitations have inhibited other parts of the country to share in the benefits of new economic opportunities. The World Bank thus adds equality to economic growth as precondition for development. This is quite a step away from the Bank's previous agenda. Together with the above mentioned new attention in the Bank for structural inequalities, such as concentrated wealth in the business sector and their negative effects on growth and development, in the end there may be an opening for some new possibilities for fair and real development.

References

Alba Vega, Carlos. 2000. 'México después del TLCAN. El impacto económico y sus consecuencias políticas y sociales'. In *México y sus perspectivas para el siglo XXI*, ed. Barbara Klauke. Münster: Westfälische-Wilhelms-Universität Münster.

Arellano, Rogelio. 2006. 'Implications of China's emergence in the global economy for Latin America: the case of Mexico'. *Integration & Trade* 24, Jan.–June: 213–50.

Basave Kunhardt, Jorge. 2001. *Un siglo de grupos empresariales en México*. México, DF: UNAM-IIE & Miguel Ángel Porrúa.

Cardero, Elena, Guadalupe Mántey, and Miguel Ángel Mendoza. 2006. 'What is wrong with economic liberalisation? The Mexican case'. *Investigación Económica* LXV (257): 19–43.

Concheiro Bórquez, Elvira. 1996. *El gran acuerdo. Gobierno y empresarios en la modernización salinista*. México, DF: Ediciones Era.

Cornejo, Romer. 2005. 'América Latina ante el Crecimiento Económico de China'. VI Reunión de la Red de Estudios de América Latina y el Caribe sobre Asia-Pacífico. Buenos Aires: Redealap / Banco Interamericano de Desarrollo.

Dussel Peters, Enrique. 2000. *Polarizing Mexico. The Impact of Liberalisation Strategy*. Boulder: Lynne Rienner Publishers

———. 2003. 'Ser maquila o no ser maquila, ¿es esa la pregunta?' *Comercio exterior* 53(4): 328–36.

———. 2004. *La Competitividad de la Industria Maquiladora de Exportación en Honduras. Condiciones y retos ante el CAFTA*. México: CEPAL.

———. 2005. *Economic Opportunities and Challenges posed by China for Mexico and Central America*. Studies 8, Deutsches Institut für Entwicklungspolitik (DIE).

———. 2007. 'What does China's integration to the world market mean for Latin America? The Mexican experience'. Paper for the 2007 Congress of the Latin American Studies Association, Montreal, 5–7 September.

ECLAC. 2004. *Foreign Investment in Latin America and the Caribbean, 2003*. Santiago: United Nations.

———. 2005a. *Foreign Investment in Latin America and the Caribbean, 2004*. Santiago: United Nations.

———. 2005b. *Latin America and the Caribbean in the World Economy, 2004. 2005 Trends*. Santiago: United Nations.

———. 2006. *Foreign Investment in Latin America and the Caribbean, 2005*. Santiago: United Nations.

Fernández Jilberto, Alex and Barbara Hogenboom. 2007. 'Latin America and China under Global Neoliberalism'. *Journal of Developing Societies* 23(4): 467–501.

Gallagher, Ken P., Juan Carlos Moreno-Brid, and Roberto Porzecanski. 2008. 'The Dynamism of Mexican Exports: Lost in (Chinese) Translation?' *World Development* 36 (8): 1365–80.

García-Herrero, Alicia and Daniel Santabárbara. 2005. *Does China have an impact on foreign direct investment to Latin America?* Documentos de Trabajo no. 517. Madrid: Banco de España.

Garrido, Celso. 1998. 'El liderazgo de las grandes empresas industriales mexicanas'. In *Grandes empresas y grupos industriales latinoamericanos*, ed. Wilson Peres. México, DF & Madrid: siglo veintiuno.

———. 2002. 'Economía, financiamiento y empresas en México. Evolución desde 1995, tendencias y desafíos'. Paper presented at the international conference Coyuntura microeconómica en América Latina. 29–30 August, CEPAL (Santiago).

———. 2005. 'Monetary policy and economic development in Mexico since 1995'. *Latin American Business Review* 6(1).

Guerrero, Isabel, Luis Felipe Lópes-Calva, and Michael Wanton. 2006. 'The inequality trap and its links to low growth in Mexico'. Draft, November 7.

Guillen, Arturo. 1994. 'El proceso de privatización en México'. *Mondes en Developpement* 22 (87): 29–39.

Hogenboom, Barbara. 2004a. 'Governing Mexico's market economy'. In *Good Governance in the Era of Neoliberal Globalisation. Conflict and Depolitization in Latin America, Eastern Europe, Asia and Africa,* eds. Jolle Demmers, Alex E. Fernández Jilberto, and Barbara Hogenboom, 91–115. London: Routledge.

———. 2004b. 'Economic Concentration and Conglomerates in Mexico'. *Latin American Conglomerates and Economic Groups under Globalisation* (guest-edited by Alex E. Fernández Jilberto and Barbara Hogenboom), special double issue of *Journal of Developing Societies* 20(3&4): 207–25.

IMCO. 2007. *Punto de Inflexión. Situación de la Competitividad en México 2006.* México, DF: Instituto Mexicano para la Competitividad.

León, José Luis. 2005. 'La Relación Económica China-América Latina Expresiones y Causas de dos Trayectorias Distintas'. VI Reunión de la Red de Estudios de América Latina y el Caribe sobre Asia- Pacífico. Buenos Aires: Redealap / Banco Interamericano de Desarrollo.

Mayer-Serra, Carlos Elizondo. 2006. 'Instituciones, competencia y desigualdad: tres caras de un mismo problema'. Conferencia Equidad y Competencia, México, DF, 28 November.

Morera Camacho, Carlos. 1998. *El capital financiero en México y la globalización. Limites y contradicciones.* México, DF: Ediciones Era.

Morley, Samuel E. and Carolina Díaz-Bonilla. 2006. 'Mexico—do the poor benefit from increased openness?' In *Who Gains from Free Trade? Export-led growth, inequality and poverty in Latin America,* eds. in Rob Vos et al., 302–28. London: Routledge

Núñez Rodríguez, Gaspar. 2006. 'Inversión pública y crecimiento económico en México'. *Perfiles Latinoamericanos* 27, Jan.–June: 11–32.

Ordóñez, Sergio. 2006. 'Captalismo del conocimiento:¿México en la integración?' *Problemas de Desarrollo* 37 (146): 51–77.

Ruiz Durán, Clemente. 2003. 'The redimensioning of sector development'. *El Mercado de Valores,* no. 1, January/February: 3–10.

Salgado Banda, Héctor and Lorenzo E. Bernal Verdugo. 2007. 'Multifactor productivity and its determinants: an empirical analysis for Mexican manufacturing'. Working paper no. 2007–09. Mexico: Banco de México.

Teichman, Judith A. 2001. *The Politics of Freeing Markets in Latin America: Chile, Argentina, and Mexico.* Chapel Hill: The University of North Carolina Press.

Transparency International. 2006. *Report on the Transparency International Global Corruption Barometer 2006.* Berlin: Transparency International

UNCTAD. 2006. *World Investment Report 2006.* New York: United Nations.

World Bank. 2005a. *World Development Report 2006.* Washington, DC: World Bank.

———. 2005b. 'Project appraisal document on a proposed loan in the amount of US$ 250 million to the United States of Mexico for an innovation for competitiveness project in support of the first phase of the innovation for competitivenesss program', 15 April.

Young, R. 2003. 'Foreign investment and democratic governance in Latin America'. In *Latin American Democracies in the New Global Economy,* ed. Ana Margheritis, 24–79. Coral Gables: North-South Center Press.

UN Tradecom. 2009. http://comtrade.un.org (accessed 20 March 2009).

Notes

1. Next to the referred literature, this chapter's analysis is based on information gathered through interviews and conversations held in June 2005 and May 2007 in Mexico with officials of the Secretaría de Economía, Secretaría de Relaciones Exteriores, Banco de México, World Bank, IDB, ECLAC, CEESP, IMCO and American Chamber of Commerce.

2. To protect their economy from unfair competition from China, members of WTO are entitled to use the so-called non-market economy (NME) methodology toward Chinese products during the first 15 years after its accession into the WTO. Since 2001, Latin American countries such as Brazil, Chile, Argentina, Venezuela and Peru have decided to grant China the status of market economy, but it is unlikely that Mexico will grant China this status before 2016.

3. This smuggling is partly related to the high Mexican import tariffs for Chinese produce as established in the Mexico-China agreements for China's entry into the WTO.

4. It needs mentioning though that Mexico had taken over that position only two years earlier from Japan.

5. Apart from strong vertical structures (brand name companies), there is also subcontracting in company networks, involving contract manufacturers.

6. Japanese investment in Mexico has recently been growing, with TNCs such as Nissan, Toyota and Bridgestone, as a result of the free trade agreement of Mexico with Japan that went into effect on 1 April 2005.

7. This section is for a substantial part based on a previous publication on conglomerates and economic concentration in Mexico (Hogenboom 2004b).

8. Much of the speed and nature of the rise of Mexican conglomerates is linked to events in financial markets (currency and stock exchange) and changing government initiatives toward banking, financial services, and exchange rates. Financial crises shake things up and may form an opportunity for change and expansion. Moreover, while leaving the public sector with an enormous debt, governmental efforts to rescue financial capital from defaulting after the financial crises of 1982 and of 1994–95 were particularly beneficial to large Mexican investors (Basave Kunhardt 2001; Garrido 2002; Concheiro Bórquez 1996; Morera Camacho 1998).

9. In 2004, I argued that the combination of neoliberal restructuring and democratisation in Mexico had given way to a market democracy (Hogenboom 2004a). The economic and political developments since then, however, have made me change my mind and I have come to agree with the suggestion of a high-level official of the Mexican Central Bank that Mexico has become a plutocracy.

10. IMCO is a private institute that was set up in 2003 with funding from the Mexican Council of Businessmen (CMHN), an organisation of Mexico's most powerful entrepreneurs. It receives (project) funding from many other sources, including USAID, OECD, World Bank, Hewlett Foundation and Mexican ministries. IMCO states that it aims at 'technifying' the issue of competitiveness in order to solve actual problems and prevent an ideological debate, and its annual overview provides a large number of data and illustrations (IMCO 2007).

11. As competitiveness is linked to a wide range of issues, the debate in Mexico is also about economic development, government policies and the political regime. Mexico's increased dependency on the US economy as a result of its globalisation-through-regionalisation strategy is not much questioned in this context; it seems that even the people who are concerned about Mexico's dependency on such an asymmetric relation see few possibilities to change this situation without Mexico paying a high price.

12. During the project's three phases, the WB (IBRD) will contribute a credit of $650 million of a projected total of $1,167 million from 2006 to 2015.

4 Neoliberalised South-South Relations
Free Trade between Chile and China
Alex E. Fernández Jilberto

The contemporary relations between China and Latin America differ radically from that of the 1980s. During that decade, the Asian giant gradually initiated its diplomatic and political offensive, aimed at creating privileged economic relations with the region. China drastically changed its strategy toward Latin America: it replaced its approach of exporting Maoism with economic pragmatism, thereby enabling itself to develop good diplomatic relations with Latin America's military dictatorships. Since then, Latin American countries generally went through processes of neoliberalisation and democratisation. Subsequently, the end of the 1990s, with the electoral victory of Hugo Chávez in 1998, marked the beginning of a prolonged cycle of access to state power for leftist politics in Latin America, which had previously been limited by the neoliberal policies of the so-called 'Washington Consensus'. This new political cycle continued with many electoral triumphs by the left or centre left (see chapter ten).

The common objective of the new left governments in Latin America is to implement economic policies that are rather different from the Washington Consensus style of neoliberalism. They want to allow more state intervention with regard to the social agenda as well as in regard to the management and regulation of the economy's globalisation. Furthermore, the leftist governments aspire to liberate Latin America from the political influence of the International Monetary Fund and the World Bank, who have been determining the economic policies in the region ever since the debt crisis in 1982. The recent institution of the *Banco del Sur* is a first step in their attempt to liberate Latin America from the World Bank.

The implementation of alternative economic strategies has been enabled by Latin America's favourable economic situation that is not merely derived from previously implemented structural reforms, but is also linked to China's economic growth. Due to China's growth, there have been substantial global price increases of raw materials that are exported by Latin America (such as petrol, copper, nickel, silver and tin). Together with the surge of China as a new market for the region's commodities, China's growth has been facilitating new economic opportunities for many of the region's left governments, while producing extra financial resources to boost social investment (Fernández Jilberto and Hogenboom 2007).

In the new political scenario of Latin America, and against the setting of the rise of China as a global political power, Chile forms a double exception. First, it is the most loyal follower of the recipe of neoliberalism, known for its hospitality to transnational capital, and a most reliable ally of the United States. The creation of Chile's free trade zone with the United States, which went into effect in 2004, is the best example of all of these characteristics. Secondly, Chile stands out for its economic pragmatism that excludes all forms of political or ideological limitations to the globalisation of its economy. This has motivated Chile to become the first country in Latin America and in the world to establish a Free Trade Agreement (FTA) with China.

This chapter analyses the background and characteristics of Chile's economic pragmatism, and its extensive relations with China. First, it briefly presents some elements of the historical Chile-China relations and contemporary data on the impressive material importance of bilateral trade and investment. Next, the political roots of Chile's economic pragmatism are discussed by focussing on the central role of the *Concertación* governments in deepening neoliberalism under 'Chilean socialism'. Chile's regionalisation and globalisation strategies are then studied extensively, showing that, to Chile, free trade with China was only a logical next step in the direction that Chile had been following for years.

Chilean Copper for China

Chile's relations with China have a long history. There have been diplomatic and commercial relations since 1845, the year in which the political and corporate elites of Chile considered it necessary to start consul relations in Canton, Hong Kong and a trade office in China. With their economically liberal mentality, Chile's elites wanted to strengthen the Chilean commercial presence in Asia and Oceania. In addition, during the 'cycle of the Chilean nitrate' in the nineteenth century, Chile's economic expansion gave way to immigration. Chinese immigrant workers were an important segment of the immigrants coming to Chile, especially those who had fled from the regime of forced labour in Peru's industrial cotton farms or sugar industry. Resulting from the War of the Pacific, the incorporation of Iquique in the Chilean territory meant the addition of the Chinese immigrants to the national population (Klein and Arenas 2000; Lin Chou 2004).

In the twentieth century, Chile was the first Latin American country to sign trade agreements with the People's Republic of China (1952), which gave way to the Sino-Chilean Trade Corporation. In 1970, for the first time in Latin America during the Cold War, Chile's socialist government, led by Salvador Allende, recognised and established official diplomatic relations with China. With the intensifying bilateral trade relations in 1971 and 1972,

30 per cent of Chinese imports of Latin American products came from Chile, while China became the third largest consumer of Chilean copper. In 1987, under the Pinochet dictatorship and with the start of 'Chinese ideological pluralism', Chile was also the first Latin American country to sign a joint venture with China, creating the Santiago-Beijing Tube Copper Company. The Chilean enterprises CODELCO and MADECO took part in this mixed company, together with the Beijing Nonferrous Metallurgical Company, and altogether they invested $9.9 billion (Gutierrez 2001).

As Chile is the world's largest copper producing country and China is the world's largest copper consuming country, this remains the key commodity in Chile's relations with China (see Figure 4.1). In 2005, China consumed almost 3.8 million tons of refined copper, of which almost 50 per cent had come from Chile. Compared with the previous year, this was an increase of 13 per cent. Especially since 2003, China's growing copper consumption has been causing a significant price raise at the London Metal Exchange, the world's largest metal market (see Figure 4.2). While in January of 2005 a pound of copper cost $143.8 cents, in December of that same year it had reached up to $207.6 cents (CODELCO 2006). The rising price and volume of Chilean copper exports have been financing the productive expansion of Chile's copper producing company CODELCO. In 2005, CODELCO established a deal with the Chinese consort MINMETALS to annually sell it 57.750 tons of copper during 15 years. In return, CODELCO received a total of $550 million, of which $110 million was to create a joint venture to operate as an intermediate between CODELCO's sales and the operations by MINMETALS: the Copper Partners Investment Company LTD. MINMETALS has invested another $100 million in this company, which is jointly managed on a 50/50 basis.

Figure 4.1. Main Refined Copper Consumers, 2005
(in thousand tons)

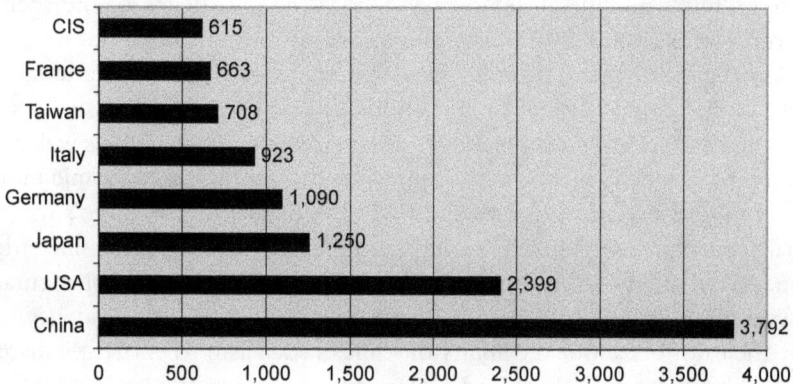

Source: CODELCO (2006)

Figure 4.2. Copper Prices at the World Market, 1990–2006

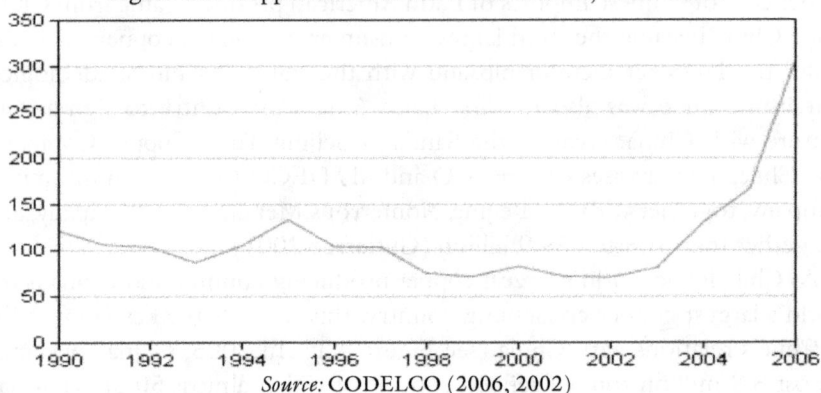

Source: CODELCO (2006, 2002)

Through these and other agreements, MINMETALS clearly aims to guarantee Chinese access to Chilean copper in the long run. Considering competition from Asia and elsewhere, China tries to have some control over the Chilean mining sector. For instance, Japan's mining companies have formulated a new strategy of expansion in Chile, which is considered to be limiting the Chinese demand in this country. Sumitomo, which is Japan's third largest producer of refined copper, agreed with the US company, Phelps Dodge Corporation, to take a 20 per cent share in the Chilean copper mine Ojos del Salado, which is 100 per cent owned by Phelps Dodge Corporation. Nippon Mining is already jointly investing with the Chilean conglomerate Lulsic in the mining company Los Pelambres, and Nippon Mining plans to invest with Korea for a total of $1.8 billion in Peru and Chile (Fazio 2006).

The Neoliberal Pragmatism of the *Concertación*

Since 1990, Chile has been governed by the so-called *Concertación*, the alliance of the Socialist Party of Chile and the Christian Democratic Party, which created Chile's neoliberal democracy. Under the presidency of the socialist Ricardo Lagos (2000–2006), the globalisation of the Chilean economy was given a major stimulus through new free trade agreements. National and transnational companies and international financial institutions such as the IMF and the World Bank applauded his economic management as well as his capacity to reconcile his socialist origin with the neoliberal economic model. What business groups mostly praised was the deepening of Chile's international economic insertion, the structural trade surpluses, and the innovations in financial markets. In their eyes, Lagos facilitated a greater complementarity between national and transnational corporate actors and his presidency took away their doubts about the ability of Chilean socialism to efficiently manage Chile's liberalised and globalised economy.

By the end of the 1990s, Ricardo Lagos had become part of the so-called Buenos Aires Consensus. This Consensus reunited the political leaders of the proclaimed *nueva izquierda* (new left), such as Cuauhtémoc Cárdenas of the Mexican opposition party PRD, Carlos 'Chacho' Álvarez of the Argentinean FREPASO, and Luiz Inácio 'Lula' da Silva of Brazil's labour party PT. Their goal was to develop a new programme for the proclamation of Latin American social democracy, founded upon the reconfiguration and compatibility of the neoliberal economic policies of globalisation, combined with a necessary reduction of social costs and democratisation. The key was a recasting of the left, including a profound political realism, to elaborate strategies and policies of progressive governability within the new social order that had emerged from Latin America's neoliberal restructuring (Korzeniewics and Smith 2000).

The Buenos Aires Consensus, however, is almost forgotten, and Chile is still considered to be the best exponent of the Washington Consensus. Nicolas Eyzaguirre, Minister of Finance under the Lagos administration, repeatedly expressed his conviction that 'the economy is neither left nor right' and that its management requires a technical capacity irrespective of any ideological interpretation. Indeed, the government of the socialist President Lagos continued to follow the line that had been adopted by the first two governments of the *Concertación*, lead by the Christian Democrats Patricio Aylwin (1990–1994) and Eduardo Frei (1994–2000). The Lagos administration thus not only represented the pragmatic continuity of the *Concertación* governments, it also exemplified the so-called 'socialist renewal' (which Lagos' socialist party had experimented with since the end of the 1980s), also known as Latin America's *neo-estructuralismo*. This neostructuralism acknowledges the legitimacy of the market economy as formulated by neoliberalism, but it also attributes a role to the state in governing the market (Fernández Jilberto 2004a; Kay and Gwynne 1999).

Pragmatism and continuity under Lagos appeared in economic policies and the state's cooperative relations with conglomerates and business groups, in order to maintain and strengthen Chile's export sectors and its neoliberal economic model (Fernández Jilberto 2004b). Previously, that model had been integrated in the Chilean Constitution of 1980 during Pinochet's dictatorship (Silva 2002, 1996; Ffrench-Davis 1999; Fernández Jilberto 2004a; Taylor 2006). In 2005, the Lagos administration presented a fiscal reform to maintain a structural surplus of at least 1 per cent of real Gross Domestic Product (GDP) in order to secure foreign debt payments. The IMF blessed this policy of prioritising debt payments over public expenses. Chile's foreign indebtedness, however, had among other things been caused by the dictatorial regime's financial support of economic groups during the privatisation processes. Nevertheless, the socialist President Michelle Bachelet, successor to the Lagos administration, also decided to continue with the fiscal policy of a surplus of at least 1 per cent of GDP.

During Lagos' presidency, Chile's economic growth and public revenue expansion were impressive, and these successes were intimately linked to copper exports and the double 'China effect': the increasing volume of China's imports of Chilean copper together with the spectacular increase of copper prices on the international markets as a result of Chinese demand. In 2005 the fiscal surplus even reached 4.8 per cent of GDP – the highest surplus in 18 years, despite the fact that the expenses of the central government for the period of 2000–2005 had increased by 50 per cent (Fazio 2006). From 2000 to 2005, the Chilean economy registered an average growth of 4.4 per cent of GDP. Even though this is lower than the average 7.8 per cent GDP growth during the Aylwin administration, it was much more than the global average growth, or that of Latin America (see Figure 4.3). Chile's GDP increased from $75.2 billion in 2000 to a record level of $125.5 billion in 2005.

Figure 4.3. World, Latin American and Chilean GDP Development, 2000–2005 (%)

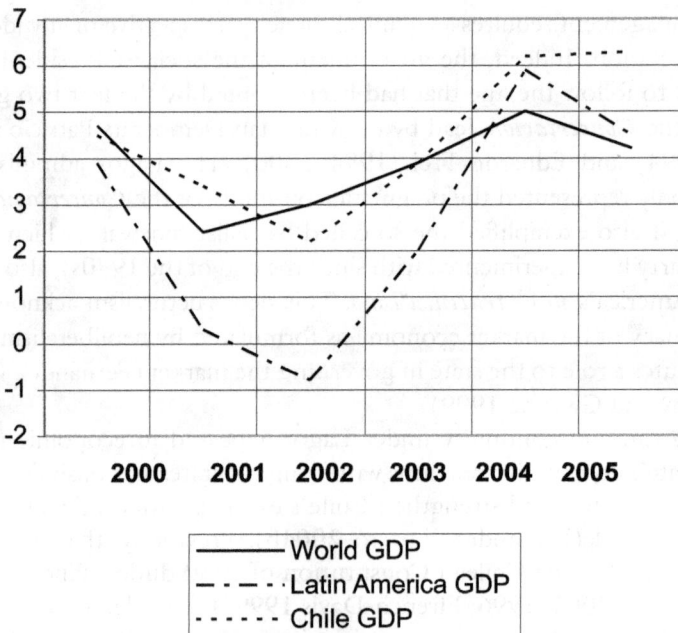

Source: CEPAL (2006)

Of Chile's total fiscal revenues of 2005, 71.2 per cent came from taxing on private mining companies, and 15.5 per cent came from the raw copper exported by CODELCO. In addition to copper, the mining and export of Chilean molybdenum also became increasingly lucrative. Total profits of CODELCO in 2005 were $4360 million, of which $3582 million went to the Chilean state and $778 million to the armed forces. As an inheritance of the dictatorial regime, armament financing takes place through funds assigned by a law (*Ley Reservada del Cobre*) that attributes at least 10 per cent of CODELCO's total sales to the armed forces (Ministerio de Hacienda 2006).

Governing Socialists and Transnationalised Business

The period of Lagos' presidency represents the remarkable reconciliation of national and transnational business with 'Chilean socialism'. His administration strengthened the relations between the state and the private sector and intensified the globalisation of the Chilean economy, particularly through the proliferation of free trade agreements, including the FTA with China. In 2000, Chile had only commercial treaties with Canada and the members of the Latin American Integration Association (ALADI). The agreements signed under Lagos are truly impressive: agreements with the European Union in 2002; the FTA with the United States in 2004; the agreements with the European Free Trade Association (EFTA) in 2004 and with South Korea in 2005; the FTA with China in 2005; and the Agreement of Partial Alliance with India in 2005 (DIRECON 2006). By the end of 2005, the president of the Chilean business organisation CPC (Confederación de la Producción y del Comercio), Hernán Somerville, concluded that the very positive legacy of the socialist President consisted of deepening the international insertion of the Chilean economy, the fiscal surplus, and the innovations on the capital market. The newspaper *El Mercurio,* which had been the official channel of communication of Pinochet's dictatorship and remained the primary newspaper for the corporate sector, stated in an editorial in December 2005 that the widespread appreciation for Ricardo Lagos among businessmen demonstrated that they were no longer worried by the high probability that he would be succeeded by another socialist, namely, Michelle Bachelet (Fazio 2006).

An important motivation for Lagos' pro-business policies was the fact that at the beginning of his presidency, the Chilean economy showed clear signs of flat growth since the Asian Crisis resulted in a 74 per cent drop of foreign investment. With the region-wide decline of foreign investment, Chilean businessmen started to invest heavily in other Latin American countries. The foreign investments of Chilean companies increased from $370 million in the first trimester of 2002 to $1818 million in the second semester of 2004 (Salazar 2006: 78). The speculative nature of these investments put at stake the political successes of Chile's democratic governments, which had been characterised by stability and economic growth.

This new scenario of economic decapitalisation made the Lagos administration decide to confront the crisis with a series of policy measures: eliminating the remaining market limitations on national capital; a further lowering of import tariffs; maintaining the state's low level of social expenses; stimulating the export of traditional and non-traditional goods; keeping low interest rates; and deepening economic globalisation by signing many free trade agreements. Taken together, it was not simply the spectacular increase of the price of copper, but this large package of macro-economic measures through which the Chilean government succeeded in re-establishing foreign investment and restoring its relations with national business. The strategy of the Lagos administration even enabled Chile to re-establish its triumphal discourse about the globalisation of its economy. By virtue of its national competitiveness, Chile appeared in the 'top ten' of global rankings as elaborated by international agencies such as Standard & Poor, the Institute for Management Development, the World Economic Forum, and J.P. Morgan.

Lagos' policy measures contributed to the high profitability of businesses in Chile. Among Chile's thirty largest business and economic groups are the transnational financial conglomerates Santander Central Hispano and J.P. Morgan Chase Bank, the French-Spanish transnational Suez-Aguas that exploits Aguas Andina, and the Spanish electricity company Endesa. Another company on the list is Empresa Minera Escondida, the world's largest private copper mine, which is controlled by the Anglo-Australian consortium BHP Billiton. In 2004 and 2005, Empresa Minera Escondida's profits rose 55 per cent and 38 per cent respectively, equalling $2.6 billion in 2005. In addition, the list of Chile's largest business and economic groups shows several Chilean economic groups, which in various degrees are linked to transnational capital, such as Matte, Angelini, Solari, CAP, Cueto-Sebastian Piñera, Consorcio Financiero, and ClaroAn (Fazio 2005; Fernández Jilberto 2004b). However, the high profitability of businesses in Chile has at least two troublesome causes. First, it is related to the very unequal national income distribution for which the country is known. Second, part of the high profits flows from the non-payment for negative effects of the extraction of natural resources, especially in the mining sector.

This 'top thirty' points at a third explanatory factor for high Chilean profits, which is the fact that Chile's democratic neoliberalism has resulted in a high level of economic concentration. This can, for instance, be observed in Chile's banking sector, which has been highly profitable from 2000 to 2005 (see Figure 4.4). Of the 40 banks that existed in 1990, 27 remained fifteen years later (Stallings 2005). Moreover, in 2005, only four banks dominated 74.4 per cent of the market: Santander-Santiago, Banco de Chile, BCI and

Corpbanca. Santander is a Spanish multinational, and the other three banks are part of Chilean economic groups: Banco de Chile belongs to the Luski Group; BCI is controlled by the Yarur Group; and CORPBANCA is controlled by the Saieh Group. In addition, Chile is among the Latin American countries with the lowest levels of participation of public property in the national financial system. The Banco Estado is the only commercial bank of the public sector, which in 2003 managed 11 per cent of the banking assets (Rivas 2004).

Figure 4.4. Chilean Bank Profits: Index of Annual Profitability, 2000–2005 (%)

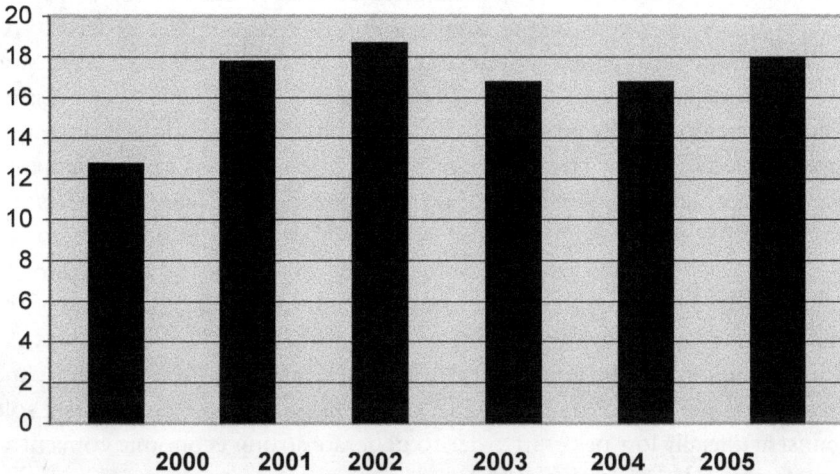

Source: SBIF (2006)

Also, Chile's transnationalisation is best reflected in its financial sector; the Chilean financial system is dominated by foreign banks. While in 1993 foreign banks managed 20 per cent of the assets, by 2000 they controlled 60 per cent of the assets and granted 45 per cent of the loans. As in many other parts of Latin America, the financial system in Chile is primarily dominated by Spanish and US banks, with 55 per cent and 30 per cent of the foreign-owned assets, respectively (Rivas 2004). Many of these transnational banks have established relations with Chinese capital. With the prospect of expanding economic relations between Latin America and China, BBVA, for instance, initiated a strategic alliance with the Chinese CITIC Group. The CITIC Group was founded in 1979, in the era of Deng Xiaoping, with the objective of channelling Chinese public investments to international markets. According to Francisco González, president of BBVA in Beijing, his bank and CITIC Group signed a strategic alliance in November of 2006, by which the Spanish bank acquired 5 per cent from the CITIC Bank and 15 per cent of CITIC International Financial Holdings (CIFH). This whole operation cost almost 1 billion. In March of 2007, BBVA decided to increase its participation within the CITIC Bank from 5 per cent to 10 per cent, and within CIFH from 15 per cent to 35 per cent. The strong presence of BBVA in Latin America was an important reason for Chinese financial authorities to decide in favour of the alliance with this Spanish financial conglomerate (Reinoso 2007).

The Chilean banking sector tripled its loans from 1991 to 2003, passing a lending mark of $15 billion to $44 billion. As a proportion of GDP, loans increased from 55 per cent to 66 per cent, and as the central government had ceased to require loans, the majority of these credits were for private companies (53 per cent of the total volume of credits). The generosity of the Chilean government and state toward the private sector once again was proven after the presentation of the report of the parliamentary commission on privatisations (Informe de la Comisión Privatizaciones de la Cámara de Diputados del 2005). The report presented the results of the parliament's research commission (*Comisión Investigadora de la Cámara de Diputados*), which stated that the Chilean state had lost $2.5 billion due to the dictatorship's privatisations, confirming earlier conclusions of the Republic's comptroller (*Contraloría General de la República*). The largest losses of the Chilean state came from the privatisation of Endesa ($895.6 million), CAP ($706.0 million), Chigener ($171.1 million), Chilectra ($96.4 million), and Banco de Chile ($66.9 million). The state companies were consciously sold against artificially low prices in order to generate strong economic concentration (Cámara de Diputados 2005).

Perversely, the neoliberal technocrats who had made the privatisations of these companies possible, not only in many cases became their new owners, but they also had used public funding, such as loans granted to economic groups, in order to finance the buying of other companies. The main other beneficiaries of this process were of course the economic groups directly benefitting from Pinochet's neoliberalism. After the presentation of the parliamentary commission's findings, the Lagos government condemned what had happened. In President Lagos' opinion, it was a challenge to his administration to deal with the commission's findings, but by the end of his presidency, the government had not formulated any proposal on how to do so.

Economic Regionalisation and Globalisation

The dilemma between the regionalisation and the globalisation of the Chilean economy already manifested itself in the first *Concertación* government under President Patricio Aylwin (1990–1994): should Chile enter MERCOSUR, or sign a FTA with the United States? This question dominated part of the debate about the need to formulate a new strategy of market opening by means of economic agreements (Butelmann 1993). Irrespective of the decision to prioritise regionalisation or globalisation, this strategy implied continuing with the model of market opening initiated by the dictatorial regime, and its implementation by a neocorporatist model of relations between the state, the government and the private sector.

The first democratic government of Aylwin began the cycle of the *Concertación* with the acknowledgement of business associations as the primary social interpreters for determining economic policies (including trade agreements) as well as for more general policies. Business associations such as the *Sociedad de Fomentos Fabril* (SOFOFA), the *Sociedad Nacional de Agricultura* (SNA), the *Cámara de Comercio de Santiago* (CCS), the *Confederación de la Producción y del Comercio* (CPC) and the *Asociación de Exportadores de Manufacturas* (ASEXMA) have since then played a strategic role within the strategic segments where Chile's economic and other policies are defined (Montero 1997; Fuentes 1997; Mönckeberg 2001; Carmona 2002; Campero 2003). And as a result of Chile's strong presidential system, inherited from the dictatorial regime, 'civil society' and parliament only played a marginal role in determining economic policies and agreements.

With its strategy to sign regional or bilateral trade agreements, the Aylwin government aimed at two essential goals. The first was Chile's re-insertion into the global economy as well as international politics, after its prolonged political and economic isolation that had been provoked by Pinochet's dictatorship. The second goal was to counter Chile's backward positioning in economic internationalisation in the context of the accelerated proliferation of regional economic blocs in Asia, Europe and Latin America. It was therefore inevitable to take part in this new trend of preferential trade, which had surged as a result of the difficulties of reaching global trade liberalisation within the framework of the GATT. In Chile's national debate on the post-dictatorship's economic model, the proponents of continuity by means of a unilateral reduction of import tariffs met resistance from groups demanding more distance from the inherited policies. The Aylwin government was able to prevent a confrontation between these two groups with its new strategy of preferential trade agreements.

Aylwin's strategy of 'open regionalism' was considered to be an efficient formula for Chile's international economic insertion. As a start, in 1991 a complementary agreement (*Acuerdo de Complementación Económica*) was signed with Mexico, involving a unilateral reduction of Chile's trade tariffs from 15 per cent to 11 per cent. This agreement had political advantages for both governments. For Chile it had the symbolic value of demonstrating the government's ability to re-integrate the country into the Latin American political and economic arena. In Mexico it enabled President Carlos Salinas to show that his government still had a profound 'Latinamericanist' vocation, which was severely questioned by opponents of Mexico's free trade negotiations with the United States. After Mexico, the Aylwin government started negotiations with Venezuela, Peru, Bolivia, Ecuador and Colombia, in order to achieve similar agreements and thereby redefine Chile's economic relations with members of the Pacto Andino from which Chile had withdrawn in 1976.

The new economic strategy of the Aylwin government and the neocorporatist relations between state and business stressed the need for an efficiently functioning state. In 1978, Pinochet's neoliberal dictatorship had created the General Office of International Economic Relations (*Dirección General de Relaciones Económicas Internacionales,* DIRECON), which was part of the Ministry of Foreign Affairs, but managed Chile's international economic relations under the direct mandate of the President. This 'Pinochetist' structure of DIRECON, including its extraordinary influence on other strategic state departments, was complicated due to the context of Chile's new democracy as well as its new international political relations. In 1992, Aylwin restructured DIRECON and created an inter-ministerial committee, the *Comité Interministerial de Relaciones Económicas Internacionales,* that had to coordinate the ministries of Foreign Affairs (in charge of economic relations with Latin America), Economy (handling relations with the Asia-Pacific region and Europe), and Finance (responsible for relations with North America). This entire structure was coordinated by the Secretary General to the Presidency (Mladinic 2000; Porras 2003). The restructuring – to enable a more effective handling of economic globalisation and regionalisation – produced a modern state management of trade and economic relations of which later *Concertación* governments were able to benefit.

Nevertheless, Aylwin's 'open regionalism' and the signing of regional or bilateral agreements for preferential trade were not applauded by Chile's private sector as a whole. On the one hand, the business organisations representing the large economic groups supported policies for greater access to the markets of industrialised countries, such as the United States and the European Economic Community. On the other hand, the business organisations representing small and medium-sized companies were in favour of better economic relations with Latin America, which had traditionally been their export market. It was, however, the large economic groups and conglomerates monopolising the interaction with the state, and they also criticised the first democratic government's trade policies. They did so in a contradictory and confusing manner, first demanding to prioritise economic opening to the North American and European markets, and then showing indifference to the negotiations with the European Economic Community. Only the agricultural association SNA clearly opposed the import of agricultural products from Europe (Saéz 1993).

In December 1990, the framework agreement between the European Community and Chile was signed, which included a wide spectrum of political and social issues, but said little about trade liberalisation since the European Community was unwilling to grant major concessions, especially on agricultural and meat products (Silva 2001). Against this meagre result, Chile searched to strengthen its trade relations with the Asia-Pacific region, which as of the 1980s had become Chile's new trade horizon. The Chilean government stressed Chile's economic capacity to function as a bridge between Latin America and Asia. Therefore, it was crucial that Chile become a member of the organisation for Asia-Pacific Economic Cooperation, APEC, in which it succeeded in doing in November 1994. However, the Aylwin government did not realise its main objective: a free trade agreement with the United States.

During the last stage of Pinochet's rule, the relations between Chile and the United States were characterised by a high level of conflict, which had partly arisen from the changed US policies toward dictatorial regimes. The US imposition of non-tariff barriers on products from Chile, especially fruits, harmed Chilean companies. The most conflicting issue between the United States and Chilean exporters took place in March 1989, with the obscure discovery of poisoned Chilean grapes in Philadelphia's port. Subsequently, the US government accepted the request by the large US trade union federation AFL-CIO to exclude Chile from the Generalized System of Preferences because of Chile's incompliance with international labour standards. As a result, the start of the Aylwin government coincided with a profound anti-Americanism among right-wing politicians, heirs of Pinochet, and the corporate followers of the dictatorial regime, who all mistrusted the new President's neoliberal faith. This surreal situation was complemented by Chile's moderate left and the democratic government both aspiring for the rapid normalisation of the political and economic relations with the United States (Porras 2003).

Initially, the Aylwin government kept hoping to achieve free trade with the United States, parallel to or immediately after Mexico's entry into the NAFTA. With his visit to the United States in May of 1992, President Aylwin attempted to reach a compromise about stepping up free trade negotiations as soon as Mexico, the United States and Canada concluded the NAFTA negotiations (which happened in August 1992). Apart from a general willingness, however, the US government made no promises and gave no deadlines. Thus, Chile entered an unknown scenario of negotiations, and depended on consultancy agencies (such as the law firm Akin, Gump, Hauer & Feld) to lobby for Chilean trade in the White House, US Congress, and US labour unions and business organisations. The subsequent election of President Bill Clinton, and the opposition of US labour organisations as well as environmental organisations, turned the Chile-US FTA into a long-term project that would only be completed during the government of President Lagos (Fazio 2004).

The priority given to free trade with the United States by the *Concertación*'s first government caused an abandonment of Chile's entry into MERCOSUR, while contributing to Chile's support for the US hemispheric initiative that was announced in 1991 by President (George H.W.) Bush. This *Iniciativa de las Américas* aimed to form the Free Trade Area of the Americas (FTAA; in Spanish, *Área de Libre Comercio de las Américas*, ALCA), stretching from 'Alaska to Tierra del Fuego'. Chile's distant relations to Latin America under Aylwin were supposed to be corrected during the presidency of Frei (1994–2000) by means of revising its relations with MERCOSUR. Yet Chile's support for the FTAA and the US strategy of establishing bilateral trade agreements with Latin American countries in order to impede collective demands from the region distanced Chile only further from Latin American initiatives for regional integration such as MERCOSUR. Furthermore, Chile did not approve of the European Union's strategy of privileging its relations with MERCOSUR as a way to weaken the US economic influence over Latin America in favour of European economic expansion in the region. Already in 1990, Chile had been invited by Brazil and Argentina to become a part of MERCOSUR, but instead Chile decided to be the first country to express full support for the *Iniciativa de las Américas,* and in return acquired credits from the Inter-American Development Bank (IDB) for private sector investments.

The second *Concertación* government was lead by President Frei (1994–2000) and adopted a policy of economic globalisation and regionalisation through the so-called 'business deals diplomacy'. Its finance minister, Eduardo Aninat, declared on various occasions that in business terms, Chileans wanted to turn into Latin America's Phoenicians, for which they relied on political and economic stability through its exemplary transition to democracy. The Frei government began with the good news that Chile had been accepted as a member of APEC. And in contrast with Aylwin, President Frei reiterated his willingness to strengthen economic relations with Latin America, calling it 'our neighbourhood in the Global Village'. However, his government was put to the test: economically by the Mexican crisis (1994–1995) and the Asian crisis (1997–1998), and politically by the arrest of Manuel Contreras, the head of the police and a political accomplice of Pinochet, and by the London arrest of the dictator himself. The Mexican crisis proved a new obstacle for Chile's desire to materialise free trade with the United States, as a result of the additional US financial support used to rescue this NAFTA partner (Lustig 1997; Fazio 1998). Unexpectedly, in the Miami meeting of the Chamber of the Americas in December 1994, Chile received an official invitation from Canada, Mexico and the United States to join the NAFTA. But the euphoria was short lived because the electoral defeat of the Democratic Party (and the AFL-CIO stating that this was linked to the effects of NAFTA), and the 'tequila crisis' of 1994–1995 made it impossible for President Clinton to achieve minimal Congressional support for the (so-called fast track) negotiations with Chile. The protectionist tendencies that arose within the Republican Party did the rest to destroy Chile's hopes.

This new failure of Chile's attempt to enter into NAFTA once again forced the Chilean government to re-orient its policy on trade agreements. It started negotiations for a free trade agreement with Canada, a major source of foreign direct investment in the Chilean mining sector; parts of Chile's agricultural and industrial sectors also supported this agreement. The Canada-Chile FTA formed the first in a series of trade treaties to be signed. The importance of Chile's entry into MERCOSUR was stressed again by proponents, but others feared that doing so would be harmful because MERCOSUR's requirements for collective negotiations with other economies would limit Chile's possibilities for reaching free trade through bilateral agreements. Moreover, in Chile there was the perception of MERCOSUR members as struggling with economic instability while lacking the capacity necessary to achieve regional integration in the long run. This view was even expressed by business organisations of the manufacturing sector (SOFOFA and ASEXMA), which was likely to be an important beneficiary of Chile's entry into MERCOSUR. Nevertheless, the extraordinary expansion of trade with the MERCOSUR economies created a generally favourable Chilean attitude toward this economic bloc.

MERCOSUR

In the negotiations for Chile's association to MERCOSUR, the main issue was the competitiveness of the Chilean economy, which had much lower trade tariffs than the ones collectively adopted by MERCOSUR. The Chilean private sector was divided, as the manufacturing sector and agricultural sector took different positions toward MERCOSUR. The SNA opposed Chile's association to MERCOSUR as it considered the association to be disadvantageous for Chile's traditional agricultural sectors. Yet SOFOFA and ASEXMA declared that it was unacceptable that the protection of such sectoral interests would stop an agreement that would be beneficial to the Chilean economy at large. A more moderate opposition was taken by the CPC, which considered the agreement that was signed with MERCOSUR in August 1996 to have little meaning in terms of trade liberalisation (Silva and Alvarez 2006). Eventually, Chile had to wait until the presidency of Ricardo Lagos (2000–2006) to reach an agreement with MERCOSUR about Chile's autonomy and its ability to decide on its national trade policy. This privileged position of association was clearly facilitated by the ideological match of President Lagos with President Fernando H. Cardoso (Brazil) and President Fernando de la Rúa (Argentina), who considered themselves to be representatives of the South American version of the Third Way. This exceptional form of association did force Chile to protect itself from the negative effects of different tariffs, different levels of economic openness, and economic instability in the other MERCOSUR economies.

The Frei government also strengthened Chile's economic ties with Mexico, the Asia-Pacific region, and the European Union (EU). The *Acuerdo de Complementación Económica* with Mexico, which had been signed by Aylwin, was implemented and extended. With the EU, the Framework Agreement of Cooperation was signed in 1996. By doing so, the European Union showed for the first time a willingness to negotiate with an individual Latin American country rather than only with the region's economic blocs. However, Chile hoped to subsequently replace the Framework Agreement of Cooperation (which had been of little significance due to the limited European willingness to regulate its agricultural sector) by a new scheme of economic relations with the EU that would lead to the establishment of a Free Trade Agreement. Eventually in 2002, during the presidency of Lagos, Chile would consolidate its economic relations with the European Union by signing the EU-Chile Agreement of Political and Economic Association. With respect to the Asia-Pacific region, in 1994, the Frei government created the *Fundación Chilena de Pacífico* to enhance Chile's economic presence in the region. In addition, several business organisations established an advisory business council to APEC. Next, President Lagos renewed the Chilean agenda of economic insertion in the Asia-Pacific region by means of bilateral negotiations with the Republic of Korea, Japan, Singapore, and China. Yet the two largest accomplishments of Chile's new agenda of economic insertion in regional and global markets would be its free trade agreements with the United States and with China.

FTA with the United States

The free trade agreement with the United States that was signed at the beginning of Lagos' presidency was one of the most important goals of Chile's trade agenda. The return of the Republicans – with George W. Bush's presidency and a majority in the US Congress – helped Chile to achieve this goal. The first round of the official negotiations was held in Santiago in January

2001. In contrast with Chile's previous negotiations with the United States, these were lead by the Chilean President (Lagos) himself, supported by the Ministry of Foreign Affairs and DIRECON. For the first time, civil society organisations such as *la Alianza Chilena para el Comercio Justo* (Chilean Alliance for Fair Trade) became active on such trade negotiations. Transnationally, Chilean groups worked together with influential US organisations such as Public Citizen, Sierra Club and Friends of the Earth, but they had little effect on the negotiations and the final agreement (Porras 2003). Another difference with previous negotiations was that business associations showed a high level of cohesion, and the CPC was invited to participate in the privileged dialogue meetings organised by the government that ran parallel to the negotiations. Chilean businessmen were very enthusiastic about the Chile-US Free Trade Agreement since they saw it as an instrument to prevent any future attempts to reform Chile's neoliberal economic model. The only business opposition came from the SNA, which considered the agreement damaging to Chile's traditional agriculture sector, especially to wheat and beet farmers. Due to the attacks of 11 September 2001, the negotiations between Chile and the United States were delayed for some time, but they were finalised in December 2002, and in 2003 the FTA was ratified by both countries.

Before the agreement with the United Sates was signed and ratified, however, Chile was put to a test of loyalty when the United States demanded Chile's support for its war in Iraq. In April 2003, US Trade Representative Robert Zoellick expressed his government's disappointment over the fact that Chile would not support the US request for authorisation by the United Nations Security Council for invading Iraq. The sanction consisted of a few weeks delay in the US signing the agreement, which eventually occurred in the absence of both Presidents. The public punishment came in a meeting on the FTAA in Puebla (Mexico, also in April 2003), where US representative Peter Allegeier declared that Chile had to understand that the US government was worried about the position taken by Chile in the Security Council (Fazio 2004). Against this background, the Chilean government decided to search for reconciliation with the United States: Chile gave its support for the sanctioning of Cuba because of its human rights situation, and supported the United Nations resolution that handed the administration of Iraq over to the United States.

FTA with China

In November 2005, Chile signed its FTA with China, which was put into effect in 2006. Already by 2005, China had become Chile's second trade partner (the United States being its first trade partner). With a bilateral trade volume of $6988 million, trade with China had become superior to that with countries such as Argentina, Japan, Brazil, or any single European economy. Chile's exports to China had expanded rapidly (see Table 4.1), and from 1995 to 2005 the bilateral trade increased by 7.04 per cent (DIRECON 2006). Chile was the first country in the world to reach a free trade agreement with China. China granted Chile an immediate elimination of 92 per cent of its import tariffs, and agreed to liberalise the rest within ten years. According to several estimates, this agreement will increase Chile's GDP by 1.4 per cent and produce 34,500 new jobs.

Table 4.1 Growth of Chile's Export to China and the World, 1997–2005 (%)

	1997	1998	1999	2000	2001	2002	2003	2004	2005
Exports to China	22.4	6.1	21.9	152.7	12.6	21.4	50.4	73.0	37.7
Global Exports	10.5	13.3	7.9	15.8	4.1	0.0	16.7	52.5	24.8

Source: DIRECON (2006)

The recently well-developed relations between China and Chile played a decisive role in the free trade negotiations. To China, it was particularly important that Chile had been the first Latin American country with which it held bilateral negotiations about the Chinese entry into the WTO. Chile was also the first to recognise China's (WTO) status as 'market economy', which is vital to China's international economic competitiveness (see also chapter one). Furthermore, Chile and China had developed intensive diplomatic contacts through the periodical meetings of the leaders of the APEC countries. In November 2004, Presidents Lagos and Hu Jintao thus announced the start of their free trade negotiations during APEC's annual meeting. The first round of negotiations (in January 2005) were about import tariffs, market access, rules of origin, customs, technical trade barriers, and resolution mechanisms. In the second round (April), a high-level joint technical group was created. During the third round (June), progress was made on the issues of services, investments, intellectual property rights, labour, environment, scientific and technical collaboration, and small business (CEPAL 2005).

In the Chilean strategy for Asia, Chile's economic activities with and in Asia evolve around strong economic relations with China, which is considered to be the central economic actor of the region. This centrality of China can be observed in Chile's FTA negotiations with China, in its diplomatic relations with China since 1970, as well as in their long history of consul relations (since the nineteenth century). Still, Chile's deepened relations with China have been part of a broad agenda for cooperation with Asia. Its Asian strategy was consolidated by the Trans Pacific Strategic Agreement founded in 2000 with New Zealand, Singapore and Brunei Darussalam. Prior to the FTA with China, Chile had established a FTA with Korea (in effect since

April 2004), which was in fact the first FTA between a Latin American and an Asian country. In addition, Chile has signed an Agreement of Partial Alliance with India and has been negotiating free trade with Japan, while studying the possibilities of FTAs with Thailand and Malaysia.

Conclusions

The effects of China's rapid economic growth and insertion into the global markets on Latin American countries vary widely. On the one hand, Mexico, Central America and the Caribbean have experienced that the massive influx of Chinese products to the United States have evaporated many of the preferential advantages of the NAFTA, the FTA between the United States, Central America and the Dominican Republic (CAFTA-DR), and the *Iniciativa de la Cuenca del Caribe*. On the other hand, South America and particularly Chile are major beneficiaries of China's demand for commodities. South American countries turned into China's most important suppliers: in 2004, soy coming from Brazil and Argentina represented 60 per cent of China's soy imports; Peru and Chile produced 80 per cent of all fish flour imported by China; 60 per cent of Chinese imports of poultry came from Argentina and Brazil; and 45 per cent of Chinese imports of grapes and wine originated from Chile. It must be noted, however, that the exports of South American countries to China are very concentrated, and in Chile's case 76 per cent of its exports to China involve one single commodity: copper (Rosales and Kuwayama 2007).

Chile's extensive relations with China, including their bilateral Free Trade Agreement, are only one ingredient of its striking economic pragmatism. This chapter has pointed out that free trade with China thus was a logic step in the regionalisation and globalisation strategies that have been applied by various Chilean governments, including those of Ricardo Lagos and Michelle Bachelet of the Socialist Party of Chile. Within the region, this economic pragmatism is exceptional – the globalisation of its economy has not been obstructed by ideological or political limitations. As a result, Chile is similarly exceptional for its long-term loyalty to neoliberalism and its hospitality to transnational capital.

Chile hopes that its Free Trade Agreement with China will enable a diversification of this highly concentrated export basket by means of the export of agricultural, meat, forestry and fish products. Many of these products are on the list of high tariffs that can still be applied in the first ten years of the Chile-China FTA. Nevertheless, it was the spectacular expansion of Chilean copper exports to China and the spectacular increase of the copper price on the world market resulting from the Chinese demand that have supported the sustainable growth of the Chilean economy over the past few years. Chile also hopes to use the FTA with China to become a regional trade platform as well as a bridge for the exchange of goods and services between Asia and Latin America's Southern Cone. For this purpose, Chile will make use of the commercial and financial possibilities of being an associated member of MERCOSUR, and from its various FTAs with Asian countries. With some stimuli to important economic sectors, Chile's FTA with China may allow for more economic diversification, for instance, through the location of the final processing of transnational production chains in Chile. Despite these Chilean ambitions to become a regional platform and a cross-Pacific bridge, for the time being most of the Chilean gains from China's economic expansion remain concentrated in the extraction of copper.

References

Banco Central de Chile. 2005. *Indicadores de Coyuntura.* Santiago: Banco Central de Chile.

Butelmann, Andrea. 1993. 'Acuerdos de Libre Comercio. ¿Que se negocia?' In Andrea Butelmann and Patricio Meller, *Estrategia Comercial Chilena para la Decada de los 90.* Santiago: Cieplan.

Cámara de Diputados de Chile. 2005. Informe de la Comisión Privatizaciones Cámara de Diputados 2005. Valparaíso: Cámara de Diputados de la República de Chile.

Campero, Guillermo. 2003. 'La Relación entre el Gobierno y los Grupos de Presión: El proceso de la Acción de bloques a la acción segmentada'. *Revista de Ciencia Política* XXIII (2): 159–76.

Carmona, Ernesto. 2002. *Los Dueños de Chile.* Santiago: Ediciones La Huella.

CEPAL. 2006. *Balance Preliminar de las Economías de América Latina y el Caribe.* Santiago: Naciones Unidas.

———. 2005. *Panorama de la Inserción Internacional de América Latina y el Caribe, 2004. Tendencias 2005.* Santiago: Naciones Unidas.

CODELCO. 2006. *Informe y Balance 2006.* Santiago: CODELCO.

———. 2002. *Informe y Balance 2002.* Santiago: CODELCO.

DIRECON. 2006. *Tratado de Libre Comercio Chile—China.* Santiago: Ministerio de Relaciones Exteriores.

Fazio, Hugo. 1998. *El 'Tigre' chileno y la crisis de los 'Dragones' asiáticos.* Santiago: LOM.

———. 2004. *TLC. El amarre del modelo.* Santiago: Universidad Academia de Humanismo Cristiano.

———. 2005. *Mapa de la Extrema Riqueza al año 2005.* Lom: Santiago de Chile.

———. 2006. *Lagos: El Presidente 'progresista'de la Concertación.* Santiago: Lom.

Fernández Jilberto, Alex E. 2004a. 'The Political Economy of Neoliberal Governance in Latin America: The Case of Chile'. In *Good Governance in the Era of Global Neoliberalism. Conflict and Depolitisation in Latin America, Eastern Europe, Asia and Africa,* eds. Jolle Demmers, Alex E. Fernández Jilberto, and Barbara Hogenboom, 38–65. London: Routledge.

———. 2004b. 'Neoliberal Restructuring: The Origin and Formation of Economic Groups in Chile'. *Journal of Developing Societies* 20 (3–4): 189–206.

Fernández Jilberto, Alex E. and Barbara Hogenboom. 2007. 'Latin American and China under Global Neoliberalism'. Journal of Developing Societies 23(4): 467-501.

Ffrench-Davis, Ricardo. 1999. *Entre el Noeliberalismo y el Crecimento con Equidad. Tres Décadas de Política Económica en Chile.* Santiago: Dolmen.

Fuentes, Luis Arturo. 1997. *Los Grupos Económicos en Chile y los Modelos de Propiedad en otros Países*. Santiago: Dolmen.

Gutiérrez, Hernán. 2001. 'Las relaciones de China y América Latina: Perspectivas desde Argentina, Brasil y Chile'. *Integración & Comercio* 14: 75–116.

———. 2003. *Oportunidades y desafíos de los vínculos económicos de China y América Latina y el Caribe*. Santiago: Cepal/Naciones Unidas.

Kay, C. and R.A. Gwynne. 1999. *Latin America Transformed: Globalisation and Modernity*. London: Arnold.

Klein, Nagel and Maritza Arenas. 2000. *Inmigrantes chinos en Chile*. Santiago: Instituto de Estudios Internacionales.

Korzeniewics, Roberto and William C. Smith. 2000. 'Los Ejes de la Tercera Vía en América Latina'. In *Chile 1999–2000. Nuevo Gobierno: desafíos de la reconciliación*, ed. Francisco Rojas Aravena. Santiago de Chile: Flacso.

Lin Chou, Diego. 2004. *Chile y China: Inmigración y Relaciones Bilaterales 1945–1970*. Santiago: Ediciones de la Dirección de Bibliotecas, Archivos y Museos.

Lustig, Nora. 1997. 'Los Estados Unido al rescate: la asistencia financiera a México en 1982 y 1995'. *Revista de la Cepal* 61: 39–61.

Ministerio de Hacienda. 2006. *Informe de Estado de la Hacienda Pública 2006*. Santiago: Gobierno de Chile.

Mladinic, Carlos. 2000. *Apertura al exterior y negociaciones comerciales: lecciones y experiencias del caso chileno*. Santiago: IICA.

Mönckeberg, María Olivia. 2001. *El Saqueo de los Grupos Económicos al Estado Chileno*. Santiago: Ediciones B.

Montero, Cecilia. 1997. *La Revolución Empresarial Chilena*. Santiago: Dolmen.

Porras, José Ignacio. 2003. *La Estratégia chilena de acuerdos comerciales: un análisis político*. Santiago: Cepal / Naciones Unidas.

Reinoso, Jose. 2007. 'El BBVA invertirá otros 1.000 millones en el grupo chino Citic'. *El País*, 3 March.

Rivas, Gonzalo. 2004. 'Opciones de la banca de desarrollo en Chile: el convidado de piedra del sistema financiero chileno'. Serie *Financiamiento del Desarrollo* no. 148. Santiago: CEPAL.

Rosales, Osvaldo and Mikio Kuwayama. 2007. *América Latina y China e India: hacia una nueva alianza de comercio e inversión*. Santiago: Cepal/Naciones Unidas.

Salazar, Gabriel. 2006. 'Ricardo Lagos, 2000–2005: Perfil histórico, transfondo popular'. In Hugo Fazcio et al., *Gobierno de Lagos: un balance crítico*. Santiago: Lom.

Saéz, Sebastián. 1993. 'Chile y la Comunidad Económica Europea'. In *Estrategia Comercial Chilena para la decada del 90*, comp. Andrea Butelmann and Patricio Meller. Santiago: Cieplan.

SBIF. 2006. *Información Financiera 2006*. Santiago: Superintendencia de Bancos e Instituciones Financieras de Chile.

Silva, Eduardo. 1996. *The State and Capital in Chile. Business Elites, Technocrats and Market Economics*. Westview Press: Colorado.

———. 2002. 'Capital and the Lagos Presidency: Business as Usual?' *Bulletin of Latin American Research*, 21 (3): 339–57.

Silva, Veronica. 2001. *Estrategia y Agenda Comercial Chilena en los años noventa*. Serie Comercio Internacional, No. 11. Santiago: Cepal.

Silva, Veronica and Ana Maria Alvarez. 2006. *Cooperación en políticas de competencia y acuerdos comerciales de América Latina y el Caribe: desarrollo y perspectivas*. Santiago: CEPAL/UN.

Stallings, Barbara. 2005. 'Financial sector development in Latin America and East Asia: a comparison of Chile and South Korea'. In *Managing Development; Globalisation, Economic Restructuring, and Social Policy*, ed. Junji Nkagawa. London: Routledge.

———. 2006. *Financiamiento para el Desarrollo. América Latina desde una perspectiva comparada*. Santiago: CEPAL.

Stanley, Leonardo. 2004. *Acuerdos bilaterales de inversión y demandas ante Tribunales Internacionales: la experiencia argentina reciente.* Santiago: Cepal / Naciones Unidas.

Taylor, Marcus. 2006. *From Pinochet to the 'Third Way'. Neoliberalism and Social Transformation in Chile.* London: Pluto Press.

5 Argentina's Relations with China
Opportunities and Challenges
Carla V. Oliva

At the beginning of the twenty-first century, China rose as a key global player with increasing political, economic and military power. China has gone through an exceptional journey, from poverty, a communist revolution and international insertion based on ideological criteria, to economic growth, political institutionalisation and international insertion based on economic priorities. This was possible due to the economic reforms carried out since 1978 by Mao's successor, Deng Xiaoping, who gave priority to economic development and modernisation based on economic and political opening. As a result, China has grown at an average annual rate of 10 per cent for more than 25 years. Likewise, major economic and social transformations have taken place, especially in the production structures and the population's quality of life.

The entry of China into the World Trade Organisation (WTO) in 2001 has particularly enhanced its importance in the world economy. China's increasing demand of natural resources and raw materials to sustain its economic growth led it to develop deeper relations with different regions in the world, among which Latin America stands out. Given its amount of natural resources, such as oil, iron and copper ore, and soy, the region has become a relevant supplier for China and a destination for its investments in natural resources and other sectors.

Since 1989, with the end of the Cold War and the start of China's economic rise, the relations with China began to be of importance to the Argentine government. Argentina's foreign policy toward China has been primarily focused on economic aspects, based on the assessment of China as a potential destination for Argentine exports and the desire to obtain Chinese investments. Simultaneously, China has been giving priority to the development of economic connections with countries that can provide natural resources. Economic interests thus have been a key element in their bilateral relations. Nevertheless, in the last few years, there has been a gradual diversification of items on the bilateral agenda, and investments and contacts in areas such as culture and education have been expanded. Apart from state officials, also businessmen, scholars and sub-national officials have come to participate in the Sino-Argentine relations.

This chapter studies various dimensions of the relations of Argentina with China with the purpose of providing a wide frame of analysis allowing for a better understanding of the evolution of this relationship. It assesses Argentina's foreign policy toward China, and subsequently looks into political-diplomatic aspects, economic dimensions and cultural exchange. Finally, the concluding remarks also discuss the relevance of these bilateral relations for the position of Argentina and China in multilateral institutions.

Argentina's Foreign Policy toward China

In 1972, 23 years after the proclamation of the People's Republic of China (PRC), Argentina established diplomatic relations with China. This took place in an international context of decreasing tensions between the United States and the former Soviet Union (USSR), following a reconsideration of the principles of containment and a redefinition of Washington's foreign strategy by Secretary of State Henry Kissinger. The Sino-American rapprochement enabled China's admittance to the United Nations and Taiwan's displacement from this organisation and the Security Council. The US recognition of China in 1971 had a remarkable influence on the Argentine military government. Headed by General Agustín Lanusse, the government decided to establish diplomatic relations with China. Not long before, in the midst of an ideological confrontation between capitalism and communism, this would have been unthinkable

Argentina's military governments laid the foundations of the ties with China. They disregarded ideological differences and focused on the political and economic convenience of strengthening these bilateral relations. Similarly, under the pragmatic leadership of Deng Xiaoping, the Chinese process of reform and opening up to the world began in 1978. China gave priority to economic relations with capitalist industrialised countries since they were in a condition to provide the country with the means to achieve economic modernisation. With Latin America, instead of emphasising the relations with countries with strong nationalist tendencies, China prioritised the development of ties with influential, politically moderate and financially more developed countries such as Brazil, Mexico, Venezuela, Chile and Argentina. Argentina fostered the signing of bilateral agreements on economic cooperation and trade. In 1980, for the first time, an Argentine president, General Jorge Videla, visited China. This Sino-Argentine rapprochement satisfied the needs of both partners at that time: China would have a Latin American partner for its economic transformation project, and Argentina would have a potential export market as well as a political ally that could mitigate its international isolation due to the accusations of human rights violations (Cesarin 2007: 2).

In 1983, before Argentina's presidential elections that marked the return of democracy, the candidate for the Unión Cívica Radical, Raúl Alfonsín, received an invitation to visit China. After winning the elections, the president-elect sent an important delegation to Beijing (Shixue, 2006: 68) and in 1988 he visited the People's Republic of China himself. On the latter occasion, the two countries signed agreements on cooperation in the Antarctic, on astronautic research and on cooperation on animal quarantine and health.

During the two presidential terms of Carlos Menem (1989–99), the bonds with China were further strengthened as China's potential as export market for Argentine products was recognised. As of 1990, China and Argentina have been holding political consultation meetings; in fact, China was the first Asian country to establish this kind of contact with Argentina. Menem visited China in 1990 and in 1995 to promote the development of political and economic relations. On these occasions, he travelled with a delegation of businessmen who took part in negotiations with Chinese counterparts in the cities of Beijing and Shanghai. Still, China did not have an important position on Argentina's foreign policy agenda, as its traditional economic relations with the United States, Latin America and Europe were Argentina's priority.

During the brief two-year presidency of Fernando De La Rúa (1999–2001), Argentina's attitude and policies toward China continued in the direction adopted under Menem. Rapprochement and mutual acquaintance were considered the first steps to gaining Chinese trust, which was seen as crucial to establish more business deals between partners coming from such different cultures. The strategy of political rapprochement clearly showed in the official meetings in 2000 and 2001. In January 2000, President De La Rúa met Chinese Vice-Premier Wu Bangguo in Davos (Switzerland), in the context of the World Economic Forum meeting. This was followed by a visit of the Argentine Head of State to China in September of 2000 and by a visit by the Chinese President Jiang Zemin to Argentina in April of 2001. Both parties expressed the importance of their bilateral relations and cooperation, and many agreements were signed, on issues such as cultural and educational cooperation, and scientific and technical cooperation in geosciences. Also, a memorandum of understanding was signed between Argentina's Energy and Mining Department and China's Ministry of Land and Natural Resources.

The opening of the Argentine Consulate General and its Commercial Promotion Centre in Shanghai in May of 2000 also clearly demonstrated Argentina's interest in China. Menem's administration had announced the centre's creation on many occasions and it was finally materialised under his successor, despite the government's budget constraints at that time. This consulate was deliberately located in an economically dynamic area from where it would be easier to identify trade opportunities and to establish contacts with Chinese companies and authorities.[1] However, while Argentina's foreign policy toward

China maintained an economic profile during the governments of Presidents Menem and De La Rúa, based on the appreciation of China's huge potential market and the opportunities to export to that destination, the statistics show that trade with China was still rather limited (see Figure 5.1). In short, the intentions and actions did not seem to produce much direct results, and the ties with China were not of great priority to Argentina, compared to its relations with Latin America, Europe and the United States.

From an economic perspective, the year 2001 was a turning point in the Sino-Argentine relations as Argentine exports to China exceeded $1 billion for the first time. Less positive, however, was the lack of diversity of these exports in which soy made up the greater part. In addition, between 2001 and 2003, Argentina experienced a profound economic, political and social crisis, as a result of which foreign affairs received less institutional attention. After Fernando De La Rúa's resignation in December 2001, several interim presidents followed until the designation of Eduardo Duhalde (from the Justicialist Party) as provisional president in January 2002, to complete the presidential term. In this period, Argentina officially defaulted, and its foreign affairs came to revolve almost exclusively around that issue. The debt restructuring process to meet the obligations to foreign creditors became the main item on Argentina's foreign agenda, prioritising the contacts with countries whose citizens were (and still are) the major Argentine bondholders, such as Germany, Italy, Japan and the United States.

In May 2003, Néstor Kirchner became Argentina's president and his policy goals included some foreign policy guidelines that had a direct effect on the relations with China (Jefatura de Gabinete de Ministros 2004: 31–32). Priority was given to negotiations with Asian countries in order to gain new markets, encourage foreign investments, enhance Argentina's international economic insertion and promote joint action with exporting companies. According to official statements, one of Argentina's strategic objectives was international insertion based on productive integration with countries with a trade profile complementary to that of Argentina (Redrado 2004a). China was considered as one of the 'seven great pivotal points of Argentine commercial policy' and Argentina aimed to creation permanent, balanced and mutual bilateral ties, based on with convergent interests (Redrado 2004b). In short, as of 2003, Argentina's foreign policy toward China focused again on economic relations, emphasising the role of this Asian country as a trade partner and fostering 'far-reaching' relations.

Visits and Agreements

Since 2000, Argentina and China have been actively intensifying their relations through a large number of visits, agreements and other initiatives.[2] In

2000, when President Fernando De La Rúa went on a state visit to China, the bilateral agreement on China's accession to the WTO was signed. In 2001, when the Chinese President Jiang Zemin and the President of the National People's Congress travelled to Argentina, agreements on bio-engineering and bio-safety and on legal assistance in civil and trade affairs were signed. During Argentina's crisis, there were no visits of high-ranking officials between China and Argentina, but in 2003 they were resumed. In November 2003, the Argentine Minister of Foreign Affairs, Rafael Bielsa, travelled to China and met with Premier Wen Jiabao (who would visit Argentina in 2004) and Foreign Minister Tang Jiaxuan. The Argentine mission included the Secretary of International Trade (Martín Redrado), the Secretary of Industry, Livestock, Fishing and Food (Miguel Campos) and a group of businessmen who came to sign business agreements. Argentina announced the decision to create an Agricultural Attaché's Office in Beijing, like the ones it had already established in Brussels, Washington, DC and Brasilia. When President Kirchner visited China a few months later, the Attaché's Office was officially opened.

In 2004, from 28 June to 2 July, President Kirchner visited the Chinese capital, Beijing, and its economically most booming city, Shanghai. He was accompanied by his wife, then Senator Cristina Fernández, who in 2007 would be elected as President of Argentina. In addition, the Minister of Federal Planning (Julio de Vido), the Minister of Economy (Roberto Lavagna), the Presidency's Legal and Technical Secretary (Carlos Zanini), the Chief of the Justicialist Deputies' bloc (José María Díaz Bancalari) and the governors of the provinces of Buenos Aires, Córdoba, Santa Fe, San Juan, Jujuy, Mendoza and Santa Cruz were also present. Kirchner met President Hu Jintao, Premier Wen Jiabao and the Chairman of the Standing Committee of the National People's Congress, Wu Bangguo. As a result of those meetings, a series of agreements were signed, with the purpose of increasing investments and encouraging the creation of Sino-Argentine companies. The main areas of interest were mining, biotechnology, bio-safety, food and agriculture, energy, chemistry, medicines, forestation, tourism, port equipment and services. Also, a delegation of over 200 businessmen was in China at the same time, and they held numerous business meetings. The Argentine government described it as 'the most important business tour in our history' (Redrado 2004c).

From 16 to 18 November 2004, President Hu Jintao visited Argentina, before going to the APEC summit in Chile. In the days prior to his visit to Argentina, the rumour was spread that Chinese officials would make an important announcement. There were speculations that in return for Argentina granting China 'market economy' status, China would pay a part of Argentina's external debt, or that it would make massive investments. While

Argentina indeed recognised China as a 'market economy', the rumours and expectations marred the real outcome of the presidential visit with regard to Chinese investment. Several letters of intent were signed on Chinese investments in Argentina, among other things in road construction, railways and the Agua Negra tunnel. A bilateral working group was created to analyse the possibilities for more economic complementarity. China also granted Argentina the status of tourist destination, which implies that Argentina was placed on the list of countries that Chinese citizens can choose from as a holiday destination.

To China, its recognition as a 'market economy' by the government of Argentina was a key issue during Hu Jintao's visit. Hu had previously gained the support of Brazil's President, Luiz Inácio Lula Da Silva, which conditioned the bargaining power of Argentine officials. The importance of this recognition lays in the role China plays in the WTO rules regarding competition and dumping (see chapter one of this volume). Without 'market economy' status, a country that can prove it has been harmed by cheap Chinese products can apply anti-dumping actions equivalent to the calculated dumping margin, which is then added to the import tariff. With China's recognition as a market economy, it would be harder for Argentine producers to be protected against such dumping (Tussie and Bianchi 2004). Therefore, Argentina's Minister of Economy, Roberto Lavagna, and potentially harmed business sectors strongly opposed granting China this 'market economy' status. During the first two weeks after Hu Jintao's visit, the private sector's worries of a possible flooding of Chinese products received extensive media attention in Argentina. Later on, however, the corporate complaints ceased, probably because the Argentine government was willing to apply other safeguards, such as quantitative restrictions or higher import tariffs.

In November 2005, the Argentine Minister for Foreign Affairs, Rafael Bielsa, visited China again. On the agenda was the purchase mechanism for Argentine debt bonds, which Argentina needed to meet its financial obligations to the International Monetary Fund (Argentina indeed paid off its debt two months later). Other issues were possible Chinese investments in the planned gas pipe from Caracas (Venezuela) to Buenos Aires, and the Chinese interest in investing in infrastructure, especially roads, railroads and power stations. Bielsa met with Foreign Minister Li Zhaoxing, Minister of Commerce Bo Xilai and former Foreign Minister Tang Jiaxuan. They agreed to take a common stance against US and European agriculture subsidies in the WTO summit in Hong Kong in December of 2005.

In 2006, Argentine Vice-President Daniel Scioli went to Beijing and Shanghai in October, and met with his Chinese colleague Zheng Qinghong, the Vice-Chairman of the National People's Congress, Wu Bangguo and the Mayor of Beijing, Wang Qishan. The Argentine Vice-President promoted a 'strategic alliance' between both countries and encouraged cooperation in the fields of politics, economics and technological innovation. A month later, Argentine Foreign Minister Jorge Taiana, together with executives from 25 small- and medium-sized enterprises made a trip to Shanghai and Nanjing with the purpose of diversifying the areas and sectors of Argentina's exports to China. The participating companies represented a range of sectors, including foodstuffs, wines, cereals, plastics, compressed natural gas, educational services, biotechnology, tobacco and pharmaceuticals. In Beijing, Taiana took part in political meetings and in the Joint Committee for Economic and Trade Cooperation, where he discussed issues such as anti-dumping, agricultural biotechnology cooperation, tourism, technology cooperation and the consolidation of the China-MERCOSUR[3] ties.

Trade Relations between Argentina and China

The centrality of economic aspects in their bilateral relations is a direct consequence of China's priorities with regard to Latin America in general, and Argentina in particular. China has encouraged relations with states around the world that can supply the natural resources necessary for its economic growth. Complementarity was a key factor in the rapid increase of trade between Argentina and China. The growing and changing Chinese consumer needs resulted in such an increase in Argentine exports that its trade deficit with China of the 1990s turned into a surplus. However, industrial exports from China to Argentina began to increase as well.

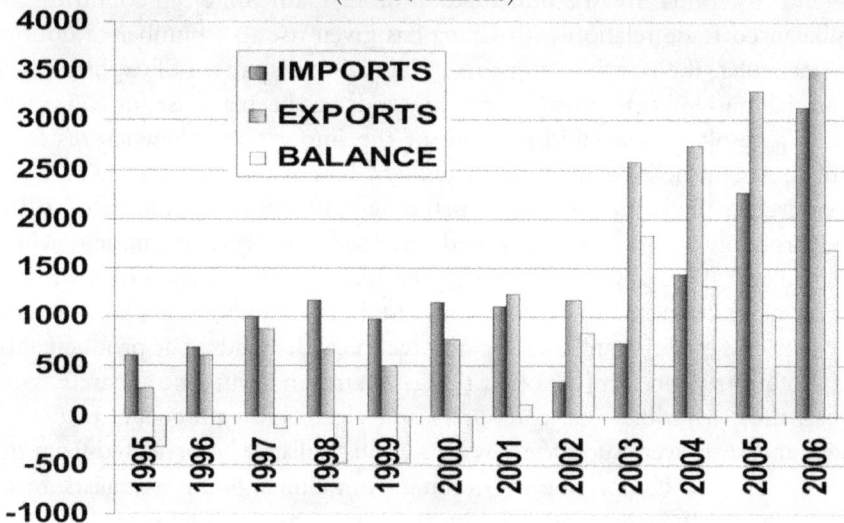

Figure 5.1. Argentina's Trade with China, 1995–2006
(in US$ millions)

Source: Centro de Economía Internacional (2007)

Since 2001, Argentina has had a trade surplus with the People's Republic of China, especially since 2003, when the trade flows in both directions started substantially to grow. In 2003, the Argentine exports to China doubled those of 2002 and valued over $2.5 billion. This was largely prompted by the increase in China's soybean demand. In 2006, China had become Argentina's fourth export destination, after Brazil, Chile and the United States, and its third supplier, after Brazil and the United States. Exports to China accounted for 7.9 per cent of Argentina's global exports, and Chinese imports made up 5.9 per cent of the total. Yet for China in that same year, Argentine imports represented only 0.4 per cent of China's total import, and its exports to Argentina 0.2 per cent of the Chinese total (Centro de Economía Internacional 2007).

Bilateral trade has been unbalanced, however, as Argentina exports primary products and agricultural manufactured goods to China while it imports manufactured goods from China (see Figures 5.2 and 5.3). In 2006, 52 per cent of Argentine imports from China were machinery and electric household appliances, whereas 84 per cent of Argentina's exports to China were concentrated in three products: soybean (41 per cent), crude oil (25 per cent) and soy oil (18 per cent). This high concentration of Argentine exports to China into the category of the so-called soy complex of soy bean, soy oil and soy flour (used mainly to feed pigs), indicates that Argentina is an important supplier of that product to China. As a result, Argentina's exports to China are very vulnerable to any variation in the demand and price of soy, as was shown in 2006 when the value and volume of soybean complex's products went down. China's soy imports originate from the world's three main producers: 60 per cent from the United States, and the rest, in equal shares, from Brazil and Argentina. In Argentina, like in other Latin American countries, the imbalanced trade relation with China has given rise to a number of doubts. In particular, the possible return to a colonial trade pattern of exporting raw materials and importing manufactured goods has been a cause for concern.

As a result of the rapid increase of the imports of manufactures from China, Argentine industrialists affected by Chinese competition began to put pressure on their government, demanding protection. In August of 2007, the Argentine government imposed restrictions on certain imports, which particularly affected Chinese goods. The restrictions consisted of the imposition of non-automatic permits and additional requirements, such as new security and quality standards and new technical demands. The products subject to quotas were, among other things, textile and synthetic apparels, footwear, tires, toys, bicycles, computers and electronic equipment. Evidently, these measures were supported by local industrialists who benefited from the limitations forced upon imports coming from China. Some specialists, however, rejected the measures, claiming that the measures closed the Argentine economy and would lead to higher prices of the affected goods (as they are produced at higher costs in Argentina).

Figure 5.2. Composition of Argentine Exports to China, 2006

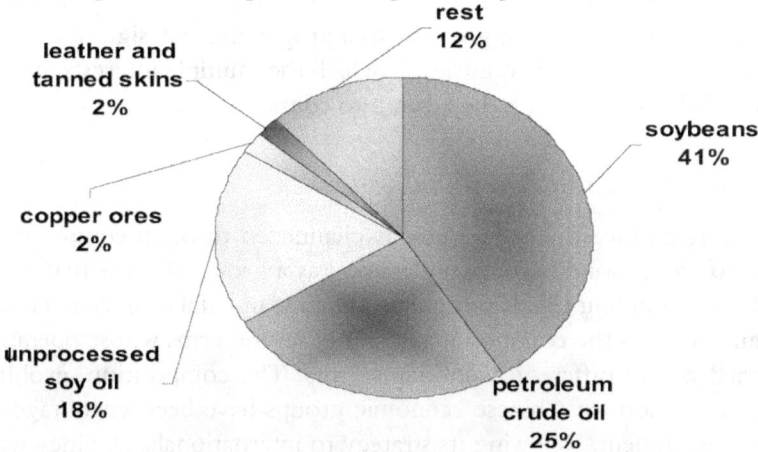

rest
12%

leather and
tanned skins
2%

soybeans
41%

copper ores
2%

unprocessed
soy oil
18%

petroleum
crude oil
25%

Source: Centro de Economía Internacional (2007)

Figure 5.3. Composition of Argentine Imports from China, 2006

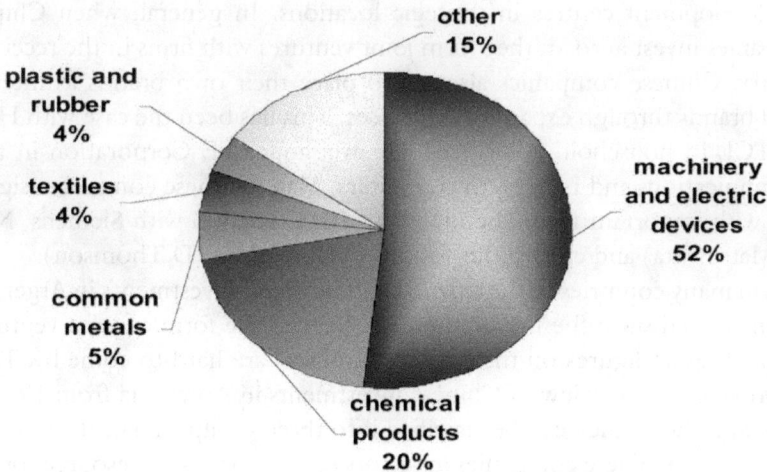

other
15%

plastic and
rubber
4%

machinery
and electric
devices
52%

textiles
4%

common
metals
5%

chemical
products
20%

Source: Centro de Economía Internacional (2007)

The Chinese government reacted formally to the Argentine measures by means of a complaint by its Minister of Trade to the Argentine Embassy in Beijing, in which he reserved 'the right to take the necessary actions' in view of Argentina's decision (Galak 2007). A few days after this announcement, it became known that Chinese customs officials applied more phytosanitary controls to ships loaded with Argentine soy, thereby delaying their admittance. Later on, meetings were held between officials of the Chinese Ministry of Economy, the Argentine Ministry of Foreign Affairs and the Chinese Ambassador in Buenos Aires, during which the tone of the dispute was softened and they agreed to work together to solve the issue. Solving these sorts of trade conflicts may over time give way to a progressive redesign of the trade relations between the two countries, in which the multiple interests involved in these relations will need to be taken into consideration.

Chinese Investments in Argentina

Chinese foreign investments are usually channelled through companies belonging to an economic group, understood as a group of firms that are related through binding bonds or capital. The fundamental characteristic of an economic group is the common managing of several firms whose operations are carried out in different economic sectors. The composition, evolution and foreign actions of Chinese economic groups have been encouraged by China's government, following its strategy to internationalise Chinese companies as part of the economic reforms as of 1978. Chinese economic groups are internationally inserted through mergers and acquisitions of already established technological companies, and through new investments in research and development centres in strategic locations. In general, when Chinese companies invest abroad, they form joint ventures with firms in the receiving country. Chinese companies also try to place their own brands as international brands through expansion processes. This has been the case with Haier and TCL in household appliances, Huawei and ZTE Corporation in telecommunications and Lenovo in computers. Many of these companies signed deals with important firms (Lenovo with IBM; Huawei with Siemens, NEC and Matsushita) and carried out fusions (TCL with DVD Thomson).

As in many countries in the world, Chinese direct investments in Argentina have increased since the mid 1990s, especially in the form of joint ventures. Although exact figures on the invested amounts are hard to come by, Table 5.1 provides an overview of Chinese investments in Argentina from 1995 to 2005, and shows they can be classified into three groups. First, there are investments by Chinese companies in sectors related to natural resources or raw materials like pisciculture, cereals and mining, including infrastructure for the export of the products to China. Second, there are Chinese investments with the purpose of supplying to new markets through local production, like in the cases of National Automobile Industry, Jincheng Group, Nanchang Railna and Sitong. Third, there are Chinese companies that, besides from gaining new markets, aim at placing their brands as international ones, such as TCL and Huawei. The geographical destination of these investments is also interesting, with many investment projects in the Argentine province of

Santa Fe. Since 2004, there has been a series of new Chinese investment plans and projects in Argentina, and Table 5.2 shows that the interests of Chinese companies have become more diverse than before, and include activities and sectors such as oil, construction, telecommunications, tobacco, infrastructure and tourism. These investment plans also indicate a wider geographical spread within Argentina.

Table 5.1. Chinese Investments in Argentina, 1995–2005

Company or Economic Group	Sector	Year	Province
Beijing Meilu Enterprises Co.		1995	Santa Fe
National Automobile Industry	vehicle assembly (trucks, minibuses, etc.)		Mendoza
Wuxi Little Swan	household appliances		
Global Fishing Co. Ltd.; Argentina Qiangua Fishing Co; Chonglu Fishing Co. Ltd.[a]	pisciculture		
Jincheng Group	motorcycle assembly	1999	Santa Fe
Nanchang Railna	motorcycle assembly	2000	Santa Fe
Sitong	textile	2002	Santa Fe
Huawei Technologies	telecommunications	2003	Buenos Aires
Noble Group	cereals commercialization	2005	Santa Fe
A Grade Trading Ltd.	mining	2005	Río Negro
TCL International Holdings Ltd.	household appliances	2005	Tierra del Fuego

a. These companies invested each in pisciculture, independently from one another.

Source: Elaborated by the author based on information from various Argentine media sources, the Argentine-Chinese Chamber of Production, Industry and Commerce, Argentina's Ministry of Economy (Foreign Trade Policy National Administration—Asia, Africa and Oceania Unit), China's Ministry of Foreign Affairs; and China's Ministry of Foreign Trade and Economic Cooperation.

Table 5.2. Chinese Investment Plans in Argentina, 2004–2007 (in US$ millions)

Company or Economic Group	Sector	Year[a]	Province	Sum appointed
China Beiya Escom International Limited; China Railway 20 TH Bureau Group	railway	2004		8.000
China National Petroleum Company; China National OffShore Oil Corp; China Pek	crude oil	2004	Continental Shelf	
New World; China Constructions	house construction	2004		6.000
	telecommunications and satellite technology	2004		260
Jiangsu Zhisi	tobacco	2004	Jujuy	20
FID[b]	infrastructure	2004	San Juan	300
COVEC	infrastructure	2005	Córdoba Santa Fe Entre Ríos	
Tianshi Group International	vitamin supplements and cosmetics	2005		
Shanghai's Chamber of Commerce	tourism-infrastructure	2006	San Juan	8
ZTE Corporation	telecommunications	2006	Santa Fe	
Huishang Group, Anhui Hui Zhang Chuangyuan, Decoration Co., Anhuio Hui Shang Fodd Inc., Anhui SZD Co.	mining, household appliances, supermarkets, construction industry and tourism	2006	La Pampa	
Anhui Winsang Group	product commercialization and distribution	2006	La Pampa	
Shinewide	sports shoes manufacturing	2007	Buenos Aires	

a. The year of the potential investment's proposal.

b. Shanghai Foreign Investment Development board (FID) is the organization in charge of advising Shanghai's companies on foreign investments.

Source: Elaborated by the author based on information from various Argentine media sources and Argentina's Ministry of Foreign Affairs and International Trade.

Note: These investment plans include different cases: announcements of intentions to invest, initial contacts and/or visits to analyze investment possibilities, declarations of interest, the signing of agreements of understanding, and the announcement of dates to start investment-related activities.

Ever since the 2004 presidential agreements, greater complementarity can be observed in Argentina's and China's strategies for investment, which has become a crucial item on the bilateral agenda. Argentina seeks to attract foreign investments due to its need to increase its productive capacity and employment, whereas China favours investing abroad due to its need to obtain vital resources for its economy. However, the expectations of multi-million dollar Chinese investments raised by the 2004 agreements have gradually vanished as the following years have shown that much of the anticipated capital did not arrive. Among the reasons for this development may also be Argentine faults, such as a lack of market research by public institutions.

Cultural Relations

The cultural bonds between Argentina and China have evolved in relation with the development of their economic ties. Since they include artistic expressions such as cinema, theatre and literature, sports, science, technology, education, as well as exchanges between all sorts of communities, the cultural dimensions are extensive and wide, and contribute to the consolidation of the bilateral relations in general. A special role is played by Chinese residents in Argentina, in particular regarding arts and education, which have contributed to the diversification and consolidation of cultural relations.

Chinese residents represent an increasingly important community in Argentina. While in the 1990s most of its Asian population came from Taiwan and Korea, from that time onward, more citizens from the People's Republic of China (mostly from the province of Fujian) began to arrive, and it turned into the main Asian migratory flow to Argentina. About 60,000 Chinese residents nowadays reside in Argentina, mainly in Buenos Aires (city and province). Working primarily in retail trade, Chinese residents play a relevant economic role in Argentina as they offer a cheaper shopping alternative to the large supermarket chains. In April, they created the Chamber of Self-service Stores and Supermarkets of Chinese Residents in the Republic of Argentina (CASRECH), which represents over 2,500 self-service stores and supermarkets. This Chamber takes part in meetings and organises conferences to enhance the sector's growth, the integration between members of the Chinese community and Argentine citizens and the fight against every kind of discrimination. As a sign of their interest to become part of Argentina's economy and society, the members of the Chamber of Self-service Stores and Supermarkets of Chinese Residents in the Republic of Argentina respected the system of fixed prices that President Kirchner designed and implemented to control the prices of basic products in 2006.

Contrary to the Maoist policies of active cultural diffusion, currently it is the increasing worldwide interest to learn about the Chinese history, culture, philosophy and language – along with the country's rise to a global player status – that is a driving force for cultural and educational bonds. Over the past few years, artistic delegations from both countries carried out visits, and the works of the renowned Argentine writer Jorge Luis Borges were pub-lished in Mandarin Chinese. In 2003, a group of China's central television stations invited by the Argentine National Department of Tourism produced a series of programmes about Argentina's tourist locations, sports, dances and food. In 2004, an agreement on (language) educational cooperation was signed, which included the decision to open a bilingual primary school in Buenos Aires, for which China would send teachers and didactic materials. The Argentine interest in the study of Mandarin Chinese showed from the increase in the number of students and in the opening of Chinese language study centres, especially in the most important universities of Argentina.

In Argentine universities and governments institutions as well as among students there are high expectations of these new connections with China. In view of the remarkable increase in the requests for scholarships to study in China, several universities in Argentina signed cooperation agreements with Chinese universities. In 2005, Argentina was the only Latin American country that took part, for the first time and with representatives from fif-teen universities, in the *China Education Expo* in Shanghai. In March 2007, representatives from 54 Chinese universities paid a visit to Argentina to in-form Argentine students and lecturers about their programmes, especially in economics and business, agriculture, medicine and engineering. Finally, the opening of a Confucius Institute in Argentina was announced, which is a prestigious institute that teaches the Chinese language in multimedia format and trains school teachers and university lecturers.

Conclusions

Apart from the various bilateral initiatives, visits, agreements and economic ties between Argentina and China, their relations are also relevant at the multilateral level, in particular in the United Nations (UN) and the World Trade Organisation. In the UN context, Argentina and China share positions regarding key matters on both countries' foreign agendas: the situation of human rights in China's case, and the status of the Islas Malvinas (Falkland Islands) in Argentina's case. Argentina does not condemn China on account of its human rights' situation. It has abstained from the yearly voting on UN resolutions to investigate China's human rights situation (proposed by the United States and successfully neutralised by China with the 'non-action' motion). As for the Islas Malvinas, Beijing supports Argentina's yearly claim in the UN Committee on Decolonisation. China's support for Argentina's position on the Islas Malvinas is consistent with its policy on Taiwan, which the PRC considers to be a rebel province that is part of its territory. In turn, Argentina (as any state that has diplomatic relations with the PRC) considers

Taiwan a part of China. In these instances, both China and Argentina refer to the International Law principles of territorial integrity, non-intervention and state sovereignty.

During the long and hard process in which China sought its reincorporation into the General Agreement on Tariffs and Trade (GATT)[4]/WTO, China engaged in multilateral negotiations with the Working Group on China's Status as a Contracting Party as well as bilateral negotiations with all of the members of the WTO. Bilaterally, Argentina agreed to support China in May 2000. In exchange, China granted Argentina exemption from customs barriers to 78 Argentine agricultural products. China's accession to the WTO in November 2001 represented a conclusion of a long process of economic reforms and negotiations, and the next phase of its integration into the global economy.

Parallel to its rise as a key global player, China has clearly strengthened its presence in different regions of the world. Also, Argentina has been establishing relations with the Asian country, based on a trade pattern in which China sells mainly manufactured goods and Argentina provides raw materials. In addition, some Chinese capital has been invested in Argentine natural resource sectors. Meanwhile, political ties have played an extremely important role as well, since the agreements on foreign and domestic policies that are relevant to both countries encourage cooperation. The high frequency of visits from high-ranking government officials and the number of signed agreements reflect a marked interest in consolidating the cooperation between the two countries, above all in economic affairs.

Although Argentina's foreign policy is generally characterised more by interruptions than continuity, its policies toward China appear to be an exception. The reasons for this exceptionality are of a political and economic nature. Politically, the absence of conflicts and the concurrence on foreign policy issues that are crucial to both states have contributed to harmony. The strengthening of cultural bonds as well as the growing knowledge about one another has also favoured understanding. Economically, the complementarity of the trade relations between Argentina and China over the past few years suggests that there is great potential for progress.

On the other hand, agreements at the macro level do not prevent conflicts from rising at the micro level, above all in the area of trade. This showed in the 2007 dispute, when the Argentine government enacted restrictions on the imports of particular industrial products that especially affected Chinese goods. In that case, the good condition of the bilateral political relations made it easier to end the trade conflict through negotiations. In other respects, Argentine sentiments about the economic relations with China went from a state of euphoria in 2004 with the Argentina's trade surplus and major Chinese investment plans, to a state of disappointment due to the trade surplus reduction and the low level of actual investments coming from China in the following years. Argentina's challenge is to find a formula to reconcile the interests of its agricultural sector, which is eager to expand its sales to China, with those of its industrial sector, which is keen for more state protection against Chinese competition. And more generally, the government of Argentina has to start implementing policies in order to realise the much needed diversification of exports.

References

Centro de Economía Internacional. 2007. Estadísticas, Ministerio de Relaciones Exteriores, Comercio Exterior y Culto, Argentina. http://cei.mrecic.gov.ar/html/estadis.htm (accessed 20 December 2007).

Cesarin, Sergio. 2007. *China-Argentina: reflexiones a 35 años del establecimiento de relaciones diplomáticas.* Buenos Aires: Centro de Estudios Internacionales, Programa Asia-Pacífico.

Galak, Olivier. 2007. 'China rechazó las restricciones y amenazó con represalias'. *La Nación* (Buenos Aires), 25 August: section 2: 4.

Jefatura de Gabinete de Ministros. 2004. 'Memoria Detallada del Estado de la Nación—Año 2004'. http://www.jgm.gov.ar/Páginas/MemoriaDetallada04/03_Ministerio_Relaciones Exteriores.pdf (accessed 20 December 2007).

Redrado, Martín. 2004. 'Hacia una integración inteligente'. *Argentina Exporta* (Buenos Aires), 7 January: 11.

———. 2004b. 'Los siete grandes ejes de la política comercial argentina'. *Clarín* (Buenos Aires), 11 April: 5.

———. 2004c. 'China, nuevo socio de la Argentina'. *Clarín* (Buenos Aires), 4 July: 28.

Shixue, Jiang. 2006. 'Una mirada china a las relaciones con América Latina'. *Nueva Sociedad* 203: 62–78.

Tussie, Diana and Eduardo Bianchi. 2004. *El reconocimiento de China como economía de mercado,* Red Latinoamericana de Política Comercial, Otros Papers no. 18, noviembre. http://www.latn.org.ar/principal/home/investigacion.php?mod=otros (accessed 20 December 2007).

Notes

1. The jurisdiction of the Consulate General in Shanghai includes the municipality of Shanghai as well as the provinces of Zhejiang, Jiangsu and Anhui. Argentina also has a consular office in Hong Kong, whose jurisdiction includes the special administrative regions of Hong Kong and Macau. In turn, China has a consulate in the city of Buenos Aires.

2. Apart from the mentioned references, information for this section has been gathered from the (electronic) newspapers *Clarín, La Nación, Infobae* and *China Today,* and the websites of the Ministries of Foreign Affairs of Argentina and of China and of the Argentine-Chinese Chamber of Commerce (Cámara de la Producción, la Industria y el Comercio Argentino-China).

3. The Mercado Común del Sur (Southern Common Market, MERCOSUR) was founded in 1991 by Brazil, Argentina, Uruguay and Paraguay. In 1996, at the initiative of the Chinese government, MERCOSUR and China established a dialogue and an alliance for cooperation.

4. China was a founding member of the GATT, but in 1950, the Kuomintang government denounced the Agreement, thereby ending China's representation. The government of the PRC considered this invalid as the authorities of the Kuomintang government did not lawfully represent the Chinese people, and in 1986, the PRC requested to be reincorporated into the GATT as a full member.

6 China and Venezuela's Search for Oil Markets

Javier Corrales

For a while now, Venezuelan President Hugo Chávez has had high hopes for relations with China. In his effort to 'soft balance' the United States (Romero and Corrales 2010; Williams forthcoming), Chávez has elevated relations with China to almost national priority. He considers deepening ties with China as vital for constructing a more 'multipolar world', lessening Venezuela's dependence on US markets for oil (Wilpert 2004), saving Venezuela from becoming the 'backyard of any empire' and accelerating Venezuela's transformation into a 'world power country'. Venezuela's strategy of 'using oil' to create a more multipolar world is not exclusively focused on China. Venezuela has proposed – to little enthusiasm in the region – the creation of a Caracas-led Latin American Petroleum bloc (Petrosur), as a Latin American version of the Organisation of Petroleum Exporting Countries (OPEC).

Chávez has (unilaterally) called relations with China a 'strategic alliance'. Chávez has visited China six times (in 1999, 2001, 2004, 2006, 2008 and 2009). Prior to Chávez, only one Venezuelan president, Luis Herrera Campíns in 1974, had visited China since the establishment of formal relations. Chávez has signed a number of cooperative agreements, among other things on telecommunication. Venezuela agreed to cooperate with China on the development of information technologies, including building a $250 million telecommunication network (Fletcher 2005) and a fibre-optic communications network. In 2007, China and Venezuela signed an agreement to create a $4 billion Joint China-Venezuela Fund for presumably development projects, the largest loan that China has given in its history to a single Latin American country (Conapri 2007).

But there is no question that the most important component of the agreements is energy. Chinese oil companies and Chinese-financed corporations have been given preferential access to new oil and gas projects in Venezuela, including exploration and production, and the construction of new pipelines, refineries and petrochemical plants. In August 2006, Venezuelan Energy Minister Rafael Ramírez announced that Chinese state-owned oil companies would invest around $5 billion in energy projects in Venezuela by 2012, up from $800 million in 2004 (Chan 2006; *Petroleumworld* 2005).

Yet, despite this seeming congruence of interests (China's growing oil demand and Venezuela's growing hope for multipolarity), I argue in this chapter that China is unlikely to offer, at least in the short term, what the Venezuelan government most actively seeks: a big enough market to lessen Venezuela's dependence on oil exports to the United States, and sufficient investments to help Venezuela expand production. Venezuela always promises grand plans for oil trade with China, but consistently falls short. There are both supply and demand side constraints to greater Venezuela-China trade, and this explains not only why Venezuela is unable to break ties with the United States, but also why ties with Iran have expanded since 2005.[1]

What Venezuela Could Offer China

With a booming economy since 1981, China has developed an enormous demand for primary commodities, especially energy resources (oil and gas) and petrochemical products. Starting in 1993, China's demand for oil has exceeded domestic production, and this demand continues to expand. China's demand for oil expanded significantly, from 4.8 million barrels per day in 2000 to 7.9 million barrels per day by the end of 2008. Demand has expanded far more rapidly than domestic production, making China the world's second-largest crude oil importing nation after the United States.

Figure 6.1. China's Oil Production and Consumption, 1981–2008

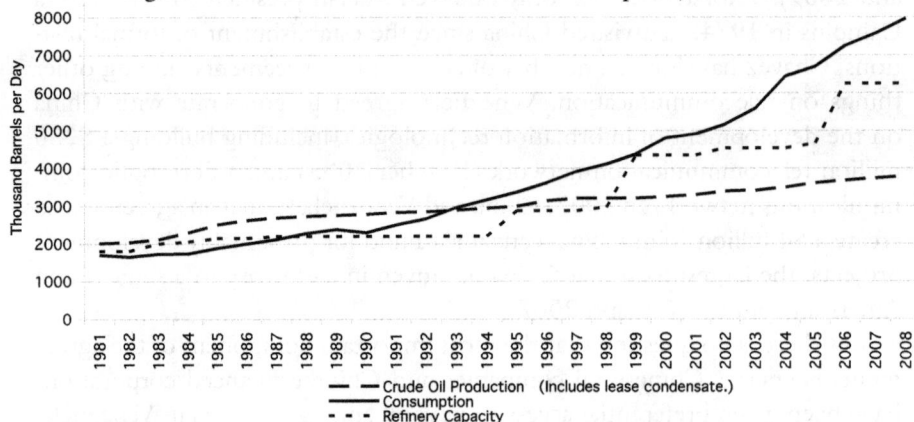

Source: Energy Information Administration (2009)

On the face of it, Venezuela seems well poised to help China meet its demand for oil. With proven reserves of 99 billion barrels of oil (excluding billions of extra-heavy and bitumen reserves), Venezuela is one of the world's largest oil exporters. Venezuela also has one of the largest natural gas reserves in the world (148 trillion cubic feet), occupying second place in the Western

Hemisphere behind the United States. However, the infrastructure necessary to export gas is not as developed as the infrastructure to export oil. Venezuela has yet to install a single gas liquefaction plant. These plants convert natural gas into liquid form, which makes gas easier to transport. Liquefaction reduces gas volume by 600 hundred times. However, liquefaction facilities can cost several billion US dollars (Suárez-Núnez 2005).

Chávez has made it clear that he has a strategic interest in selling more oil to China in order to lessen dependence on the United States. Venezuela sells approximately two-thirds of its oil exports to the United States, a historical average of about 1.5 million barrels per day, far lower today, but still significant for Venezuela. This level of trade with the United States places Venezuela in a contradictory position. Venezuela is one of the world's loudest critics of the United States, accusing President Bush of conducting genocide abroad and planning 'magnicide' at home.[2] But Venezuela is also making huge profits by selling to the United States, which makes Venezuela not just too dependent on the United States (in the event the United States decides to suspend imports), but also it appears hypocritical.

Figure 6.2. Venezuela's Oil Export Economy Compared

Average Barrels Per Day (Thousands)

Estimated exports to Cuba in 2007	92
Exports to China in 2008	380
Targeted Exports to China for 2008	500
Venezuela's Domestic Consumption in 2008	810
Targeted Exports to China for 2013	1,000
Venezuela's Exports to the U.S. in 2007	1,360
PDVSA's share in 2008	1,820
Venezuela's Total Production in 2008	2,642
Venezuela's Total Production in 2000	3,461
Mexico's Total Production 2008	3,185
Iran's Total Production 2008	4,174
Venezuela's Production Target for 2012	5,800
Saudi Arabia's Production 2008	10,782

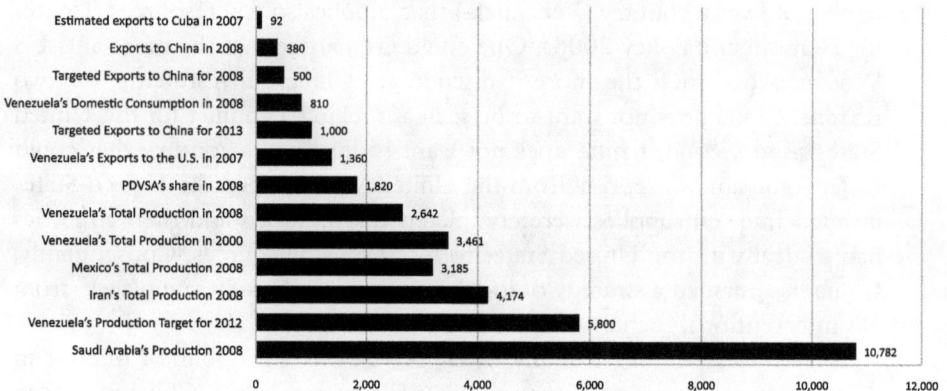

Source: Energy Information Administration (2009); Espinaza (2009); Noticias EFE (2009).

China, on the other hand, does not share Venezuela's desire to fight globalisation, reduce trade dependence on the United States, or even lessen the economic weight of the United States in the world economy. China has realised that its own prosperity depends on the prosperity of the United States. As Guy Pfeffermann and Bernard Wasow (2005) argue, exports are a key to maintaining China's industrial momentum, representing fully one-third of the country's total output (GDP). And one-quarter of these exports go to the United States (accounting for 30 per cent of all US imports, second only to Canada). This means that the economic health of the United States is of vital interest to the Chinese leadership.

On energy, China and the United States have mostly compatible and some incompatible interests. The most important common interest is to keep oil prices low and supplies plentiful, as would any oil-importing nation. The most important conflict of interest is differences about regime tastes. The United States often prefers to isolate certain oil suppliers deemed unacceptable for security reasons, such as Iran. China does not allow regime type of suppliers to interfere with its interest in diversifying its oil supply (Bremmer 2005). The common interest pushes China away from closer political collaboration with Venezuela, whereas the incompatible interest encourages China to seek closer ties to Venezuela.

Yet, Venezuela is still not a major trading partner for China. It does not even rank among the top oil suppliers to China. This low level of economic importance contrasts sharply with the importance of other Latin American countries to China. For instance, Brazil represents China's third largest supplier of iron ore, Chile and Peru combined provide 50 per cent of China's copper ore imports and Argentina is China's third-largest supplier of soy bean imports (Deutsche Bank 2008).

There is a political reason for China's hesitation with Venezuela. China has no desire to enter into an unnecessary conflict with the United States, certainly not over a country (Venezuela) that supplies so few resources (Center for Hemispheric Policy 2006). One could even argue that the more anti-US Venezuela becomes, the more it discourages Chinese investments, for two reasons. China does not want to be seen as fuelling a conflict for the United States. And second, China does not want to invest in a country that could suffer some kind of reprisal from the United States. When the United States invaded Iraq, oil supplies were completely discontinued and then countries had to deal with the United States to recover its oil sources. Consequently, China has pursued a strategy of looking for oil in relatively safe places (from US intervention), such as Africa and Central Asia.

Nevertheless, China, like any rising power, has a geopolitical interest in diversifying and securing energy supplies (Bremmer 2005). China may even be interested in more than diversification. Conservative strategists in China think in terms of resource back-ups. These conservatives seek, not so much the capacity to carry out a punitive action against the United States (as Venezuela might), but to be prepared in the event of a punitive action on the part of the United States. A rapprochement with Venezuela thus conforms to a doctrine of energy diversification and back-up. This may explain why Venezuela is today the largest recipient of Chinese foreign investment in Latin American and the Caribbean, most of it focused on energy.

The question still remains whether China stands ready to absorb Venezuela's oil exports in the event of a disruption of oil shipments to the United States. Some speculate that were China to declare itself ready to absorb such exports, Chávez will be more inclined to end or disrupt its oil trade with the United States (think Cuba-US-USSR sugar politics in 1959–1960) and turn more radical in its foreign policy. However, absorbing the bulk of Venezuela's oil exports to the United States will be economically and technically costly for China, as the next sections show.

The Problem of Selling Venezuelan Oil to China

Placing more oil on China's market will not be easy for Venezuela. Venezuela always promises to deliver record-level supplies of oil, only to fall short. The most recent promise was in 2009, when Venezuela promised to deliver 1 million barrels per day by 2013, up from the 380 thousand barrels per day of 2008 (see Figure 6.2). However, these goals, as previous ones, seem unrealistic. To understand this, it helps to compare Venezuela's oil supply with South America's overall food supply. China has a pressing need for both oil and food, especially soybeans. South American nations are ideally suited to meet China's demand for food relatively rapidly since most Latin American countries have been experiencing a boom in agricultural commodity production since the 1990s. Between 1997 and 2004, for instance, Argentina doubled the amount dedicated to soy production, from 17 million to 34 million acres. Brazil is working to double its acreage of soy plantations, from 32 million to 57 million. According to the US Department of Agriculture, South America will produce 62 per cent of the world's soybean exports in 2004 and 66 per cent by 2010 (*Stratfor* 23 December 2004). Furthermore, South America's commodity surplus has few new markets. The refusal of the EU, the United States, Japan and Canada to liberalise agricultural markets leaves Latin America with agricultural production surpluses. China is therefore a natural and immediate trading partner with South America on agricultural markets.

On the other hand, Venezuela's oil production, unlike South America's soybean production, is neither expanding nor devoid of markets – the United States alone could absorb most of Venezuela's oil. To alleviate its dependence on the United States, Venezuela must either expand production and generate oil surpluses, or divert to China oil that is currently exported to the United States. Both options entail onerous technical and economic difficulties.

Supply Restraints

The first option – expanding domestic production – faces numerous constraints. Under Chávez, Venezuela has announced ambitious production goals. In August 2005, for instance, the state-owned oil company of Venezuela, *Petróleos de Venezuela, S.A.* (PDVSA), unveiled its strategic plan for 2006–2012, calling for $56 billion in investments to raise Venezuela's production capacity from 1.7 million to 5.8 million barrels per day (bpd) in six years (4.1 million bpd produced by PDVSA). However, despite abundant reserves, Venezuela does not offer the right institutional climate to achieve this expansion. There are four major obstacles: the government's anti-technocracy approach to the oil sector; increasingly insecure property rights across the economy, not just in the oil sector; continued political unrest in Venezuela; and Venezuela's policy toward OPEC.

First, Venezuela under Chávez has shown little regard for maximising the managerial competence at PDVSA, the state oil company, leading to a significant decline in productive capacity. In 2001, PDVSA was producing close to 3.2 millions barrels per day. Venezuela's political unrest in 2002, culminating with the oil strike in the winter of 2002–2003, caused a serious decline in oil production. Average production declined to 2.6 million and 2.3 million barrels per day in 2002 and 2003. Although the Venezuelan government claims that oil production has recovered to 2001 levels, no serious analyst believes this claim. International agencies place Venezuela's current production at no more than 2.36 million of barrels per day, which is the same level as the record-low level of 2003, the year of the strike (see Espinasa 2009). Experts estimate that approximately 1.0 million of this total crude production is being produced by 'third' parties rather than PDVSA. The government fired 20,000 PDVSA employees during the oil strike and replaced them with staff appointed for political reasons, depriving the company of technical and managerial know-how. In addition, the government hardly invests in PDVSA. PDVSA also faces enormous credit constraints to raise non-government capital, since private creditors simply refuse to offer lending to a firm that hardly discloses credible financial statements. In short, Venezuela's oil sector is in the midst of a serious investment crisis, which, in turn, is yielding a production crisis.

Secondly, increasingly insecure property rights in Venezuela's oil sector have created an unfriendly business environment, which compounds the oil sector's productivity crisis. Although Venezuela, unlike Mexico and other Latin American countries, is technically open for private investment in oil exploration and production, the country's insecure legal environment is putting the brakes on private investments. In 2004, oil companies expressed an interest in investing $30 billion in Venezuela (Bloomberg News Service 2004), but today, little of this investment has materialised, mostly because Venezuela is also creating all kinds of obstacles for *private* international oil companies. If anything, Venezuela has experienced capital flight every year that Chávez has been in office, and more surprisingly, even during the boom years of 2004–2008, which is remarkable for a booming economy. The 1999 Constitution is unclear about the security of private property rights in the oil sector. The 2001 Hydrocarbon Law calls for the now-decaying PDVSA to own at least 51 per cent stake in any project regarding exploration, production, transportation and initial storage of oil. A 2004 Presidential decree unilaterally raised royalties on four heavy oil production projects along the Orinoco Belt from 1 per cent to 16.67 per cent and imposed a 30 per cent royalty on excess output. In the spring of 2005, the government raised taxes on companies that run 32 oil fields for PDVSA from 34 per cent to 50 per cent. Minister of Energy and Oil Rafael Ramírez gave those 22 companies until year-end to convert the oilfield contracts into joint ventures that are 51 per cent owned by PDVSA. And tax auditors began to carry out raids against several foreign oil companies. There is no question that the industry can afford this level of taxation. The issue is the level of arbitrariness that accompanied the change: the government consulted neither the sector nor the legislature. Furthermore, the decree violated the 1993 law governing joint ventures in oil. Some foreign companies have reported cheating by the state, in the form of discriminatory tax treatment and non-compliance with payments. The former refers to the fact that Venezuela has begun to collect taxes retroactively on foreign operators.[3] This may explain why there were no major contracts with foreign firms on gas and liquid hydrocarbons between 1999 and 2004 (*Veneconomía* January 2005). Whereas foreign direct investments in South America increased by 48 per cent between 2003 and 2004, in Venezuela, they declined by 60 per cent during the same period and they are currently three-fourths below the annual average during the 1996–2000 period (CEPAL 2004).

It seems that the government has been trying to push out private oil companies, such as Shell and Exxon Mobil, in favour of state-owned companies.[4] Chávez has a strong preference for making business deals with state-owned companies from mostly authoritarian regimes than with private companies. There is a reason for this. State-owned companies from autocracies do not disclose their operations to the public, in contrast to large private multinationals, which are subject to all forms of scrutiny by government officials, rating agencies and creditors. It is simply easier to keep secrets among autocrats. But these secrets come at a high economic cost: few state-owned companies have the pockets and technologies that Venezuela requires to fix its decaying oil sector.

A third obstacle to expanding Venezuela's oil production is heightened political unrest and criminal activity. Although the government's impressive electoral triumphs of 2004 (in the recall referendum and the gubernatorial and mayoral elections) demoralised the opposition – generating a period of political calm not seen since 2001, which lasted until 2006 – the underlying causes of the political unrest of 2002 and 2003 have not dissipated. The government continues to deny political space to the opposition, and the opposition continues to find the government unacceptable and threatening.

Furthermore, clashes with the ruling forces are on the rise, mostly between leftist civilians and nationalist military leaders, both of whom support Chávez but mistrust one another. The government's defeat in the 2007 referendum to reform the constitution, and the opposition's ability to win various governorships and mayoralties in the 2008 mid-term elections has galvanised the opposition again and maybe even the radicals within the government. And since 2008, the decline in oil prices put an end to Venezuela's magnificent consumption boom of 2004–2008, generating discontent across the population.

Furthermore, criminality, already high in the 1990s, has skyrocketed under Chávez. Annual homicides went from 4,550 in 1998 to 12,257 in 2006. In terms of homicides per 100,000 inhabitants, this represents an increase from 19.4 to 45.3 (Briceño-León 2007). Drug traffic passing through Venezuela has almost tripled since the early years of the Chávez administration. As much as one-third of total world cocaine traffic goes through Venezuela (Shifter 2007). Because cooperation between Venezuela and US drug enforcement agents have declined to near zero, Venezuela has become, in the last two years, a perfect haven for drug trade – a place where drug dealers can operate without fear of interdiction. Furthermore, Colombia's insurgents and gangsters, who frequently seek refuge on Venezuelan territory (often encouraged and sheltered by Venezuelan officials), could begin to target oil interests. Venezuela thus has all the right conditions for further insecurity: political polarisation, a corrupt state, blind eye toward drug operations, contacts with a neighbour experiencing war and drug trade, and an abundance of arms and ammunitions.

The fourth major obstacle to expanding domestic production is Venezuela's post-1999 OPEC policy. Chávez himself is personally opposed to expansion in oil supplies so as to avoid price declines. Chávez spent his first four years in office fighting overproduction – at home, but mostly abroad – as a way to bolster OPEC. He criticised (unfairly) the previous administration and PDVSA managers for being too concerned with oil expansion and thus undermining OPEC's efforts to keep prices high. In 2000, Chávez was instrumental in getting OPEC members to address the issue of overproduction, thus contributing to a rise in OPEC prices. Expanding oil production to sell to China might thus clash with Venezuela's OPEC policy of restricting supply. This works for Venezuela: low production helps keep prices high, yielding higher revenues for the government while simultaneously diminishing the government's need to court private investors, since there is little interest in expanding production.

Yet, Venezuela's policy toward OPEC carries costs. It alienates energy-dependent nations, who are hurt by high oil prices. This group of countries includes China. Chávez's solution to this conflict with oil-importing nations has been to offer subsidised oil to small, oil-importing nations located mostly in the Western Hemisphere and the Caribbean basin (Corrales 2009). For China, Venezuela's solution has been to give China access to the lucrative oil-extraction business – that is, to allow China to make some profits from Venezuela's oil trade with the United States. For the Chinese, the opportunity to make money from the Venezuela-US relationship is even more appealing than actually buying oil directly from Venezuela.

This unfriendly investment environment has taken its toll. *Veneconomía* (18 October 2007) has calculated that between 2002 and 2007, the average foreign direct investment in Venezuela was $500 million annually or approximately $16.60 per capita. In comparison, China received $662,000 million in foreign direct investment in 2006, or approximately $510 per capita. These are two booming economies, with Venezuela's petroleum boom ranking first, and yet Venezuela received significantly less foreign investment per capita. This is all the result of the government's unfriendly policies toward private multinationals.

This decline in Venezuela's business climate in general and the oil sector in particular affects prospects of oil trade with China in two ways. Firstly, Venezuela has lost one its pre-1999 competitive advantages vis-à-vis other petrostates: a stable and pro-business institutional climate. Secondly, for investors who are risk averse, who do not have much capital to invest and who want more autonomy in investment decisions, Venezuela is not an attractive investment site.

During much of the 2000s, China in Latin America seems to have been a risk averse, low capital, autonomy-seeking investor. For instance, when asked to explain why President Hu Jintao did not visit Venezuela during his December 2004 Latin America tour (whereas President Jiang Zemin visited Venezuela in 2001), the Political Counsellor to the Chinese Ambassador in Venezuela, Mr. Zhang Bolun, answered with an argument that exuded risk aversion: 'the political conditions in Venezuela were too unstable and uncertain to permit a Presidential visit.'[5] This was an odd comment – the end of 2004 was a stable period in Venezuela, relative to the past three years. The political conditions in Venezuela could only appear 'unstable and uncertain' to a leadership that is risk averse. Furthermore, when asked to explain why there is no more Chinese investment in Venezuela (as Chávez would want), Mr. Zhang Bolun replied: 'there is too much risk for little return.' This time, he was referring not so much to the political situation, but to the enormous obstacles to investments, including the degree to which PDVSA (that is, the government) wants to be part of (control) oil investments. China has been able to negotiate more autonomous oil business deals in countries that are closer to its borders.

Obstacles to Processing Venezuela's Oil in China

Another obstacle to deeper oil trade between China and Venezuela has to do with the type of Venezuelan oil, which is hard to place in world markets. Most of Venezuela's oil reserves fall under the category of heavy crudes (with an average API gravity of 20 degrees).[6] Heavy crudes are cheaper than light crudes, but more difficult to extract and refine. Furthermore, Venezuela's heavy crudes in particular have the added problem of containing very high levels of impurities – an excess of sulphur, nickel and vanadium. For these reasons, Venezuelan oil requires special refineries designed to process heavy, sulphur-rich, low-grade oil. Much of the world's refining capacity, especially in China, cannot easily generate gasoline and heating oil from heavy, sulphur-rich petroleum (Zellner 2004). That is why most of the oil that China currently buys from Venezuela gets traded in Singapore to third markets. To have oil exports to China reach the level of 500,000 bpd, as Chávez wants, would require China to invest heavily in this type of special refineries. China wants new refineries, but so far, it has shown no signs of building refineries that can handle Venezuelan crude. Saudi Arabia and Kuwait are willing to invest in new refineries in China, but not refineries for Venezuelan heavy and sour crude (Houser, Rosen and Voght 2006). Venezuela does not have the cash to make such investments in China.

The reason that Venezuela became a major oil exporter to the United States, despite the quality issues of its oil, has to do with the special attributes of US-Venezuelan bilateral relations and smart business decisions by the Venezuelan government prior to 1999. These were, firstly, low transportation costs, due to short maritime distance between Venezuelan and US ports. Secondly, there has been a very close political relation between both countries since 1959, with a commitment on the part of the United States to expand the bilateral oil trade, as a way to bolster and showcase Venezuela's nascent democracy during the Cold War. Thirdly, there was the smart decision, in 1986, to acquire CITGO, a US-based oil refining and marketing firm that in 2007 controlled 10 per cent of the US oil retail market (13,500 gas stations), thereby granting Venezuelan oil easy access to US retail markets. Venezuela has the enviable position of being both a wholesaler and retailer of oil in the United States, lessening the impact of price-induced changes in demand (when oil prices are high, Venezuela wins on the wholesale side; when oil prices decline, Venezuela wins by selling more oil on the retail side). Finally, CITGO is the third largest refinery in the United States; it refines about half of Venezuela's oil sales to the United States, and is well suited to refine Venezuelan heavy, sulphur-rich crudes. In fact, PDVSA acquired CITGO precisely because of the difficulty of finding refineries and markets for its extra-heavy oil, which, back then, was forcing Venezuela to sell its oil at a discount (Campoy and Lubnow 2007; Campbell 2004).

If Venezuela were to divert oil sales to China, it would need to find ways of refining large amounts of oil. China and Venezuela would also need to finance the higher transportation costs of shipping 1.5 million barrels per day to China: it would take 40 days or more for Venezuelan oil to reach China (compared to 4–5 days to reach the United States), which would push transportation costs to prohibitive levels. Furthermore, most Venezuelan vessels are small, designed to travel the short distance between Venezuela and the Gulf Coast. To reach China from Venezuela in an economically viable way, PDVSA would need to acquire much larger vessels (Contreras and Gunson 2005). Typically, long-haul routes (e.g., Persian Gulf to Europe, the Americas to East Asia) are handled by ultra-large crude carriers (ULCC), which have a cargo capacity of 300,000 to 500,000 deadweight tons. To reach the figure that the Venezuela government has targeted for China would require at least three trips of ultra-large crude carriers per month (*El Universal* 23 August 2005). Furthermore, the Panama Canal is not an option, since only medium-sized vessels carrying less than 75,000 deadweight tons are allowed to cross the Canal. To reach China, shipments from Venezuela would need to go through Africa, which would take 44 days. The Venezuelan government has begun to focus on this transportation problem, and there are reports that a team of transportation experts from PDVSA received training in London by Iranian experts on how to ship oil to Asia (*El Universal* 11 March 2005).

China seems to be quite aware of these costs and does not seem eager to absorb them. Mr. Zhang was emphatic: 'Venezuela's oil business deals with the United States are more lucrative than any possible oil business deal with China, because of the heavy costs entailed.' In the words of Mr. Zhang: 'we don't need it; we have other sellers.'[7] In fact, most of the oil that China is acquiring from Asia and Africa, unlike Venezuelan oil, matches closely in terms of weight and sulphur content to Chinese refining capacities. That is why China to this day is not a main buyer of Venezuelan oil.

In addition to the problem of expansion constraints and committed supplies, the prospects of deepening Sino-Venezuelan oil trade are hindered by technical constraints within China's refining industry. China's refining capacity is ill suited to keep up with the country's energy demands, let alone to absorb Venezuela's oil. Luis Giusti (2005), a former president of PDVSA, lists the following technical problems with China's refining capacity. First, refineries are insufficient: China has 57 refineries, but no more than six are sufficiently large. Giusti estimates that China's installed refining capacity can cover no more than 70 per cent of China's energy needs. Secondly, inconvenient location: most refineries in China are remotely located in the North and Northeast region of the country, far from the coastal areas in the South, where Venezuelan oil shipments would disembark and where oil demand is highest. Venezuelan oil imports would thus face a double transportation cost within China: the cost of shipment from the ports to the refineries in the North, and the cost of distribution from the refineries in the North to the urban centres in the South. Finally, incompatibility issues: most Chinese refineries are unsuitable for sulphur-rich crude oil.

In short, for China to rival the US market for oil, both Venezuela and China will need to make enormous investments. Venezuela will need to produce more light crudes. Otherwise, it will have to build new refineries to process the amount handled by CITGO. Alternatively, China will need to upgrade old refineries in the North and create new refineries in the South. And both countries will need to absorb the cost of transporting nearly 1.5 million barrels from Venezuela to China (a 40-day sea journey).

Competing Demands and Insecurities

Have Venezuela and China made the necessary commitments to cover the high costs of expanding bilateral oil trade? Thus far, the answer seems to be no. The bilateral agreements cover some costs, but not the most important ones. The agreements are predicated on an oil-for-investment notion. China has obtained more opportunities to participate in the oil extraction business. In addition to expanding China's existing oil operations in Intercampo and Caracoles oilfields, China obtained the rights to expand operations (from six to 13 oilfields) in the Zumano region, with reserves of 400 million barrels of oil (maybe as much as 1 billion) and 3 billion cubic feet of natural gas. It seems that investing in these oilfields is profitable only as long as PDVSA maintains its current customer base: business with the United States. China also obtained more opportunities to import gas and oil products. For China, only fuel oil and orimulsion are worth importing in large quantities. In return, China commits to making investments in the oil sector.

In general, the agreements address two important costs. The first is the cost of property rights insecurity. Venezuela agreed to allow China to continue to operate the investments in place since 1998. In addition, Venezuela committed to continue Chinese-financed investments in Orimulsion (in 2003, PDVSA was considering discontinuing production of orimulsion). During his December 2004 visit to China, Chávez went out of his way to assure Chinese investors that his Office, rather than lower-level entities such as the Ministry of Energy and Petroleum or PDVSA, will manage all oil investment decisions – a way to ease Chinese concern about insecure property rights.

Nevertheless, the agreements between Venezuela and China say little about subsidising the more onerous transportation costs (crossing the Pacific), acquiring new vessels, granting Venezuela distribution facilities in China and more importantly, producing new and upgraded refineries in China. Mr. Zhang even said that an 'agreement' to build pipelines is nothing more than just 'talk', for now.[8] Furthermore, the firmness of Chinese investment commitments in Venezuela is unclear. China has agreed to make infrastructure investments in Venezuela. But these investments will not occur as direct disbursements, typical of traditional foreign direct investments, but rather, as conditional loans with favourable interest rates to interested Chinese firms. Chinese firms do not have a long tradition of aggressive investments abroad, in part because Chinese investors are risk averse and in part because China's vigorous domestic economic growth absorbs most surplus capital.

Finally, there is the classic problem of international relations of 'asymmetrical interdependence': China is more important to Venezuela than vice versa. Just as Venezuela is committed to diversifying its oil markets, China is committed to diversifying its oil supplies. To that end, China is actively increasing investments in domestic oil and natural gas exploration, and signing joint ventures in other countries (OPEC and non-OPEC). In particular, China is aggressively working with Vietnamese, Russian, Middle Eastern and Central Asian governments to secure oil access (Kozyrev 2007). Even in Latin America, China has been diversifying its source and investment portfolio. In Brazil, for instance, Petrobras and China National Offshore Oil are exploring joint operations in refining and pipelines, with a $1 billion agreement with Sinopec to build a gas pipeline in Brazil. China has also expressed strong interests in investing in oil in Ecuador, Peru and Colombia, and gas in Bolivia. China also has the largest oil concession in oil-rich southern Darfur, Sudan.

Taken together, it seems that China can count on alternative oil suppliers that are geographically closer and provide more autonomy than Venezuela. From the point of view of conservatives in China, who presumably worry about developing 'back-ups' in case of US aggression, oil trade with Venezuela would be China's least appealing back-up. The reason is that, to reach China, Venezuelan oil must cross various zones of US influence: the Caribbean basin, the Panama Canal (or Colombia, if a pipeline were created) and the Pacific Ocean. For conservatives, securing oil from the east (Central Asia, the Middle East) or the North (Russia) seems safer. It is unclear, therefore, whether China needs Venezuela as much as Venezuela needs China to promote a 'multipolar' oil policy. That might be the reason that China has not been as eager as Venezuela to call its new bilateral agreements, however potentially profitable, as a strategic alliance.

Scenarios

Since heavy crudes are abundant worldwide, and thus cheaper, oil companies are actively improving the technology necessary to extract, refine and up-grade orimulsion. Orimulsion is a special emulsion developed in Venezuela's Orinoco belt, comprised of 70 per cent natural bitumen (a very solid form of fuel) and 30 per cent water. Orimulsion is used as a power station fuel in heavy industry and as boiler fuel. In 2001, China National Petroleum Corporation (CNPC) and PDVSA signed an agreement to develop orimulsion through a joint venture 70 per cent owned by CNPC. Venezuela could either convert extra-heavy crudes into orimulsion or upgraded petrol. The latter can be sold at a higher price than orimulsion, but it is costlier to produce (*Veneconomy Daily* 12 April 2005). Recently, there have been advances in the capacity to process this type of extra heavy fuel. A Total (French)-PDVSA consortium by the name of Sincor has been able to extract bitumen and upgrade it to oil by use of a new technique. These technological improvements would make Sino-Venezuelan oil trade more economically viable in the medium term.

Unlike the cost of diverting heavy crudes, China seems prepared to absorb the costs of developing orimulsion. Venezuela holds almost 20 per cent of the extra-heavy tar-like oil that is suitable for orimulsion. Venezuela wants to expand orimulsion production, at a cost of $40 billion. This business seems more appealing to China, which has already made significant investments in this sector. China may or may not be able to afford more investments in Venezuela's orimulsion, but if it does, the result would not necessarily be negative for the United States. As Houser, Rosen and Voght (2006) argue: larger imports of orimulsion in China would ease Chinese demand for crudes from Africa and the Middle East, thereby lowering energy prices.

Because China is unable to act as Venezuela's buyer of last resort for the bulk of its oil exports, Venezuela has increasingly turned to Iran. Chávez has visited Tehran three times and was awarded Iran's highest state medal for supporting Iran's nuclear standoff with the international community (Farnsworth 2007). The primary purpose of ties with Iran is to push oil prices up, in addition to exchanging and developing weapons. There is some concern that Iran is helping Venezuela explore the nuclear option. There are rumours that Iranian scientists and engineers are prospecting for uranium ore in the granite bedrock under the south-eastern jungles of Venezuela, a region rich with mineral deposits. It is difficult to see why Chávez would want nuclear technology for peaceful, energy-producing ends: Venezuela has the largest hydrocarbon reserves in the Americas, and it already makes good use of its ample hydroelectricity generation potential.

There are two ways in which a Venezuela-Iran alliance can promote oil price increases. The first strategy is out in the open: increase the number of hawks within OPEC. Hawks are countries interested in price increases (through oil production cutbacks) rather than price stabilisation (through production increases). Iran and Venezuela are the second and fifth largest producers in OPEC, thus partnering up makes them powerful within the oil cartel to counteract Saudi Arabia's attempt to keep production high. They are courting Libya and perhaps the new member, Ecuador. The other reason that an alliance with Iran could help promote price increases is a bit more sinister. Venezuela knows that a confrontation between Iran and the United States could produce a crisis in the Middle East, which would boost the price of oil. If so, one could argue that Venezuela has an interest in encouraging such a crisis. Chávez has said that he expects a US invasion of Iran to increase the price of oil to \$200 a barrel, more than doubling the current price, and essentially erasing Venezuela's need to address productivity problems at home. Venezuela could be developing ties with Iran for no other reason than to encourage Iran's bad behaviour, and thus, bring on a crisis in the Middle East.

Table 6.1 shows the crucial actors in the international political economy of oil from the point of Venezuela, and the actual, tacit and potential alliances. Venezuela and Iran share similar policy goals: strengthen OPEC and oil prices. The United States and China share the opposite goals: dilute the power of OPEC and keep the price of oil low. Saudi Arabia is the intermediate player: it sides with Venezuela and Iran on the issue of strengthening OPEC, and is somewhat sympathetic to the United States and China on the issue of avoiding oil price increases by boosting oil production. Technically, then, Venezuela is at odds with OPEC's official position of price stability and moderation. In the words of OPEC's secretary general, 'We at OPEC don't want extremes, prices that are too high or too low. What we do want is a stable price' (Follath and Kraske 2008).

Table 6.1. Actual, Tacit and Potential Alliances

	Policy Preference toward OPEC	Policy Preference toward Oil Prices
Venezuela and Iran	Strengthen[a]	Raise
Saudi Arabia	Strengthen[a]	Moderate and Stable
United States and China	Weaken	Lower

[a]Grey areas: common interests.

This distribution of powers and preferences means that the United States is not alone. Insofar as the United States can keep China and Saudi Arabia on its side, it will preserve an international political economy that can contain some of Venezuela's foreign policy goals. However, a confrontation between Iran and the United States may bring China closer to Venezuela. China has significantly increased it oil ties with Iran in the last decade. Iran is China's second largest source of imported oil, and China dominates about 8 per cent of Iran's oil market. If a confrontation between Iran and the United States were to occur, leading to an increase in the price of oil or a disruption in Iranian oil to China, the alliance between China and the United States might become strained. At the very least, China will want to find new suppliers. Venezuela might suddenly become appealing to China.

Having said that, the United States remains far less dependent on Venezuela than vice versa. Venezuela provides approximately 13 per cent of US oil imports. In contrast, the United States provides the bulk of Venezuela's export revenues (70 per cent) and thus government revenues (almost 50 per cent). Economically speaking, the United States is in a better position to absorb an increase in oil than Venezuela is to survive a collapse in oil sales to the US. Provided some conditions hold (inflation stays low, oil exporters continue to send their dollars to the United States), many analysts feel that the United States could survive further increases in oil prices given that current prices today are still 25 per cent below in real terms the prices in 1980.

But politically, for the United States to unilaterally end trade with Venezuela would be a serious public relations disaster and a boom for *chavismo*. Hugo Chávez is interested in a provocation with the United States. A confrontation with the United States will allow him to blame all of his economic foes on the United States, to concentrate more power and crackdown on enemies by declaring a state of emergency and to gain even more international sympathy than he already has. Far from containing chavismo, a confrontation with the United States will embolden it.

Conclusions

China needs energy, Venezuela has energy, and both countries have an interest in diversifying their energy markets. Yet, this trade compatibility and congruence of political interest has not yielded a booming bilateral energy trade. Placing Venezuelan oil on China's markets is costly, requiring new investments in light crude production in Venezuela, upgrading and creating new refineries in China and absorbing high transportation costs. Venezuela may have the political interest in making these investments, but lacks the resources to do so. It no longer has the most optimum institutional climate to attract supplementary foreign investments, even from China. China's strong demand for oil will no doubt force it to think seriously about increasing investments abroad, even in Venezuela, but it also has other potential oil suppliers that are geographically closer than Venezuela. It is unclear whether the new agreements between China and Venezuela, on their own, will generate the policy objective (a more diversified oil sector) that each country seeks for itself.

Consequently, China seems content with the opportunity to make modest investments (big for Latin America, modest for the oil industry) in Venezuela's marginal fields, to continue the operations in Intercampo and Caracoles oilfields (signed in 1997 between the state-owned China National Petroleum Corporation, CNPC, and PDVSA) and to continue the Chinese-financed development of Orimulsion. China has not openly expressed a huge interest in large oil investments in Venezuela (compared to its investments in Kazakhstan) or in making large oil purchases from Venezuela.

Nevertheless, politics can trump all economic costs. While China will not be an eager consumer of Venezuelan oil for now, China could still help Venezuela politically in the event of a disruption in US-Venezuelan oil trade by acting as a seller in secondary markets. For instance, China could purchase Venezuelan oil and trade it with countries that have the capacity to refine heavy, sulphur-rich oil, such as Singapore. In fact, Venezuela has a similar type of deal with Cuba, which apparently consumes only about half of the oil it imports from Venezuela, and resells the surplus to third countries. These surplus barrels do not even go through Cuba: Cupet, the Cuban state-owned oil company, negotiates directly the sale of these barrels between PDVSA and third countries. Cuba may be pocketing as much as $1 billion annually, paying no cash to PDVSA (*El Miami Herald* 21 February 2005). If China were also to become a secondary market seller, it could certainly lower the costs for Venezuela of disrupting oil trade with the United States. But it will also give China a new political cost – that of upsetting the United States. Nothing to me suggests that China loves the Bolivarian Revolution that much.

In short, the Venezuela case is a perfect example of how countries can have multiple foreign policy objectives, each of which are incompatible with at least one other objective. Venezuela values five different foreign policy objectives: easing dependence on US markets; developing the Chinese market; maintaining heavy spending at home and abroad; keeping the price of oil high; and strengthening OPEC. This chapter tried to show how each policy comes with an important sacrifice. Unilaterally ending US dependence means sacrificing social spending. Developing the Chinese markets means sacrificing social spending and would ease pressure on oil prices, thus undermining the goal of price maximisation. Maximising the price of oil means alienating China and weakening or dividing OPEC. And maximising social spending means preserving dependence on the United States. For now, Venezuela has chosen to prioritise the latter strategy. Whether it decides to prioritise any of the others will depend on how much it is willing to absorb any of the costs involved.

References

Bloomberg News Service. 2005. 'Venezuela's Chávez Squeezes Oil Companies with Taxes, Raids', 24 August. http://www.bloomberg.com (accessed 20 September 2006).

Bremmer, Ian. 2005. 'China and America's common energy interests'. *The Financial Times,* 15 March.

Briceño-León, Roberto. 2007. 'Violence in Venezuela: Excess Homicides and Social Pact.' Laboratorio de Ciencias Sociales, LACSO and Observatorio Venezolano de Violencia.

Campbell, Oliver L. 2004. 'We look forward to greater transparency from PDVSA', 12 December. http://www.vheadline.com (accessed 20 September 2006).

Campoy, Ana and David Lubnow. 2007. 'Citgo Scales Back in US to Fund Chávez's Goals'. *Wall Street Journal,* 16 November.

Center for Hemispheric Policy. 2006. *Findings and Recommendations of the China-Latin America Task Force,* Policy paper. Miami: University of Miami.

CEPAL. 2004. 'La inversión extranjera en América Latina y el Caribe'. Santiago de Chile: CEPAL.

Chan, John. 2006. 'China's oil diplomacy: Hugo Chavez makes high profile visit to Beijing', September, World Socialist Website. http://www.wsws.org/articles/2006/sep2006/chavs06.shtml (accessed 20 September 2006).

Conapri (Consejo Nacional de Promoción de Inversiones). 2007. 24 November, http://www.conapri.org (accessed 7 November 2007).

Contreras, Joseph and Phil Gunson. 2005. 'Balance of Power: President Hugo Chavez is fighting the "imperialist" United States with his most formidable weapon – oil'. Newsweek, 14 February.

Corrales, Javier. 2009. 'Using Social Power to Balance Soft Power: Venezuela's Foreign Policy'. *The Washington Quarterly* (Fall).

Deutsche Bank. 2008. 'China's Commodity Hunger'. 13 February. http://www.dbresearch.de (accessed 20 February 2008).

Energy Information Administration. 2007. China, Country Analysis Briefs. Washington, DC: Energy Information Administration, US Government. http://www.eia.doe.gov/emeu/cabs/China/pdf.pdf (accessed 20 February 2008).

———. 2008. Venezuela, Country Analysis Briefs. Washington, DC: Energy Information Administration, US Government. http://www.eia.doe.gov/emeu/cabs/Venezuela/pdf.pdf (accessed 20 February 2008).

Espinasa, Ramón. 2009. 'The Performance of the Venezuelan Oil Sector 1997-2008: Official vs. International and Estimated Figures'. Coral Gables, FL: University of Miami, Center for Hemispheric Policy.

Farnsworth, Eric. 2007. 'The Company We Keep'. *Poder,* 47, November.

Fletcher, Pascal. 2005. 'China Boosts Role in Venezuela's Oil, Gas Sector'. Reuters, 31 January.

Follath, Erich and Marion Kraske. 2008. 'Opec Secretary-General: "International Oil Companies Are The Real Dinosaurs"; Interview with Salem el-Badri'. *Spiegel,* 20 January.

Gerencia de Asuntos Públicos. 2005. 'Avances de la nueva PDVSA'. Ad published in *El Universal,* 20 February: I–3.

Giusti, Luis E. 2005. 'Refinación en China'. *El Nacional,* 20 February: A10.

Houser, Trevor, Daniel Rosen and David Voght. 2006. 'Chávez-China Oil Deal May Produce Unsuspected Winners'. *YaleGlobal Online,* 7 September. http://yaleglobal.yale.edu/ (accessed 20 September 2006).

Kozyrev, Vitaly. 2007. 'China's Contiental energy Strategy: Russia and Central Asia' (mimeo).

Noticias EFE. 2009. 'Tres objetivos petroleros centran la visita trabajo de Hugo Chávez a China'. 7 April.

Petroleumworld. 2005. 'Venezuela, China Ink Raft of Energy Agreements Over Weekend'. 1 February. http://www.petroleumworld.org (accessed 20 September 2006).

Pfeffermann, Gay and Bernard Wasow. 2005. 'The US and China: The Global Economy's Odd Couple'. *The Globalist,* 1 March. http://www.theglobalist.com (accessed 20 September 2006).

Romero, Carlos and Javier Corrales. 2010. 'Relations between the United States and Venezuela, 2001-2009: A Bridge in Need of Repairs'. In *Contemporary U.S.-Latin American Relations-Cooperation or Conflict in the 21st Century?* eds. Jorge I. Domínguez and Rafael Fernández de Castro. London and New York: Routledge.

Shifter, Michael. 2007. 'Internal Dynamics of the Venezuela Domestic Drug Problem'. Presentation in Key West, FL.

Suárez-Núñez, José. 2005. 'Batalla por la búsqueda del gas sube la adrenalina de las transnacionales'. *El Nacional,* 7 March: A–16.

Taylhardat, Adolfo. 2005. 'Los fusiles rusos'. *El Universal,* 23 February: 1–17.

Williams, Mark E. Forthcoming. 'International Relations Theory and Venezuela's Soft Balancing Foreign Policy'. In *The Revolution in Venezuela,* eds. Jonathan Eastwood and Thomas Ponniah. Durham, NC: Duke University Press.

Wilpert, Gregory. 2004. 'Venezuela Offers China Greater Access to Oil To Reduce Dependency on US Market'. 28 December. http://www.venezuelanalysis.com (accessed 2 January 2005).

Zellner, Wendy. 2004. 'Crude Lessons About Oil'. *Business Week,* 9 November.

Notes

1. I am grateful to Roberto Bottome, Peter DeShazo, Gustavo Coronel, Francisco Monaldi and Moisés Naim for comments on earlier drafts. I am also grateful to Daniel Mogollón and Andrew Slutsky for their research assistance.
2. Chávez's anti-globalisation and anti-US rhetoric escalated after November 2004. At a large meeting with cabinet members, ruling party legislators, governors and mayors, and the high command of the armed forces, Chávez unveiled his new government program – the 'The New Phase: The New Strategic Map of the Bolivarian Revolution'. It includes ten priority objectives, one of which was to attack the US-dominated 'axis in the Andes', comprised of 'Bogotá-Quito-Lima-La Paz-Santiago', and entails, among other things, a new campaign to train the armed forces for a 'non-conventional' war in response to Plan Colombia.
3. See the US government's Energy Information Administration (EIA), at http://www.eia. doe.gov/emeu/cabs/Venezuela/Oil.html.
4. While the government is raiding private oil companies, it is offering very favourable deals exclusively to seven state-own companies (Brazil's Petrobras, Iran's Petropars, India's ONGC, Russia's Lukoil and Gazprom, Spain's Repsol, China's CNPC) to develop reserves of extra-heavy oil from the Orinoco Oil Belt (*Veneconomy Weekly* 24 August 2005).
5. Interview with author, 22 February 2005, Embassy of the People's Republic of China, Caracas, Venezuela.
6. API gravity is a measure of oil's 'heaviness'. Oil with API gravity greater than 30 degrees is termed light; between 22 and 30 degrees, medium; below 22 degrees, heavy; and below 10, extra heavy. Asphalt on average has an API gravity of 8 degree; Brent Crude of 35.5; and gasoline of 50 degrees.
7. Interview with author, 22 February 2005, Embassy of the People's Republic of China, Caracas, Venezuela.
8. Interview with author, 22 February 2005, Embassy of the People's Republic of China, Caracas, Venezuela.

7 Bridging the Pacific
Peru's Search for Closer Economic Ties with China
Rubén Berríos

Relations between Peru and China can be traced to the mid nineteenth century, when Chinese labourers in huge numbers arrived to work in Peru's sugar plantations and on the Guano islands during the boom years (Chang-Rodriguez 1958; Rodriguez Pastor 2000). This was to be the first wave of immigration from China to Latin America. Commercial contacts and a friendship agreement were signed in 1874. The Chinese have been in Peru for over 150 years and comprise one of the major foreign communities in the region.

A key link in the development of stronger ties with Asia has been the significant presence of both the Chinese and Japanese communities in Peru. These communities have served as networks in international trade and investment ventures and have played a key role in the establishment of business contacts. In 1990, the Chinese community in Peru was estimated to be half a million (Poston and Yu 1990). Many individuals from these ethnic communities have become quite prosperous and a number of them have held public office in recent years.

Since Peru has a natural outlet to the Pacific and is a fishing nation, it has been re-evaluating its foreign policy priorities since 1968 and, in recent years, focussed more attentively on the Pacific Rim. Thus, it was only natural that it should take a more active role in strengthening its diplomatic ties with China. Bilateral relations have been primarily based on the geographic imperative and their respective worldviews: both countries face the Pacific and they maintain similar views on international issues such as non-intervention, non-alignment and foreign debt. In addition, China has sought Peru's support for its 'One China' policy.

As China has assumed a greater global presence in the past two decades it has become more engaged in international diplomacy and has made cultivating economic and diplomatic ties with the Latin American region a foreign policy priority. Latin American countries, especially those that can provide China with much needed resources, have gained a significant stature in Chinese foreign policy. China no longer supports wars of liberation, stresses diplomacy based on non-interference and has gradually been opening to the world. In December 2001, China was admitted to the World Trade Organisation (WTO) and has gone out of its way to assure the world that it is now a market economy. Over the past twenty-five years, China has undergone substantial economic transformation. Its economy has been growing at an average of 9.5 per cent annually. Its participation in world trade has been impressive, particularly in manufacturing. China also has attracted most of the direct foreign investment flows to the developing world. Perhaps the most significant change is that China has pulled more than 400 million of its citizens out of poverty. While twenty years ago the financial press was more preoccupied on how the world would affect China, today the emphasis seems to be on how China is affecting the world (Kynge 2006).

This chapter examines Peru's China policy, how it has evolved and the present trend in the face of monumental changes that have occurred in Asia's giant. Is Peru prepared to deal on an equal footing with the new China? What can Peru offer China beyond primary exports? Is Peru's membership in the Asia-Pacific Economic Cooperation forum (APEC) and China's admission into the WTO of any significance in their trade relationship? Does a more active diplomacy and access to these organisations result in official recognition that would elevate Peru to a new status as an economic player? And what is the significance of the free trade agreement that Peru and China signed in 2009? These are the main questions that this chapter addresses.

The Evolution of Diplomatic Ties

Diplomatic and commercial ties with the People's Republic of China were established in the early 1970s. The nationalist government of Velasco Alvarado (1968–75) sought to expand Peru's relations with socialist countries. Peru became the third Latin American country to establish diplomatic relations with China (after Cuba and Chile). China in turn was interested in generating Latin American support as part of its South-South cooperation strategy. China also was of value to Peru's foreign policy because the former supported the non-aligned movement, of which Peru was an active member, sympathised with Peru's demand for restructuring foreign debt and supported Peru's territorial claim of 200 miles of maritime waters. Peru's positions on various international issues also coincided with those of the Chinese. Peru supported China's admittance to the United Nations, took a nationalist position on US-owned multinational firms and sympathised with China's view on the principle of self-determination.

In the almost four decades of diplomatic relations between Peru and China, the two countries have found common ground both bilaterally and multilaterally (Maúrtua de la Romaña 2005). In the early 1970s, the Peruvian government launched a series of state-sponsored development projects and received lines of credits and some technical assistance from China (Berríos 2003). Although Peru experienced economic stagnation in the 1980s due to its large foreign debt, resulting in structural adjustment, diplomatic ties with China remained cordial and trade continued to increase. By the end of the decade, Peru had taken notice of the economic success of some Asian countries and particularly the rise of China as an emerging economic power.

During the 1990s, China put forth a more active policy in Latin America. There was an increase in diplomatic visits by China's leaders and reciprocal visits by their Latin American counterparts. There also was a renewed interest on both sides in securing access to new markets and the PRC also increased its development assistance to some Latin American countries. Aid was used to seek or strengthen alliances or to achieve political credibility. As the Soviet Union collapsed in 1990, China sought to fill the vacuum and at the same time isolate Taiwan, which had been actively seeking a growing commercial presence in the region. That same year, China's president, Yang Shangkun, visited five Latin American countries with the purpose of securing resources and reinforcing and consolidating diplomatic and political ties. In 1993 and in 1997, President Jiang Zemin visited the region, and Premiers Li Peng and Zhu Rongji visited Latin America separately in 1992, 1995, 1996 and 1998. Then, in 2004, President Hu Jintao paid an official visit to the region. All of these contacts have bolstered economic ties between China and Latin America, but China's interest has been motivated mainly by its desire to have access to much needed resources. For the most part, China has shown more interest in boosting trade than promoting foreign investment. China has been able to rapidly expand and diversify its export markets and has only slowly diversified its investments in extractive industries (Devlin et al. 2006; Li 1991, 1998, 2007; Kurlantzick 2006; Mann 2006).

During the 1990s, diplomacy between China and Peru intensified, resulting in high-profile visits by Chinese and Peruvian officials (see Table 7.1). Peru's renewed interest in Pacific Asia was largely influenced by President Alberto Fujimori (1990–2000). Fujimori is of Japanese descent and he visualised Pacific Asia, especially Japan and China, as promising market outlets for Peru's exports. During his ten years as president, he made four official visits to China. In 1991, President Fujimori became the first Peruvian head of state to visit the People's Republic of China. Soon after, China's minister of foreign affairs visited Peru. In 1995, then-Prime Minister Li Peng paid an official visit to Peru.

Although Fujimori had a particular interest in having closer relations with Japan, he perceived China as the upcoming star of the Asia Pacific region. His Japanese roots did not affect the Sino-Peruvian relations. Fujimori was impressed by China's economic success and wanted to explore the opportunities offered by such a large expanding market. Under his administration, large purchases of machinery and equipment were made. Years later, some of this equipment, such as tractors and motorbikes, became unusable due to the lack of service and parts.

Table 7.1. Diplomatic Exchange between Peru and China, 1986–2005

Year	Purpose of visit
1986	President of Council of Ministers and Minister of Economics & Finance Luis Alva Castro visits China and meets Deng Xiaoping.
1987	Foreign Minister Wu Xuaqian visits Peru and meets President Alan Garcia.
1988	Peruvian Foreign Minister Alan Wagner visits China and meets Acting Premier Li Peng , Foreign Minister Wu Xuaqian, and Minister of Foreign Economic Relations and Trade Zheng Tuobin.
1990	Chinese Foreign Minister pays visit to Peru and meets President Alberto Fujimori.
1991	Vice-President San Roman visits China heading a congressional delegation and meets Chinese President Yang Shangkun and Foreign Minister Qian Qichen.
1991	President A. Fujimori travels to China in April and November, signs agreements on friendship and cooperation, and visits economic zone Shenzen.
1994	President A. Fujimori and Premier A. Bustamante sign an agreement of mutual protection of investments in Beijing. Peru obtains a credit line from Bank of China for $120 million to import Chinese machinery and equipment.
1994	President A. Fujimori travels to China to participate in The World Conference on Women, and meets Chinese officials.
1995	President A. Fujimori and Vice-President R. Marquez travel to China to participate in APEC meeting.
1996	Vice Chairman of NPC Standing Committee Chen Muhua pays official visit to Peru as head of NPC delegation, and meets Fujimori and other top officials.
1997	Peruvian President of the Congress Victor Joy Way visits China, meets Chinese President Jiang Zemin and other top Chinese officials.
1998	Vice premier Wu Bangguo pays an official visit to Peru at the head of a government delegation and meets top government officials.
1998	Defense Minister Gen. Julio Salazar signs an agreement on shipping, economic, and technological cooperation in Beijing.
1999	Presidents Jiang Zemin and Fujimori meet at the sixth and seventh APEC meeting (in 1998 and 1999).
2000	Peruvian Foreign Minister F. Treguiezes pays an official visit to China.
2000	Deputy Minister of Foreign Affairs of PRC Yang Jiechi visits Peru and meets President of Council of Minister Javier Perez de Cuellar.
2001	PRC President Jiang Zemin meets President Alejandro Toledo at the ninth APEC meeting held in Shangai.
2001	Vice-Foreign Minister Manuel Rodriguez Cuadros visits China.
2002	Foreign Minister Diego Garcia Sayan visits China and meets Li Peng.
2005	PRC Vice President Zeng Qinghong visits Peru and eight protocols are signed.
2005	President Alejandro Toledo travels to China on an official visit.
2007	Peru's Vice-Foreign Minister visits China. There is a fifth round of trade negotiations.
2009	Peru's President Alan Garcia visits China. Relations are elevated to 'strategic partners'.
2009	China's President Hu Jintao attends APEC Summit held in Lima. Confirms FTA is to be signed.

Source: Collected by the author from press releases and other information of the Ministry of Foreign Affairs of the People's Republic of China, and the Ministerio de Relaciones Exteriores, Peru (various years).

Although Fujimori had a strong interest in promoting closer relations with China and other Pacific Rim countries, neither his staff nor the business sector was fully prepared to take the relationship one step further. Initially, there was no clear plan or policy consensus on Asia because the continent was geographically distant and was relatively unknown to Peruvian diplomats, businessmen and scholars. There were no research centres that dealt with Asian affairs. To make matters worse, in 1992, Fujimori also dismissed more than 100 diplomats, including his very seasoned diplomat and ambassador in Japan: Luis Macchiavello. He replaced him with his brother-in-law and confidant, Victor Aritomi. Fujimori did establish PROMPERU, a commission to promote Peru abroad, but its sole purpose was to serve as a public relations entity to promote investment and tourism. The idea was to counter the negative image of Peru because of political violence, drug trafficking and the backlash of Fujimori's *autogolpe* in April 1992. Although Peru's trade policy regime at the time was undergoing some reforms to compete in world markets, the government had not yet been able to promote an effective trade policy to upgrade and diversify its exports. The Ministry of Trade, for instance, as a more dynamic and autonomous institution to forge policy formulation and implementation, was not created until a decade later.

Despite Peru's slow government institutions and lags in policy formulation and implementation, some diplomatic gains were being made in the Asian front. As Peru worked to enter the Asian market, diplomats attended a series of meetings and succeeded in getting the country admitted to the Pacific Business Economic Council (PBEC) in 1990 and to the Pacific Economic Cooperation Council (PECC) in 1991. The Fujimori government opened embassies in Malaysia, Indonesia, Singapore and Thailand as well as a trade office in Taiwan. Early on, Peru also expressed an interest in joining the Asia Pacific Economic Cooperation forum (APEC) and sent diplomatic representatives to various meetings. Membership in the PBEC and PECC served to set the groundwork for the entrance of Peru, along with Russia and Vietnam, into APEC in 1998. Peru's active diplomacy in Pacific Asia finally paid off. Admission to APEC initially was lauded as a diplomatic achievement and was cause for much optimism, even if Peru had little to offer (Ferrero Diez Canseco 2000). Because of Peru's geographic location, Fujimori reaffirmed that Peru would be a gateway for Asian products to South America and stressed that it also would be a vehicle to expand Peruvian exports across the Pacific.

Although Fujimori was forced to resign from office in 2000 due to allegations of corruption and human rights abuses, there has been little change in the policy toward China. On 20 October 2001, President Alejandro Toledo had a meeting with President Jiang Zemin during the APEC summit meeting in Shanghai. In 2002, President Toledo met with President Hu Jintao at an

APEC meeting held in Mexico and they met again later in Bangkok in 2003 and Santiago in 2004. In 2005, President Toledo visited China for the last time to sign more protocols and discuss ways to increase trade, investment and tourism between the two countries (Castro Obando 2005; Ly 2005).

With the fall of Fujimori, some diplomatic tension ensued from Japan's refusal to extradite the former President of Peru to face accusations of human rights abuses and corruption under his administration. Trade between the two countries slowed and investments dried up. China's economic presence, on the other hand, continued to expand. One could argue that to some extent, China's economic success has prompted the Peruvian government to examine its own trade strategy and to learn from the success of its Asian partners. Peru is slowly realising that trade alone will not boost the economy, but it must be done with a set of complimentary policies and incentives that will shape its long-term growth. A more outward looking approach to development requires adequate institutional support to properly manage the opportunities and minimise the costs trade is likely to cause.

The Economic Importance of China in Peru's Foreign Affairs

In recent years, trade between Peru and China has grown remarkably (see Figure 7.1), and this has contributed to Peru's rapid economic growth. From 2000 to 2005, Peru's total exports increased from $9 billion to $17 billion and much of that was due to exports destined for the United States and China. As Table 7.2 shows, from 2003 to 2007 the value of its exports to China more than quadrupled (from $677 million to more than $3 billion). Spurred by rising world market prices for commodities, mainly due to China's increased demand, Peru's export revenues have risen sharply these last few years (see Figure 7.1). So far, Peru has maintained a trade surplus, but that may change since its exports show some volatility, while China's imports continue to rise at a steady rate.

For Peru, China has become the major entryway into the Asian market. Since China has had one of the highest sustained growth rates in the world, Peru sees China as an important player in international trade and realises the importance of its role as a member of APEC; the export sector has experienced a boost from increased demand and higher prices for its commodities from China. Since 2004, more than half of Peru's exports are destined for Asia, and primarily China. As of 2005, China has become Peru's second largest trading partner as trade between the two countries steadily rose (Gallardo 2006; Mincetur 2007).

Figure 7.1. Evolution of Peru's Trade with China 1987–2007
(in US$ millions)

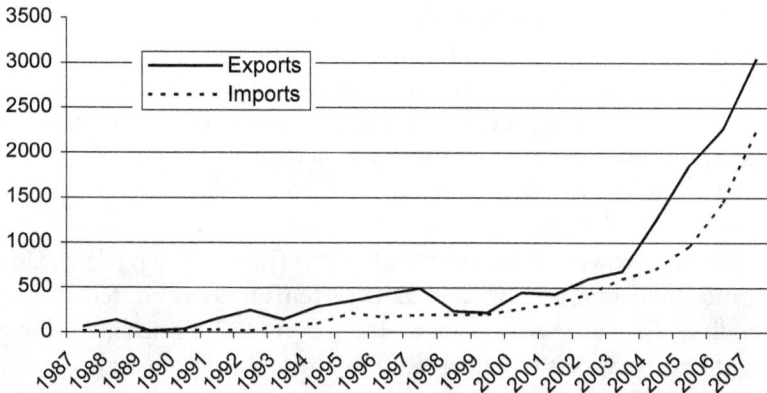

Source: Aduanas, MINCETUR, SUNAT (various years).

Table 7.2. Peru's Trade with China, 1987–2007 (in US$ millions)

	Exports	Imports
1987	60.0	19.6
1988	134.1	2.6
1989	11.3	13.3
1990	34.6	15.8
1991	149.5	26.4
1992	243.5	17.1
1993	140.5	76.3
1994	284.8	94.3
1995	349.4	209.2
1996	419.4	166.6
1997	491.2	195.9
1998	233.2	191.5
1999	215.5	201.4
2000	442.7	260.6
2001	425.2	321.1
2002	597.6	426.6
2003	677.0	597.8
2004	1235.3	699.8
2005	1860.9	956.6
2006	2267.3	1447.5
2007	3041.3	2251.1

Source: see Figure 7.1.

For Peru, China has become the major entryway into the Asian market. Since China has had one of the highest sustained growth rates in the world, Peru sees China as an important player in international trade and realises the importance of its role as a member of APEC; the export sector has experienced a boost from increased demand and higher prices for its commodities from China. Since 2004, more than half of Peru's exports are destined for Asia, and primarily China. As of 2005, China has become Peru's second largest trading partner as trade between the two countries steadily rose (Gallardo 2006; Mincetur 2007).

Despite the growth of Peruvian exports to China, they represent low diversification and low added value as they remain concentrated in primary commodities such as metals (copper, lead, iron) and fishmeal. As Table 7.3 shows, of Peru's exports to China in 2006, the first ten product groups represented almost 95 per cent of the total value. Although the basket of Peruvian goods in demand by the Chinese market has grown to include wood, canned seafood and paper, in terms of volume and value, minerals and fishmeal consist of about 85 per cent of total exports. Because of its vast market and rapid growth, China promises to absorb a growing number of Peruvian goods, but so far Peru has not had a coherent trade strategy and the marketing skills to maximise further gains. China's exports to Peru, on the other hand, show great diversification: recording, image and sound equipment, telephones, memory devises, motorcycles, machines, chemicals and textiles. In 2006, no single product accounted for more than 4 per cent of the Chinese exports to Peru (see Table 7.4).

Table 7.3. Main Peruvian Products Exported to China, 2006 (in US$)

No.	Products	Value[a]	%
1	Copper minerals & concentrations	926 897 887	40.88
2	Fish meal	427 164 681	18.84
3	Lead minerals & concentrates	271 739 920	11.99
4	Molybdenum & concentrates	103 724 013	4.57
5	Raw oils or from bituminous	99 770 480	4.40
6	Iron ore & concentrates – aglomerates	86 281 868	3.81
7	Cathodes & cathode-sections of refined copper	84 218 303	3.71
8	Iron ore & concentrates	70 981 713	3.13
9	Canned seafood	36 804 231	1.62
10	Pine planks for parquet, unassembled	36 011 381	1.59
	Total (of 1 to 10)	2 143 594 477	94.54
	Other products	123 682 487	5.46

a. FOB

Source: SUNAT (2007)

Table 7.4. Main Chinese Products Imported in Peru, 2006 (in US$)

No.	Products	Value[a]	%
1	Telephones	51 929 615	3.27
2	Parts & machine accessories	46 709 016	2.95
3	Automated machines & data processing equip.	40 734 610	2.57
4	Motorcycles	37 218 611	2.35
5	Recording, sound & image equipment	33 557 748	2.12
6	TV reception devices	29 602 509	1.87
7	Input-output units, case memory included	29 034 576	1.83
8	Memory units	23 514 097	1.48
9	Radio receptors & recording equipment	22 781 617	1.44
10	Footwear	20 362 134	1.28
	Total	335 444 533	21.15
	Other products	1 250 232 196	78.85

a. FOB

Source: SUNAT (2007)

Over the past few years, Chinese leaders have sought closer commercial ties with Latin American countries as well as the (WTO) recognition by Latin American governments of China as a market economy. China's leaders also stressed their country's interest in investing more in the region, but it has been rather slow in materialising. Peru is a case in point. In 1996, the first major investment was the purchase of Hierro Peru by the Shougan Corporation for $122 million. In 2004, Sapet (a subsidiary of the China National Petroleum Co.) bought a 45 per cent stake in PlusPetrol Norte, for $200 million. In 2006, the Chinese Fisheries Group bought one of Peru's largest fisheries, Pesquera Alexandra, for $100 million. And in 2007, China's state-owned Aluminium Corporation of China (CHINALCO) announced the planned purchase of Peru Copper for $792 million. The company also has announced that it plans to invest $2.2 billion to develop the Toromocho copper project owned by Centromin Peru. In addition, Chinese companies are reportedly interested in investing in timber (EIU 2007).

The first trip by President Alejandro Toledo to China in 2001 was intended to push for more bilateral economic agreements and to promote cooperation in areas of culture and tourism. As the two governments intensified high-level contacts, the business communities of both countries have shown interest in expanding business opportunities. In 2002, Peru opened a consulate and a commercial office in Shanghai. Toledo also expressed interest in Chinese firms bidding for rebuilding and upgrading Peru's ports on the Pacific coast. Another area of interest is Chinese tourism. However, despite the fact that, in 2005, the Chinese government declared Peru an approved tourist destination, the number of Chinese tourists travelling to Peru has been low.

China is not a major aid donor, but to solidify its economic presence, China has provided some foreign aid to Peru in the form of small low-interest loans, small donations and technical assistance (Berríos 2003). Still, Chinese foreign direct investment in Peru has been slow in coming and is concentrated in mining. However, in recent years, Chinese companies have shown more interest and have conducted preliminary studies to invest in infrastructure (roads, ports, railways). During the 1990s, the Chinese were reluctant to invest in Peru due to the country's political instability. Recent visits by Peruvian officials to China have not resulted in any significant investment despite the rapid increase in trade, but high-ranking Chinese officials have pledged to invest more in the future.

In March 2008, Peru's President Alan Garcia made an official visit to China to speed up trade negotiations and encourage China to invest in Peru. As a result of the visit, a so-called strategic partnership protocol was signed and various rounds of trade negotiations have taken place. In November of 2008, Chinese President Hu Jintao came to Lima to attend the APEC Summit. Some 12 ministers and about 600 Chinese businessmen and other support staff came with the president. The large Chinese presence was seen by the press as a signal of the growing economic importance of Latin America to China. At his arrival, Mr. Hu announced that trade flows between Peru and China had reached $6 billion for 2008. During his extended visit in Lima, a number of agreements were signed to facilitate trade and to show his strong support for the free trade agreement between the two countries.

Unresolved Issues

Since the beginning of the new millennium, China has had considerable success in expanding its economic presence in Latin America. To boost trade relations, China has been pursuing free trade agreements. At the end of 2005, it signed a trade accord with Chile. In February 2007, President Alan Garcia announced that Peru was engaged in negotiations with China to establish a free trade agreement (FTA). To accelerate the process, a high-ranking Chinese official, Li Chanchung, went to Peru in March to follow up on negotiations as a way to increase economic cooperation between the two countries, and both countries conducted a joint feasibility study. The trade talks continued in 2008. The FTA was signed in April 2009 and went into effect in March 2010.

Despite the optimism displayed by the Peruvian authorities at the time of the trade talks with China, some analysts urged Peru to carefully evaluate the possible consequences of a free trade agreement (Kleinwechter 2007). They argued that while Peru could certainly boost its exports to China primarily with agricultural products and minerals, the Andean country is no match for China's competitive strength in manufactured goods, and particularly in textiles and footwear, because of its large pool of cheap labour. This would exert downward pressure on prices: domestic producers would not be able to compete with a large inflow of cheap Chinese imports. Although there is a consensus among economists that trade is good and that it is an important instrument to build goodwill, in this instance, only a few sectors of the Peruvian economy would benefit from a free trade agreement and it is likely that the economic benefits promised by political leaders would fall short. Peru's domestic market is small and too fragmented to generate significant revenues. An additional problem is that more than half of Peru's labour force is in the informal sector and would not benefit from the agreement.

Whereas Peru remains a predominantly primary producer and exporter, the country faces stiff competition from China in manufacturing. According to WTO figures, 74 per cent of Chinese total exports are manufactured goods (WTO 2006). The FTA with China is likely further confine Peru to an extractive economy that produces and exports primary goods and relegates it to a net importer of manufactured goods. Even the investments promised by China are directed mainly toward the mining sector and oil extraction. Free trade with China is unlikely to promote more diversified and balanced development in Peru because it only opens a window of opportunity for those sectors exporting natural resources. It is therefore equally unlikely that it will generate much more employment and encourage production of more value-added goods. For Peru's part, its commercial policy still requires research to identify areas where it can compete with China beyond the sale of fishmeal and minerals.

When the signing of the free trade agreement with China neared, it was intensely debated in Peru. In general, much was said about Chinese trade policies, such as keeping their currency low to boost their exports, government subsidies for their exporting industries, widespread abuse of intellectual property and even 'slave labour' inside their large factories (Fallows 2007). China was accused by Peru's trade enforcement agency Indecopi (National Institute for the Defence of Competition and Protection of Intellectual Property) of dumping. According to one report, 'incidence of antidumping investigations by country of origin of imports shows that the main country reported was China with 28 per cent of total cases' (Webb et al. 2006). Many of these cases involved textiles, clothing, shoes and other goods. Peru raised concerns about unfair trading practices and has issued formal complaints on China's commercial interest office in Lima (Berríos 2003). In addition, the Chinese export boom was said to be facing a quality crisis. Some Chinese goods have been of substandard quality, with Peruvian importers often complaining about the poor quality of some Chinese products (such as pharmaceuticals), and other items such as small tractors and vehicles have not performed well in Peru's terrain (Pintado 2001a, 2001b; *El Comercio* 2001). More cases involving substandard Chinese products, for instance, tainted toothpaste and lead paint in toys, could create a backlash against Chinese imports. Some high-profile recalls raised questions about the quality and safety of some Chinese goods. China was also blamed for widespread piracy of music and movies. But the major complaints were directed at the Chinese practice of dumping. Although the complaints increased, the Chinese insisted that their internal cost structure and prices are significantly lower, which is why they offer goods at such low prices. But the growing presence of low priced Chinese goods has caused serious concern for some local manufacturers who fear that the Chinese are driving them out of the market.

The plans for a FTA with China gave cause to serious concern in Peru. On the one hand, Peru saw in China an opportunity to consolidate a trade relationship of vital importance, on the other hand, it also perceived it as a threat because of the impact that Chinese imports would have on some sectors of the Peruvian economy (Mathews and Bákula 2005). China could become a competitor to Peru's producers of footwear, textiles and other light industry goods. There also was increasing concern that with China's entry into the WTO and with the collapse of the multifibre agreement, Peru's textile export sector would suffer – China is capable of dominating the market. In other sectors such as light manufacturing, China could also cause a threat to countries such as Peru that are seeking to compete in a more global economy. Most troublesome for Peru's local entrepreneurs was whether they could compete in garments and apparel. Fully aware of the problem, the Ministry of Economy and Finance as well as Indecopi issued decrees and safeguards to protect certain local products against cheaper Chinese goods that enter the market (Castro Obando 2007; Ministerio de Comercio Exterior 2006). Still, since China has a comparative advantage in many areas because of its higher productivity and efficiency, the question remains: Can Peru be competitive enough if Chinese costs are so much lower? China's superior competitiveness is based on lower production costs, particularly labour and some inputs (for instance, electricity), greater efficiency and diversification in manufacturing, as well as better infrastructure to expedite exports.

Even though Peru's production capacity is limited, the country could still increase exports to China. However, as Chinese demand for commodities such as fishmeal increased rapidly, Peruvian companies at times were not able to satisfy the demand or meet the export target for reasons that were not under their control. For instance, the climatological phenomenon *El Niño* can wreck havoc and negatively affect production. Under those circumstances China has had to turn to Chile, which is a more reliable supplier. Peru can benefit from an enhanced trade relationship with China, but it needs to reassess its Asia policy. The government has had a relatively weak capacity to formulate a forward-looking policy. There also needs to be a stronger part-nership with the private sector to generate greater collaboration and to cre-ate a more focused policy. Furthermore, Peru needs to identify competitive strengths and opportunities to increase export diversification

The presence of Peru in APEC is of paramount importance because this group of 21 countries seeks to promote economic integration along the Pa-cific and represents about 57 per cent of the world's GDP. Peru, Chile and Mexico are the only Latin American members. In recent years, nearly two-thirds of Peruvian exports and more than half of its imports were to and from country members of APEC. Even though Peru is small relative to other APEC members, in particular the United States, China, Japan and Russia, it has yet to take full advantage of the opportunity as a member (Mexico and Chile have been more successful in doing so).

To improve its chances and as a way of raising its levels of productivity, Peru has also been seeking free trade agreements with some other APEC members such as the Unites States (signed in 2006 and implemented in Feb-ruary 2009) and Japan. One thing is certain: some sectors would not be able to compete with the levels of productivity of those countries, but could compete on products that have low value-added (agriculture and mining). The problem with an FTA is not the agreement itself, even if it reflects an economic policy dictated by special interests. Previous administrations touted other bilateral and sub-regional agreements as the sure path to development, but their effects have in general been mixed or disappointing. Peru's agree-ment with China may turn out not to be any different unless the govern-ment provides clear and effective commercial policy goals and development objectives.

Conclusions

Peru and China have historical links and over the years they have had many reasons to strengthen economic ties. As Peru has sought to diversify its mar-kets, it has become increasingly aware of the importance of the Asia-Pacific region. Today, regional economic cooperation and free trade agreements have gained widespread support. Peru has, in some sense, 'rediscovered' the Asia-Pacific region; it has expressed admiration for the economic success and transformation of Asia's newly industrialising countries. APEC, which was created to advance economic cooperation, has fostered diplomatic rela-tions and extensive discussions among the member countries. Although trade among the members remains partly on a small scale because of geographical distance and some complementarity, there is potential for growth.

However, obstacles for completing the cross-Pacific bridge remain. They include insufficient knowledge of markets, different ways of doing business and transportation costs. In the case of Peru, it lacks the vision to capitalise on its potential as a trade partner; it remains an extractive economy. China, for its part, has capitalised on its ability to sell cheaper goods, but has been hesitant to risk large-scale investment initiatives in Peru. Investment in sectors other than mining has been slow in coming, and in that sector, there are issues that still need to be resolved. For example, the purchase of Hierro Peru by Shougan has led to disputes over workers' rights. Peruvian miners traditionally have been militant and have frequently clashed with Chinese management over low wages, long working hours and unsafe working conditions.

Better understanding and analysis of the Asian market could make Peru a player at the trans-Pacific economic table, and recognition of the potential of Peru could spur Asian countries to be more aggressive in capital investment in Peru. There is no doubt that increased diplomatic and business contact can facilitate the expansion of trade and lead to greater economic cooperation. But Peru's private sector will need to link up with Asian firms to engage in business ventures. Peru's diplomatic missions also need to begin providing more information on what the nation can offer. The opening of a consulate and commercial office in Shanghai was a first step. But the fundamental challenge facing Peru today in the Asia-Pacific region is how to develop and implement an outward-looking policy that is not simply a derivative of what others are doing. Peru has begun to conceive of itself as a Pacific country. But this self-image is the result of diplomatic achievements such as joining APEC, which so far has brought few concrete results. If Peru wants to go further, it needs to promote the study of Pacific Asia to understand the region better; it must be more engaging in entrepreneurial matters; and it needs to look into possible public-private alliances to explore the vast possibilities of the Chinese market, as Chile has done (Faust 2004).

In a broader sense, Peru needs to begin taking a more coherent and comprehensive approach to China. Despite Peru's rising interest in improved economic links, attempts at diversification of external links have been only partially achieved. Diplomatic contacts and economic transactions have increased, but the relative weight of Asia, and particularly China, in Peru's foreign policy is still modest. There has been no systematic policy network involving the state, domestic businesses and academic institutions to design and promote an Asia-Pacific policy. If Peru is to sustain and increase its links with the Asia-Pacific region, it must have a coherent policy of active engagement and coordination with its new trading partners to the East. Its domestic actors (businessmen, academics and policymakers) must be more engaged and must help to create an effective approach for successful strategy with Pacific Asia, and especially China.

The optimistic view for Peru is that China represents a source of expand-ing trade, investment and tourism. In recent years, China has had a more visible economic presence in Peru. From a realist perspective, China courts Peru by seeking commercial and strategic gains. China's economic goal is to secure extractive resources necessary for Chinese companies. China's foreign interests are no longer motivated by an ideology, but by a well-defined com-mercial strategy; it sees Peru and the rest of Latin America as a new kind of global partner (Santiso 2007). Regarding the recently implemented bilat-eral free trade agreement, it still needs to be seen whether Peru's gains will outweigh its losses. Businessmen, some academics and government officials in Peru have seen China as threatening because it can stifle Peru's efforts to re-energise its light manufacturing industry. Peru, as well as many Latin American countries, has seen a flood of Chinese products, both legal and contraband. This has been taken very seriously and the government is look-ing at ways to ameliorate the problem.

China's thriving economy is reflected in its pragmatic approach in generat-ing investment incentives to propel exports and thus growth. For instance, about 60 per cent of foreign investment going into China is channelled to the manufacturing sector. As China now has a highly dynamic and diversified market, its success story does offer some lessons for countries such as Peru. China has had the ability to forge effective policy to upgrade and diversify exports, and to deliver specialised goods. In contrast, Peru has weak govern-ment institutions that are unable to formulate and implement a consistent policy. Peru needs to create a better framework for competition, and Peru's policymakers need to address public-private alliances and a strategically com-petitive approach to trade. Peru is likely to benefit from its free trade agree-ment with the United States, which ensures a stable supply of products for the US market. However, this FTA also requires Peru to reform legislation on labour, safety standards and other issues. Furthermore, to boost its com-petitiveness as markets open up, Peru needs to improve its infrastructure and modernise its ports to lower costs.

In sum, what implications do the Sino-Peruvian relations have in terms of Peru's broader macro-economic development? A major concern for Peru is China's export expansion and how it affects Peru's prospects for export growth. Another issue is to what extent China's emergence as a large player in world markets threatens Peru's manufacturing sector (Mesquita Moreira 2006). Finally, it is important to assess the effects of China's growing pres-ence in the US market on Peru's exports to the United States, which is Peru's main export market.

Peru is a natural resource abundant country, and the logic of compara-tive advantage states that the country should follow that path. Others would argue that in spite of past poor performance, a country such as Peru should diversify and move into a more manufacturing-based strategy. But even after trade liberalisation, the manufacturing share of GDP has not grown to any significant degree. Although there are advantages in diversification, Peru is still at a disadvantage because of its low technological capabilities and level of human capital. So far, natural resources have been the main source of higher growth rates and the future of its manufacturing sector is not encouraging. China, on the other hand, has emerged as an exporter of labour-intensive technology products and increasingly of higher technology end products. In a broader context, while Peru's macro economy has been better managed in recent years, it needs to sustain stability and limit distortions (budget deficits, high inflation).

China's ascension has proven to be a real test for Peru. It provides a great opportunity in that it is a huge market. Yet China is a threat because it could overwhelm the very manufacturing industries that Peru has been trying to diversify, especially apparel, textiles, footwear and light assembly goods. Sino-Peruvian relations have developed progressively since the early 1970s. China's growing profile reflects a policy of engagement that is driven mainly by economic interests to secure reliable resources sustaining its economic growth. The result of Chinese diplomacy has been a better competitive position in Latin America. China is not only buying more, but it is also investing in extractive resources and infrastructure. Peru has benefited from China's booming demand for commodities, but there is unease among Peruvian trade officials and entrepreneurs about China's emergence in global manufacturing, where the Asian giant is making the most gains. As Peru takes advantage of the FTA with the United States by boosting exports of light manufactured goods, China could diminish that market.

References

Berríos, Rubén. 2003. 'El Perú y la República Popular de China: otro puente de entrada a Asia'. *Agenda Internacional* (Lima) 9 (18): 145–60.

Castro Obando, Patricia. 2005. 'Toledo anuncia invesrsiones asiaticas en carreteras, puertos y aeropuertos'. *El Comercio* (Lima), 4 julio: A9.

———. 2007. 'El Perú no tendrá un TLC tradicional con China pues se excluiría sectores sensibles'. *El Comercio* (Lima), 4 julio: B3.

Chang-Rodriguez, Eugenio. 1958. 'Chinese Labour Migration into Latin America in the Nineteenth Century'. *Revista de Historia de América* 46: 375–97.

Devlin, Robert, Antoni Estevadeordal and Andres Rodriguez-Clare, eds. 2006. *The Emergence of China: Opportunities and Challenges for Latin America and the Caribbean*. 375–397. Washington, DC: Inter-American Development Bank.

EIU. 2007. 'Peru/China Industry: Mining for Copper'. *Economist Intelligence Unit*, Country Briefing EIU, 13 June: 7–9.

El Comercio. 2001. 'Un centenar de tractores chinos estan inservibles'. *El Comercio* (Lima), 12 junio: A10.

Fallows, James. 2007. 'China Makes, the World Takes'. *The Atlantic*, July/August: 48–72.

Faust, Jörg. 2004. 'Latin America, Chile and East Asia: Policy-Networks and Successful Diversification'. *Journal of Latin American Studies*, 36: 743–70.

Ferrero Diez Canseco, Alfredo. 2000. 'APEC y Peru: estableciendo nuevos vínculos con Asia Pacífico'. *Apuntes* 46: 77–100.

Gallardo, Carlos. 2006. 'Análisis de los flujos comerciales entre el Perú y China con miras a la firma del acuerdo de alcance parcial'. In *Tópicos de negociaciones comerciales internacionales: metodologías y aplicación relevantes para el Perú*, eds. Fernando Gonzalez Vigil, Alvaro Henzer Vernal, Carlos Rueda Heredia and Diego Urbina Fletcher, 63–92. Lima: Universidad del Pacífico.

Kleinwechter, Uli. 2007. 'Una receta mágica? Por qué el TLC con China no significa desarrollo para el Perú'. *Bilaterals.org*, 1 May. http://www.bilaterals.org/ (accessed 9 June 2006).

Kurlantzick, Joshua. 2006. 'China's Latin Leap Forward'. *World Policy Journal* 23 (3): 33–41.

Kynge, James. 2006. *China Shakes the World: A Titan's Rise and Troubled Future*. NY: Houghton Mifflin.

Li, He. 1991. *Sino-Latin American Economic Relations*. Westerport, CT: Praeger.

———. 1998. 'Economic Diplomacy: Chinese Policy Toward Latin America'. *Problems of Post Communism* 45 (2): 33–42.

———. 2007. 'Red Star Over Latin America'. *Nacla Report on the Americas*, September–October: 23–27.

Ly, A. 2005. 'Abriendo una asociación de cooperación integral'. *Revista Oriental* (Lima) 895, enero-febrero: 6–7.

Mann, Stefanie. 2006. *Peru's Relations with Pacific Asia: Democracy and Foreign Policy under Alan Garcia, Alberto Fujimori, and Alejandro Toledo*. Berlin: LIT Verlag.

Mathews, Juan Carlos and Anibal Bákula. 2005. 'China: amenaza y oportunidad'. *Punto de Equilibrio* (Lima) 14 (88): 26–27.

Maúrtua de la Romaña, Oscar. 2005. 'Perspectivas de las relaciones sino-peruanas'. *Punto de Equilibrio* (Lima) 14 (88): 19–21.

Mesquita Moreira, Mauricio. 2006. *Fear of China: Is There a Future for Manufacturing in Latin America?* INTAL-ITD Occassional Paper 36, April.

Mincetur. 2007. *Reporte de comercio bilateral: Perú-China*. Lima: Ministerio de Comercio Exterior y Turismo (Año 06, No. 083).

Ministerio de Comercio Exterior. 2007. *Consideraciones para negociar un acuerdo commercial con China*. Documento de Trabajo, Septiembre.

Pintado, Henry Rafael. 2001a. 'Se invirtieron mas de 28 millones de dolares en medicinas chinas'. *El Comercio* (Lima), 2 agosto: A2.

———. 2001b. 'Ambulancias rurales donadas por Fujimori ya no sirven'. *El Comercio* (Lima), 4 agosto: A12.

Poston Jr, D.L. and Mei-Yu Yu. 1990. 'The Distribution of the Overseas Chinese in the Contemporary World'. *International Migration Review*, 24 (3): 480–508.

Rodriguez Pastor, Humberto. 2000. *Herederos del dragón: historia de la comunidad china en el Perú*. Lima: Fondo Editorial del Congreso del Perú.

Santiso, Javier, ed. 2007. *The Visible Hand of China in Latin America*. Paris: Organization for Economic Development and Cooperation.

SUNAT. 2007. Customs Information, Superintendencia Nacional de Administración Tributaria, Peru. http://www.sunat.gob.pe/aduanas/version_ingles/index.html (accessed 7 December 2007).

Webb, Richard, Josefina Camminati and Raul Leon Thorne. 2006. 'Antidumping Mechanisms and Safeguards in Peru'. In *Safeguards and Antidumping in Latin American Trade Liberalization*, eds. J. Michael Finger and Julio J. Nogues, 247–77. London and Washington, DC: Palgrave and World Bank.

WTO. 2006. *China Trade Profile*. Geneva: World Trade Organization.

8 Bolivia and China
Indirect Relations in a Global Market
Pablo Poveda

Since the mid 1990s, Asia has rapidly risen as an important trade zone for Bolivia, with Japan as Bolivia's primary Asian export destination. For a long time, Bolivia's trade and investment relations with China remained remarkably low compared to other Latin American countries. While Bolivia and China have had diplomatic relations since 1985, it is only since 2003 that their bilateral economic relations have become a priority for the two governments. This showed most clearly in January 2006, when Evo Morales visited China shortly before his inauguration as president. At this occasion, the Bolivian president-elect met with President Hu Jintao and State Councillor Tang Jiaxuan and expressed Bolivia's interest in investments by Chinese state companies, especially in the hydrocarbon and mining sector. As it is China's policy to diversify its sources of raw material imports, Chinese investments in Bolivian mining and hydrocarbons can indeed be expected to expand. Generally, the trend of trade with China becoming increasingly important to Bolivia is likely to continue in the near future due to China's growing influence in the world economy and the intensified Sino-Bolivian relations.

China has shown a remarkable level of economic development over the past few decades, which is partly related to changes in global production structures. With its enormous and relatively young population, China has an abundance of cheap labour. These characteristics became particularly relevant when the global crisis of Fordist production gave way to a globalisation of industrial production based on sub-contracting. This sub-contracting enabled multinational companies to both lower labour costs and raise productivity, thereby increasing their profits. Initially, Chinese industrial production was concentrated in basic segments such as clothes and food production, but increasingly more complex processes such as machinery production and chemical industry have become based in China as well. China's insertion into global productions structures has also been the result of its adoption of economic principles of capital accumulation and capitalist exploitation. Although China's economic structure still has a high level of production of basic manufactures compared to industrialised countries, the shift from agriculture to industrial production and services in the distribution of Chinese GDP in the last thirty years shows that China has gone through a fast economic transformation. Still, the working conditions to which its large workforce are subjected to are extreme: low wages and long working days, which indirectly puts pressure on lowering wages internationally and exacerbates the negative elements of capitalist accumulation.

The rapid development of China's productive base has raised its demand of raw material to such an extent that it has become the world's largest importing country of raw materials. Between 2000 and 2004, China was the first consumer of metallic minerals such as steel (31 per cent), tin (23 per cent), copper (13 per cent), lead (21 per cent) and zinc (19 per cent) (CEPAL 2006). As global raw material supply was insufficient to accompany the growing demand to which China was an important contributor, prices started to rise. Another effect of China's industrial development is the transfer of production from the United States to China, which affects global capital flows and contributes to unbalanced US production and consumption. As the decrease of China's productive apparatus has been compensated by the United States with monetary mechanisms, China has exported its inflation and indirectly added to the rise of international prices on raw material.

This chapter assesses the ways in which the rise of China has affected the Bolivian economy. In the first part, Bolivia's economic insertion into the world economy will be assessed. Bolivia has a long history of economic dependency, mainly exporting raw materials: first silver and tin, and more recently gas. The Development Plan of the government of President Morales was announced as a break with this history and the start of a new stage in Bolivia's development. We will critically analyse Bolivia's economic development and the possibilities of this Development Plan to meet its aims. The second part will study Bolivia's recent relations with China and other Asian countries. Since Bolivia exports raw materials and China requires vast volumes of these materials, their economic relations have gained importance. We will look into these recent trends and discuss the likelihood of these relations to be widened and deepened in the near future.

Bolivia's Economy and Morales' Development Plan

Within the global system of capitalist production, Bolivia has not been able to achieve a satisfying economic development. Bolivia's role is limited to the supply of natural resources, and as an exporter of a few commodities, it is highly dependent on the world market. Bolivia's insertion into the global economy may be characterised as an umbilical relation in which most of the production processes in its national economy are subordinated to the world market. The perverse effects of producing a limited number of raw materials are primarily due to the accumulation system and conditions created by the industrialised countries (CEDLA 2007a).

Until 1985, the insertion of Bolivia into the world economy was based on the mining enclave of silver and tin. From then onward, coinciding with the beginning of the neoliberal period, this insertion became based on the production of other commodities such as natural gas, poly-metallic concentrates and soy (CEDLA 2007b). As shown in Figure 8.1, mining and hydrocarbons dominate in the Bolivian export production. In 2006, 48 per cent of its exports consisted of hydrocarbons ($1,671 million), 25 per cent of mining ($1,060 million) and 18 per cent of non-traditional primary products ($767 million), such as soy, soy oil, chestnuts, wood, clothing and jewellery.

Figure 8.1. Bolivia's Export Sectors, 1980–2006 (%)

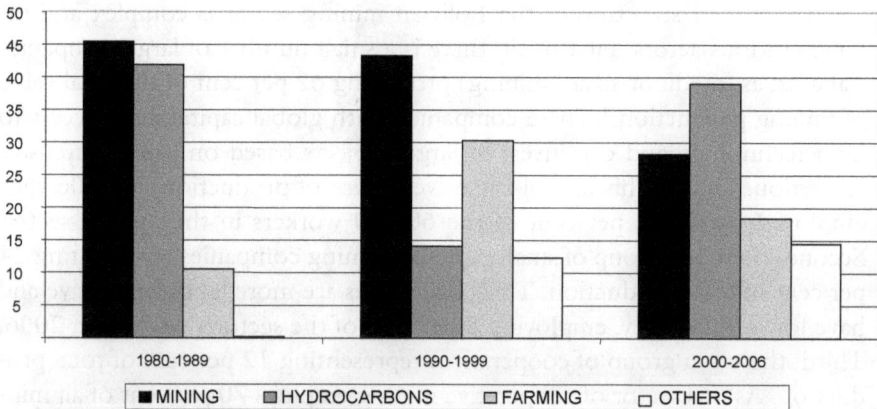

Source: Energy Information Administration (2009); Espinaza (2009); Noticias EFE (2009).

Contrary to the claims that the neoliberal policies imposed in 1985 would diversify Bolivia's export model through the expansion of manufacturing, the result of its economic opening was an ongoing dependence on the primary sector. In combination with the precarious internal economic situation, this dependency on the primary sector for export became a source of profound social and political unrest. From 2000 onward, it gave way to massive popular mobilisation against the neoliberal economic model. Social movements demanded that natural resources be used to benefit the Bolivian people at large, in particular by means of the nationalisation of natural gas, which is Bolivia's main hydrocarbon.

The democratic government of President Evo Morales, which resulted out of Bolivia's political crisis and is to govern from 2006 to 2010, is the trustee of those aspirations of its people. In its plans, this government has suggested that it will part from the neoliberal policies and the primary export model. Instead, it aims to introduce an Andean capitalism based on harmonic relations between the small 'communitarian' property holders and the large monopolist property holders. With respect to the extraction of hydrocarbons and other minerals, there is thus an important new orientation of economic policies under Morales.

Mining Sector and Policy Reform

As several Latin American countries benefited from the commodity boom and the revenues from increased exports to China, it is interesting to look also into Bolivia's mining sector. For centuries, extractive activities have been central to Bolivia's economic development and its insertion into global markets. Under the new international economic circumstances it is important to see what benefits, if any, this sector has received.

The internal structure of the Bolivian mining sector is complex and involves various actors. First of all, there is a small number of large companies (labelled as 'medium-sized' mining) producing 62 per cent of the total value of mining production.[1] These companies, with global capital, have access to high technology and can invest in large projects based on capital-intensive extraction. Due to this capital-intensive nature of production, in 2006 they employed barely 12 per cent of the 60,000 workers in the mining sector. Second, there is a group of small capitalist mining companies representing 24 per cent of total production. Their operations are more labour-intensive and have low productivity, employing 8 per cent of the sector's workers in 2006. Third, there is a group of cooperatives representing 12 per cent of total production. As this sector of cooperative mining employs 70 per cent of all miners, it is socially very important. The cooperatives were created after the state enterprise Corporación Minera de Bolivia (COMIBOL) ceased most of its operations; in order to avoid the social load of having to fire 25,000 workers in the crisis decade of the 1980s, the government gave marginal deposits to these workers. Lastly, the state is in charge of Bolivia's largest tin mine, the Huanuni deposit. In the Huanuni mine, the state company produces 2 per cent of the total mining production with labour-intensive methods and 5,000 workers (7 per cent in 2006). These workers successfully stopped the government from granting the deposit to a private enterprise, and prevented the implementation of the policy of eliminating cooperatives in that zone (CEDLA 2007a).

The cooperative mining sector is very heterogeneous. On the one extreme, there are cases, known as the 'most developed', in which the cooperative relations have disappeared and a few landlords exploit the salaried work force. On the other extreme are the most precarious cases, where the cooperative relations still exist. Apart from former workers of the state mining enterprise, small and impoverished rural owners have also moved into this last sector.

These workers have little chance of finding work elsewhere as they lack the knowledge of the high technologies used in modern mining, or in other economic sectors. Whereas the 'developed ones' rather seek alliances with private capital, these small owners demand government policies to improve the situation of cooperative mines through access to credit and markets. Meanwhile, the mainly rural communities that surround the mining deposits have been suffering from Bolivia's crisis of small-scale agriculture and demand a share of the mines, work in the mines, or both (rent and work).

Even after centuries of extraction, Bolivia still has a high mining potential, especially if modern extraction and concentration methods were to be applied in its poly-metallic deposits of zinc, silver, lead and tin. In addition, there are gold alluvial deposits in the Amazon region of the country, and there is the iron ore deposit of El Mutún, with 40 billion tonne reserves of medium-grade (51 per cent) iron ores. However, due to its complex structure, Bolivia's mining sector tends to react slowly to opportunities, such as the latest rise in international prices. As a consequence, these higher prices caused higher export values, but production volumes actually went down. Between 2000 and 2004, Bolivia was the fourth tin producer at world level (5.6 per cent), the eleventh silver producer (2.3 per cent) and the thirteenth zinc producer (1.6 per cent), but this position could be improved (Sánchez-Albavera and Lardé 2006).

The government of President Evo Morales presented a peacemaking policy plan on Bolivia's complex mining sector, claiming to favour all of the different actors: it does not want to affect the transnational enterprise's property; it aims to improve the conditions of the cooperative and rural miners; it grants a more prominent role to the state enterprise; and it aims to increase the public sector revenues from mining activities. This policy is a reaction to the Mining Code of 1997, which served to liberalise the entry of foreign capital in the sector, similar to neoliberal reforms in neighbouring countries such as Chile and Peru. This code eliminated the statal mining sector and transformed state company COMIBOL into an administrative entity. In addition, it provided conditions to ease and attract direct foreign investment; it eased the fiscal system; and it introduced a low tax (1 to 7 per cent of the gross production value). To change this policy, the National Development Plan of Morales' government contemplates four pillars for the mining sector: first, strategic state control of Bolivia's resources through a new formation of COMIBOL, including a recovery of deposits that were privatised; second, expanding Bolivia's mining potential by making a geological assessment of the territory and promoting foreign investment; third, diversifying mining activities and raising the added value of production; and fourth, support for small and cooperative mining.

Evidently, the aim of a strategic recovery of natural resources by the state is contradictory to the aim of promoting foreign direct investment (by private companies), but in practice, Morales' government has done more to strengthen foreign investment than to convert mining into a strategic sector for the state. For example, it has signed a contract with the Indian multinational company Jindal Steel and Power for the extraction of the El Mutún iron deposits, and has given the Canadian multinational Atlas Precious Metals control of the Karachipampa poly-metallurgical operations. Meanwhile, the so-called nationalisations of the tin deposits of Huanuni and the metallurgical plant of Vinto were made because the government was forced to do so – the private companies operating there did not comply with the contractual requirements, and the workers effectively mobilised against the entry of another private company. Indigenous rural communities that have protested against mining activities, claiming ownership of the natural resources in their territory, have been presented with plans for a redistribution of mining revenues, assigning a percentage of the revenues to these communities. This solution leaves the Mining Code intact, which rules that mining is the most important economic activity and that the sub-soil belongs to the state, and not to the communities, but which may be expropriated if the mining interests would require this.

The government of Evo Morales also planned to raise the tax rates on mining. Initially, it presented a plan to increase the Complementary Mining Tax to 20 per cent (from 7 per cent), and to create an additional 12.5 per cent net profits tax for mining companies. However, due to pressure from the workers of cooperative mines, the reform was limited to establishing the 12.5 per cent tax on net profits above a certain amount. Taken together, the government of Morales basically follows the previously established mining policy that favours foreign capital. Nevertheless, since this government emerged from a profound political crisis, it is forced to make some accommodations toward Bolivia's impoverished masses, like providing support to the small-scale production of the people of the cooperatives, and sharing some of the mining revenues with the local communities.

Hydrocarbon Sector and Policy Reform

Considering Latin America's energy crisis and China's need for energy, the rich hydrocarbon resources of Bolivia are already of regional importance (especially for Brazil) and may become of international importance in the future. Until 1996, Bolivia's hydrocarbon sector was dominated by the state-owned company Yacimientos Petrolíferos Fiscales Bolivianos (YPFB), which controlled both upstream (exploration, extraction and transport) and downstream (refining) operations. The privatisation of YPFB started in the upstream operations, although only partly: the Bolivian state kept 50 per cent of the shares, while a private company could buy the other 50 per cent in exchange for handling the operations. In the exploration and extraction, two companies were created: Chaco S.A., which was bought by British Petroleum; and Andina S.A., which was bought by the Spanish Repsol YPF. For the transport of the resources through pipelines Transredes S.A. was created, which was funded by US investors. Later on, in 1999, downstream operations were privatised by selling Bolivia's two main refineries to the Brazilian enterprise Petrobras.

Parallel to these privatisations, a new hydrocarbons law was adopted in 1996. It stated that foreign companies could be the owners of Bolivian hydrocarbons from the deposits onward, thereby violating Article 139 of the Constitution that holds that 'no concession or contract can bestow the property of the hydrocarbon deposits' (*Gaceta Oficial* 2004). The new law lowered the royalties from 50 to 18 per cent of the hydrocarbon production. It also stated that YPFB should sign production contracts with private sector parties, instead of being involved in production operations itself. In addition, the law established that, in the internal market, international prices should be applied, and it eased exports by ending the preference for producing for the internal market.

During Bolivia's political crisis of 2003, which gave way to the resignation of President Gonzalo Sánchez de Lozada, the Bolivian people identified hydrocarbons as the main sector that could solve the country's economic crisis caused by neoliberal policies. Nationalisation of Bolivia's gas was hoisted as a rebel flag. The subsequent process of reformulating Bolivia's hydrocarbons policy took some time. In 2004, under President Carlos Mesa (who had been Vice President under Sánchez de Lozada), there was a binding referendum on the future of the country's natural gas reserves in which a large majority agreed that the state should recover ownership over all hydrocarbons. This was followed by a debate in the Congress about a new law based on the referendum's outcome. In 2005, the new Hydrocarbons Law was approved by the Congress, and this whole reform process was concluded in November 2006, under the presidency of Evo Morales, with the signing of new contracts with the private investors.

The new law recovers the state's ownership of the hydrocarbons at the wellhead, which means that they belong to the Bolivian state as soon as they have come to the surface. However, after they have been measured and made suitable for transport through pipelines, they are handed over to private companies. For many Bolivians, this measure is not the nationalisation that was expected: it only means that the state has obtained better control of the hydrocarbons that are extracted. Regarding taxation, the new Hydrocarbons

Law returned to the level of 50 per cent royalties that had existed before the privatisation, and it created a 32 per cent direct tax over the production of hydrocarbons. It also enabled YPFB to again participate in productive activities, but only in such a way that it does not compete with the transnational companies that appropriated its patrimony during the privatisation. Finally, the law did not bring a change to the domination of export over the development of an internal market, nor to the application of international prices in the internal market.

President Evo Morales, who came into office after the new Hydrocarbons Law had been approved, tried to show that he went beyond this law when on 1 May 2006, he presented a decree that establishes the nationalisation of Bolivia's gas. This decree raises the tax and royalty level for private companies operating in Bolivia's two largest natural gas fields from 50 to 82 per cent. However, the decree character was transitory (six months) and was rather meant to force the companies in question to sign new contracts in accordance with the new law. The contracts that these companies signed in November 2006 were subject to the law and not to the decree, establishing mechanisms so that the companies were to pay only 50 per cent tax and royalties while favouring intensive extraction and export.[2]

The nationalisation decree has also changed the execution of hydrocarbon policies for the internal market. It assigns YPFB to take control over the production, transport, refining, storage, distribution, commercialisation and industrialisation activities. Accordingly, the state carries the burden of attending exclusively to the internal market, which would be very favourable if the whole of the economy was not ordered along free market principles (CEDLA 2006). Regarding the internal market, in Bolivia there is a permanent risk of not having sufficient fuel, despite the fact that it has one of the largest reserves of natural gas in South America. In view of the limited amount of natural gas available for the generation of electricity, the government has started a programme on domestic energy saving. Bolivia may even have to import liquefied petroleum gas (LPG) in the near future because there is not enough capacity in Bolivia's refineries. Meanwhile, diesel has already been imported at international prices from Venezuela.

Although the new Hydrocarbons Law has been implemented, transnational companies still control the hydrocarbons' production and export, and they continue to put the government under pressure for better deals (CEDLA 2006). These powerful transnational companies are Petrobras from Brazil, Repsol from Spain and Total from France. Despite the generally known fact that Latin America's Southern Cone region is facing a latent energy crisis since the start of this century, these companies have not made any efforts to deal with this crisis. In 2006, the governments of Bolivia (which supplies natural gas to Brazil, Argentina and Chile) and Argentina signed a long-term (twenty years) natural gas supply agreement, thereby assuming the political risk of gas extraction. Yet the transnational companies have not invested in solutions for the region's energy crisis.

In the end, the so-called nationalisation of hydrocarbons has been little more than a media stunt of Evo Morales' government. While the transnational companies continue to control the hydrocarbons extraction in Bolivia, the government's gain is limited to spending some extra fiscal income from natural gas exports on social assistance, such as bonuses for the elderly and children. The proposal presented in the National Development Plan to 're-cover national sovereignty over the hydrocarbon resources, reinstall YPFB as the main agent of the productive chain, and thereby assume the state's power to decide over volume and price' (Ministerio de Planificación y Desarrollo 2006, translation by the author) has thus not materialised.

Bolivia's Economic Relations with China and Asia

Following the global tendency of forming trade blocs, in the 1990s, Bolivia developed a dynamic foreign policy of signing trade agreements with various blocs and countries from around the world in order to open markets for its exports. Bolivia already took part in the Andean Community (CAN), and initiated processes to establish free trade agreements with Mexico and with the Southern Common Market (MERCOSUR). It established bilateral agreements with Chile and Cuba, and received unilateral preferential treatment from the United States and the European Union.

MERCOSUR and the CAN are Bolivia's main trade regions in Latin America (see Table 8.1). The Andean Community is an economic integration agreement between Bolivia, Colombia, Ecuador and Peru, while Venezuela ended its membership in 2006 to enter MERCOSUR. The CAN members apply low tariffs on most imports from the other members (with the exception of petroleum and its derivates). The CAN also aims at a common agricultural policy and seeks integration with other blocs and countries. As shown in Table 8.1, in 2006, the CAN represented almost 10 per cent of Bolivia's exports as well as imports. This Andean market is important for Bolivia's soy export sector, but the free trade agreement between Colombia and the United States may cause Colombia to import more US soy. Similarly, the cooperation agreement between CAN and MERCOSUR is a threat to Bolivian soy production, as it cannot compete with Brazil and Argentina due to bad production conditions. MERCOSUR is a regional trade agreement between Brazil, Argentina, Uruguay and Paraguay, and its new member Venezuela. Like the other CAN members and Chile, Bolivia is an associate member. MERCOSUR is Bolivia's primary trading partner: 52 per cent of its exports go there, predominantly natural gas to Brazil and Argentina.

Table 8.1. Main Trade Regions of Bolivia, 1996 and 2006 (%)

Regions	1996		2006	
	Export	Import	Export	Import
MERCOSUR	14.59	20.04	52.14	39.57
Asia	0.32	13.65	9.87	15.39
CAN	20.12	8.75	9.78	9.37
US	25.01	28.09	9.74	12.15
EU	24.50	14.56	5.82	8.63
Total ($ millions)	1,307.00	1,634.00	4,245.00	2,804.00

Source: INE (2007, elaborated by Centro de Estudios para el Desarrollo Laboral y Agrario, La Paz).

At a bilateral level, Venezuela and Chile are important Latin American trade partners. In 1993, Chile and Bolivia signed an agreement on fixed trade tariffs, and a list of 115 Bolivian and 200 Chilean products that could be imported tax-free. More recently, Bolivia and Venezuela, together with Cuba, might form an anti-imperialist trade bloc, as has been proclaimed in various political speeches. From the moment that Evo Morales assumed the presidency, Venezuela has assisted his government in education and health programmes. However, Venezuela has made no investments in Bolivia, despite the announcement of an alliance between their state petroleum companies to invest in hydrocarbons to support nationalisation.

The importance of the United States and the European Union for Bolivia's trade has significantly decreased: while in 1996 nearly half of Bolivia's total exports were directed to these regions, in 2006 it was only 16.5 per cent (see Table 8.1). The United States established the Andean Trade Preference Act to apply no import tariffs on most goods from Bolivia, Ecuador, Peru and Colombia in exchange for the eradication of coca cultivation. As a large share of Bolivia's exports of manufactures is directed to the United States, a suspension of this act would seriously affect this sector. Although the European Union is not one of its major export destinations, Bolivia benefits from the EU trade preference system that applies low tariffs on imports from the least developed countries.

Asia is the region that in the few last years has become of great importance to Bolivia. As Table 8.1 shows, Bolivia's export growth to Asia was especially spectacular from 0.32 per cent in 1996 to 9.87 per cent in 2006, while its imports increased from 13.65 to 15.39 per cent in the same year. As a result, Asia has become Bolivia's second most important trade region. Within that region, most of Bolivia's bilateral trade is with three countries: Japan, Korea and China, respectively. Japan is by far Bolivia's largest Asian trade partner. In 2006, Bolivian exports to Japan valued $378 million, representing 77 per cent of its exports to Asia (see also Table 8.2). South Korea followed with $66 million (13 per cent), and China came third with $35 million (7 per cent). Of Bolivia's exports to the three countries, 99 per cent corresponded to minerals: 93 per cent zinc, silver and lead concentrates exported to Japan and South Korea, and 6 per cent tin exported to China. Japan is also Bolivia's main source of Asian imports. In 2006, Bolivia's imports from Japan valued at $222 million (45 per cent of total Asian imports), followed by China with $102 million (21 per cent) and South Korea with $22 million (4 per cent). These are mostly manufactured products, in particular machinery and transport equipment, textiles and shoes, chemical products and plastics (INE 2007).

Table 8.2. Bolivian Exports to Selected Asian Countries, 2006 (in US$ millions)

Japan	**377.9**
Common metal minerals and their concentrates	330.5
Precious metal minerals and their concentrates (except gold)	34.2
Other products	13.2
South Korea	**48.8**
Precious metal mineral and their concentrates (except gold)	34.9
Common metal minerals and their concentrates	11.2
Other products	2.7
China	**35.5**
Common metal minerals and its concentrates	17.2
Laboured wood and wood beams for train rails	8.7
Other products	9.6

Source: INE (2007)

While trade with Asia has rapidly increased, the region has not yet become an important source of foreign direct investment (FDI) in Bolivia. Of the $7.5 billion FDI in Bolivia over the period 1996–2005, only 1 per cent was Asian. Korea was the main source with $79 million; Japan contributed only $4 million. Although being the third Asian country in trade with Bolivia, China practically did not have registered direct investments in Bolivia: in 2000, 2004 and 2005, Chinese FDI was approximately $40,000 annually (INE 2008). This shows that so far there has not been a direct relation between China's need for raw material and making investments in Bolivia. This was about to change in 2005, when their two governments were to start talks about Chinese investments and a bilateral free trade agreement, but these talks were then cancelled because of the political unrest in Bolivia. Still, in

2006, when President-Elect Evo Morales visited China and met President Hu Jintao, he invited Chinese companies to come and invest in Bolivia's key economic sectors: hydrocarbons, mining and agriculture.

There are two recent projects of Chinese investment in Bolivia. The first is an agreement for a joint venture between the Chinese company Shengli and YPFB and the Bolivian Ministry of Hydrocarbons, in which Shengli would invest almost \$2 billion in the assessment, extraction and processing of petroleum and natural gas in the north of the La Paz region (Ministerio de Minería e Hidrocarburos 2005). The second is a project of the governments of the two countries to invest in the elaboration of a geological map of Bolivia. In January 2008, the Department of Exploration and Development of Geological Resources and Minerals of China (Depgeomin) signed a treaty with the National Mine Geology and Technical Service of Bolivia (Sergeotecmin), in which they agreed that Depgeomin will invest \$60 million in the elaboration of 70 per cent of Bolivia's geological map (*El Diario* 9 January 2008). Both projects are important because they could raise Bolivia's development of hydrocarbon and mining resources, in which China would then have a preference in the extraction, thereby giving a boost to Chinese investments in Bolivia.

Conclusions

There is an interesting recent link between Bolivia and China in the large investment by an Indian transnational company in the iron mine of El Mutún. In 2006, the Bolivian Congress granted a forty-year concession to Jindal Steel and Power for the extraction of half of Mutún's iron deposits, which is one of the largest deposits in South America. With \$2.3 billion, Jindal is making the largest investment ever by an Indian company in the region. An analysis of international iron markets shows that the deposits of El Mutún will especially serve to satisfy China's increased demand for steel. The global steel industry is highly concentrated. Historically, its development was closely linked to that of the heavy industry of industrialised countries, and it was highly protected, with the whole production chain of steel (from the deposits to the steel machinery production) being integrated as much as is possible. However, since the 1970s, these industries faced stagnation as the technological evolution improved the efficiency of iron use and gave way to substitute materials. In addition, in the 1990s, the steel industry in the former socialist countries (in particular Russia and Ukraine) reoriented their production toward the global market, thereby increasing the production surplus.

This long-term crisis of the steel industry ended with the rapid development of China's economy and its demand for iron. As China came to consume more iron than any other country, global supply became insufficient and the international price significantly increased. So far, Latin America's primary iron producing country, Brazil, has been the main beneficiary of China's appetite for iron (Poveda and Guachalla 2006). China's largest steel producer, the state-owned company Boasteel, has thus been seeking deals with large mining multinationals, such as Brazil's state-owned company Vale. As the Bolivian mine of El Mutún is located near the border with Brazil, and Brazil has a dominant position in the regional and global iron, Jindal will have to relate to this market in order to produce and to be a competitor, for instance, in the construction of all of the new infrastructure in Bolivia. In short, the large foreign investment in the deposit of El Mutún will contribute to meet the Chinese iron demand, thereby linking China's industrial development to Bolivia's iron exports and public sector revenues.

References

CEDLA. 2006. *Legitimando el Orden Neoliberal: 100 días de gobierno de Evo Morales.* La Paz: Centro de Estudios para el Desarrollo Laboral y Agrario.
———. 2007a. *¿Nuevo auge de la minería? Análisis y perspectivas,* Documento de Coyuntura 15. La Paz: Centro de Estudios para el Desarrollo Laboral y Agrario.
———. 2007b. *Plan trienal de investigación 2007–2009.* La Paz: Centro de Estudios para el Desarrollo Laboral y Agrario.
CEPAL. 2006. *Panorama de la Inserción Internacional de América Latina y el Caribe, 2005–2006.* Santiago: Naciones Unidas.
Gaceta Oficial. 2004. 'Constitución Política del Estado'. La Paz, 12 noviembre.
INE. 2007. Información Estadística. La Paz: Instituto Nacional de Estadística. http://www.ine. gov.bo (accessed 25 January 2008)
———. 2008. 'Las exportaciones bolivianas se incrementaron en 17,2 per cent'. Boletín de Prensa Nº 6. La Paz: Instituto Nacional de Estadística.
Ministerio de Minería e Hidrocarburos. 2005. 'Convenio de compromiso de Inversión'. La Paz. http://www.hidrocarburos.gov.bo/Ministerio/Acuerdos/Convenio%20Bolivia-China.pdf (accessed 08 January 2008).
Ministerio de Planificación y Desarrollo. 2006. *Plan Nacional de Desarrollo.* La Paz: Ministerio de Planificación y Desarrollo.
Poveda, Pablo and Osvaldo Guachalla. 2006. 'Contexto Mundial del Acero: China motor del Crecimiento Económico Mundial'. *Boletín El Observador* no. 2. La Paz: Centro de Estudios para el Desarrollo Laboral y Agrario (CEDLA).
Sánchez-Albavera, F. and J. Lardé. 2006. 'Minería y Competitividad Internacional en América Latina'. Santiago: CEPAL, Serie de Recursos Naturales e Infraestructura, no. 109.
Viceministerio de Minería. 2008. Estadísticas, Ministerio de Minería y Metalurgia. http://www. mineria.gov.bo/Estadisticas.aspx (accessed 25 January 2008).

Notes

1. This percentage is an average of the period from 2000 to 2007 based on various reports of the Vice Ministry of Mining and Metallurgy.
2. Companies can recover up to 50 per cent of the costs of total production, including all kinds of costs that are not related to the proper activities of extraction. In addition, a formula establishes that in cases of higher production, the additional taxation levels are lower, which encourages massive export.

9 Central America between Two Dragons
Relations with the Two Chinas
Gabriel Aguilera Peralta

The countries of Central America are an important group among the nations that still hold diplomatic relations with Taiwan Province of the Republic of China, also known as the Republic of China, or simply Taiwan.[1] Even though this is economically unfavourable to Central America, the governments of the Isthmus have maintained their policy of recognising Taiwan and fostering the political and economic links with Taiwan instead of establishing bonds with the People's Republic of China. This occurs on a bilateral as well as multilateral level within the framework of Central American integration initiatives. The reasons for this pro-Taiwan policy are complex and include historical antecedents, political motives and the cooperation programmes from Taiwan. However, the decision of Costa Rica to establish relations with the People's Republic of China (PRC) may be a first step in the process of reviewing Central America's policy toward the two Chinas.

In general, we can define foreign policy as the public policy developed by a state for its relations with other states or actors in the international arena. The purpose of foreign policy is to reach objectives based on national interests while it is framed in a broad ideological vision of the world. There are usually three central elements in every foreign policy: the principles that guide it, the interests that are intended to be satisfied and the objectives that are to be reached. The case studied in this chapter, which is the relations of Central America with Taiwan and the PRC, allows us to assess these elements and understand their dynamics from a historical perspective of half a century.

A Brotherhood from the Cold War

Until 1949, when the revolution in China triumphed, the Central American countries had relations with the Republic of China. However, in general those bonds were merely formal due to the international political situation, communication technologies, the relatively minor Chinese immigration to Central America and the limitations of the countries' foreign policies at that time. Their consular and diplomatic relations had, in most cases, been established in the 1930s and the 1940s, respectively.

After World War II and the triumph of the revolution led by Mao Zedong, China's nationalistic government moved to the island of Taiwan. As allies of the United States, the Central American governments followed its political decision to maintain relations with the regime of Chiang Kai-shek and ignore the People's Republic of China. The governments of Central America accepted the international community's recognition of the legitimacy of the Chinese government in Taiwan, which had been one of the founders of the United Nations. In effect, they denied legitimacy to the government of Mao Zedong located on the continental territory of China. Evidently, this decision was partly based on the anti-communist ideological current during the Cold War. Under the mostly authoritarian governments of the Isthmus and with the region's civil wars as of the 1960s, Central America's position on Taiwan was further consolidated.

The recognition of the Chinese government in Taiwan fit well with the general principles of foreign policy of the Central American countries at that time. It served the governments' interests to retain support from the United States. For the states with authoritarian governments, relations with Taiwan also responded to the interests of regime preservation. For example, during the 1970s, the government of Guatemala was internationally isolated due to the many human rights violations occurring there, but it could count on the endorsement and military cooperation of Taiwan in the field of security and defence. The Taiwanese school for political warfare, the Fu Hsing Kang College, provided formation to Central American military officials involved in counterinsurgency operations. To Guatemalan military officers, this was valuable training for the civil war. In addition, there was an exchange of students from the schools for officials of Taiwan and Central America.

Although initially the other Latin American governments took the same position toward Taiwan as Central America, this changed after the visit by US President Richard Nixon to mainland China in 1972 and the recognition by the United States of the People's Republic as the representative of the Chinese nation. In due time, most Latin American countries switched their diplomatic recognition to the PRC. In contrast, in Central America the only change occurred with the triumph of the *Sandinista* revolution in Nicaragua in 1979. Based on its revolutionary principles, the new Nicaraguan government tended to align itself with socialist countries in the context of the Cold War, thus ending Nicaragua's relations with Taiwan. When the *Sandinistas* lost power in the elections of 1990, the new President, Violeta Chamorro, reversed the decision and recognised Taiwan once again.

With the demise of the Cold War in the 1990s, the region's pacification and transition to democracy by means of the Contadora and Esquipulas processes, the peace negotiations in El Salvador and Guatemala, and the shift of power in the elections in Nicaragua, the military-political relations with Taiwan lost importance for Central America.[2]

New Priorities in the Post-Cold War Era

Since the end of the Cold War, mainland China has experienced extraordinary economic growth and has become a central actor in international relations. China's economic globalisation and its entry into the World Trade Organisation (WTO) have increased its global influence. The PRC's foreign policy of 'One China' prevents states from simultaneously having relations with Beijing and Taipei. The inflexibility of this policy is part of the PRC's strategy to isolate Taiwan in order to achieve the incorporation of the island of Formosa. As a result, the international isolation of Taiwan has increased and Taiwan has managed to maintain a group of only 23 nations that still recognise it (see Table 9.1). Sustaining these relations is therefore of utmost strategic importance for the island.

Table 9.1. Countries Maintaining Diplomatic Relations with Taiwan

Central America	Belize, El Salvador, Guatemala, Honduras, Nicaragua, Panama
The Caribbean	Dominican Republic, Haiti, St. Kitts and Nevis, St. Lucia, St. Vincent and the Grenadines
South America	Paraguay
Africa	Burkina Faso, Gambia, Sao Tome & Principe, Swaziland
East Asia and Pacific	Kiribatu, Marshall Islands, Nauru, Palau, Solomon Islands, Tuvalu
Europe	Vatican City (the Holy See)

Source: Ministry of Foreign Affairs, Republic of China (Taiwan) (2008)

Despite these trends, the Central American countries have largely maintained their relations with Taiwan. Although anti-communism no longer plays a role in Central America's general foreign policy principles, the main reasons for relations with Taiwan are Taiwan's cooperation programmes and the strengthening of economic relations in order to promote Central America's development. The Taiwanese government has developed various resources to fortify these bonds, the objective of which is to demonstrate the privileged character of these bilateral relations. Taipei gives a high priority treatment to each of its allies; a service that some of them would not find with other counterparts. It includes the creation of friendly relations with people from the governments and civil society, including the political parties and the media. The Taiwanese embassies are very efficient in public relations; they offer ample programmes for those invited to visit the island, which has been sustained for decades. In effect, many of Central America's elites have visited Taiwan, where they were generously welcomed. This has generated a positive Central American attitude toward maintaining diplomatic relations with Taiwan. Cultural exchange is also important in this respect. In addition, despite the diminished importance of the dimension of defence, Taipei continues to cultivate close relations with security and defence institutions in the region.

The central axis of the contemporary relations of Taiwan with Central America is that of bilateral and multilateral cooperation. Although Taiwan's programmes are not as extensive as those provided by large donors such as the European Union or the United States, they are comparatively 'soft' when it comes to their conditions. Taiwan's bilateral cooperation is focused on two areas. First, there is the technical cooperation by means of seminars, workshops and scholarships. This includes Technical Agricultural Missions promoting the improvement of farming production, and provides experts and volunteers in development projects. The main areas of this cooperation are commercialisation and agricultural diversification, development of small enterprises, advisory services and computer science technology, and infra-structural improvements. Second, there is substantial financial support in the form of donations and credits with soft conditions, or long-term credits with very low interest rates. This cooperation is mainly directed to infrastructure and development, but also covers support in cases of emergency, such as after natural disasters. Table 9.2 shows the variety of Taiwanese donations and credits to Nicaragua.

Table 9.2. Donations and Credits from Taiwan to Nicaragua, 1996–2000 (in US$ millions)

Project	Amount
Donations (total)	29.8
Building of the Presidential Palace	7.0
New building of the Ministry of Foreign Affairs	2.0
Remodeling of the National Assembly	1.0
Equipment and furniture of the office of the Vice-presidency of the Republic	0.2
Funds for social emergencies	12.5
Fabrics and accessory for the Army	2.0
Fabrics and accessory for the Police	1.0
Eradication of the disease of Chagas	0.5
Construction of houses for victims of hurricane Mitch	3.0
Zinc roofs for homes of teachers	0.6
Credits (total)	101.4
Rehabilitation and modernization of the port of Corinto	17.2
Delimitation of the border between Nicaragua and Honduras	1.0
Irrigation plan in the western regions	20.2
Loans to farmers	3.0
Projects for small enterprises	35.0
Improvement of livestock	25.0

Source: Embassy of the Republic of China (Taiwan) in Nicaragua (2007)

In addition, there are advisory missions to foster investment and trade in which Taiwanese officials share their experience on matters of economic development. These missions aim at creating conditions in Central America to attract more investments from Taiwan. All together, Taiwan's bilateral cooperation with Central American countries covers a broad field of issues. In the case of Guatemala, for example, bilateral cooperation in 2006 involved the provision of programmes for farming and mining techniques, and professional training, but there were also agreements signed on cultural affairs, the promotion of investments and trade. Moreover, the Guatemala-Taiwan Free Trade Agreement that was signed in 2005 came into force on 1 July 2006.[3]

A dimension of bilateral cooperation that was not transparent concerned Taiwan's financial support for the political campaigns of presidents, such as Alfonso Portillo of Guatemala, Mireya Moscoso of Panama and Miguel Alemán of Nicaragua (Figueroa 2005). These financial transfers, known as 'dollar diplomacy', were often the subject of rumours and criticism. In several cases, they even led to (the start of) lawsuits against former Central American presidents for their acceptance of large donations (of up to millions of dollars) that were supposedly for development or cultural foundations, but which, in reality, were put to personal use. The reaction of Taiwan was that certain resources had been donated to certain people selected by the president in question, and that those people were responsible for the use given to the donation, which in those cases was not audited. However, the Taiwanese government of the Democratic Progressive Party ended this practice of personal donations, declaring that it disapproved of this policy by Kuomintang governments (Larra 2007).

The strategy of Taiwan has not only allowed it to keep up active bilateral relations with the Central American countries, it has also played a role in Central America's regional integration. Taiwan is a non-regional member of both the System of Central American Integration (SICA) and the Central American Bank of Economic Integration (BCIE), and enjoys observer status at the Central American Parliament. This multilateral cooperation is channelled by the BCIE, the Inter-American Development Bank (IDB), and the combined Commission of the Chancellors of the Republic of China and Central America. Established by the Forum of China-Central America Cooperation in 1991, this Commission meets biannually and occasionally meets with the presidents present (cf. Portillo 2003). Since 1985, Taiwan has approved 85 projects for regional cooperation in Central America on social and economic development, environmental protection and infrastructure, valued at $137 million. Among other things, most of the Ministries of Foreign Affairs have received donations from Taiwan for the construction or renovation of their buildings. This practical aid has also benefited organisations for regional integration such as SICA and the Secretariat for Central American Economic Integration (SIECA).[4]

In return for its bilateral and regional relations of cooperation and friendship, the Taiwanese government expects the Central American countries to defend its position in international political arenas. Taipei especially expects their support in the United Nations (UN) in the form of endorsing its aspiration to be re-admitted as a member.[5] Prior to the annual inaugural meeting of the UN General Assembly, Taiwan each year requests that the Presidents and Foreign Affairs Ministers of its Central American counterparts mention the endorsement of Taiwan to enter into the UN when they address the General Assembly.

The Achilles Heel: Weak Economic Relations

Despite the many forms of Taiwanese cooperation and support, in a world of globalised markets, economic relations are decisive. And that is precisely the weak point of Taiwan's strategy for the region. The economic relations between both actors are unfavourable for Central America as the region has a major negative trade balance with Taiwan. In 2007, Central America's imports from Taiwan were valued at $419 million, while its exports to the island were only valued at $126 million (SIECA 2008). This disparity is the reason for ongoing Central American initiatives to look for means to achieve more balanced economic relations. Among these has been the establishment of the Fund for Economic Development in 1998, through which Taiwan has committed to support Central America's development with an amount of $240 million over a period of twelve years. Another initiative has been the creation of a Central America office in Taipei for the promotion of trade, investments and tourism to the region. As Taiwan has argued that the unbalanced economic exchange has been caused by market conditions, the office aims to stimulate Taiwanese investments in Central America and assist the countries in improving their capacity to penetrate the island's market. As shown in Table 9.3, Taiwan has offered to create several mechanisms to advance investments in the Isthmus.

Another initiative in the same direction is Taiwan's Mission for Servicing Trade and Investment in Central America. Founded in July 2001 in Guatemala City, the mission aims to share the economic experience of Taiwan with its counterparts in the Isthmus, to provide technical support to Taiwanese businessmen who want to invest there and to provide companies in the region with information on investing in Taiwan. This mission has a broad agenda. Among other things, it has provided expertise for the cultivation of tropical fish for export in Escuintla, Guatemala; conducted an evaluation on agrarian industries in El Salvador and Nicaragua; offered technical support to furniture industries in San Juan Sacatepéquez, Guatemala; created a digital centre for schoolteachers; assisted in the recruitment of personnel for the school 'Republic of China'; and provided technical support to sweet shops and artisans enterprises (Misión de Taiwán 2007).

Table 9.3. Mechanisms to Promote Investments of Taiwan in Central America

Objective	Mechanism	Purpose
Promotion of investments	Establishment of the Research Centre of Central and South America	To offer assistance to enterprises interested to invest in Central America
Financial support	Creation of the Joint Investment Fund to offer financial support at low rates	To help enterprises with limited capital for investment
Support in human resources	Vocational training of business cadres, and resources for alternative diplomatic services	To support companies to solve problems of human resources
Technical assistance	Creation of mechanisms of consultation for industrial development, and 'spin off' mechanisms for members of technical missions	To achieve technical improvement in the allied countries

Source: Wu (2005)

Another initiative in the same direction is Taiwan's Mission for Servicing Trade and Investment in Central America. Founded in July 2001 in Guatemala City, the mission aims to share the economic experience of Taiwan with its counterparts in the Isthmus, to provide technical support to Taiwanese businessmen who want to invest there and to provide companies in the region with information on investing in Taiwan. This mission has a broad agenda. Among other things, it has provided expertise for the cultivation of tropical fish for export in Escuintla, Guatemala; conducted an evaluation on agrarian industries in El Salvador and Nicaragua; offered technical support to furniture industries in San Juan Sacatepéquez, Guatemala; created a digital centre for schoolteachers; assisted in the recruitment of personnel for the school 'Republic of China'; and provided technical support to sweet shops and artisans enterprises (Misión de Taiwán 2007).

Another way of solving the unbalanced trade relations with Central America and increase Taiwanese investments is the creation of free trade agreements. The agreement of the United States with the region, the Dominican Republic-Central America Free Trade Agreement (DR-CAFTA), has served as an example. Taiwan has managed to sign free trade agreements with five Central American countries: Panama (in effect since January 2004), Guatemala (in effect since July 2006), Nicaragua (in effect since January 2008), El Salvador (in effect since March 2008) and Honduras (in effect since July 2008). Panama is Central America's primary recipient of Taiwanese capital: in 2005 it amounted to $197.7 million (Wu 2005). The large amount of investment in Panama is related to the large service sector and to activities linked to the Panama Canal. Most investments from Taiwan are concentrated in industries and services, as Table 9.4 shows for Guatemala.

Table 9.4. Direct Investments of Taiwan in Guatemala, 2005 (in US$ millions)

Sector	Companies	Investments
Hotels	2	35.3
Export-import	29	20.4
Manufacturing	6	11.4
Computers	1	0.9
Restaurants	2	0.3
Total	40	68.3

Source: Embassy of the Republic of China (Taiwan) in Guatemala (2007)

The Attractiveness of the Other Dragon

For Central America, the negative side of its adhesion to relations with Taiwan is the difficulty in strengthening its links with the People's Republic of China, because the PRC does not allow countries to hold relations with both. This aspect has developed in the context of the increasing importance of the People's Republic of China and its immense and rapidly expanding market. In 2006, Central American exports to the PRC valued at $608 million, which was five times as much as to Taiwan. Simultaneously, the region imported four times as much from the PRC as from Taiwan (SIECA 2008). Central America's lack of relations with the PRC contrasts with the PRC's increased efforts to deepen and strengthen relations with Latin America. However, from an economic point of view, the PRC's development and growth presents interesting opportunities for Central American companies, such as the rising Chinese consumption of coffee. Although the Central American economies are very small, the PRC may show an interest in some of the region's natural resources, and has expressed willingness to invest in the generation of hydraulic energy.

Panama is definitively attracting the attention of the People's Republic of China. The extension of the Panama Canal is an especially huge project, with an estimated budget of $5 billion. As the second user (after the United States) of this aquatic lane, China has a particular interest in participating in the works of widening the Panama Canal, as the construction of new infrastructure will enable more and larger ships to move goods from the Pacific to the Atlantic. Chinese enterprises, such as the China Ocean Shipping Company (COSCO), are participating in the bids for the construction of a megaport on the Pacific side of the Canal. Other enterprises, such as the China Harbour Engineering Co. (CHEC), have opted for a contract in the projects for enlarging the Canal.

The rise of China has forced Central American countries to reflect on whether it serves their national interests to continue having relations with Taiwan. This is especially the case for Panama, which has a trade office in China, as it has been taking some steps to distance itself from Taiwan. For example, Panama did not receive the President of Taiwan, Chen Shui-bian, during his tour through Central America and the Caribbean in 2005, and it refrained from asking for Taiwan's entry into the World Health Organisation in 2007. Other countries have tried to establish economic relations with China in order to take advantage of its major trade and investment opportunities, while at the same time maintaining their diplomatic relations with Taiwan. Such an arrangement, however, is difficult to achieve. In 2005, Guatemala sent a ministerial mission to Beijing to talk about a proposal for expanding their trade relations, but subsequently China delayed its authorisation for the implementation, thereby indicating that it prefers Guatemala to first end its relations with Taiwan. The private sector in Central America, which has a strong influence in most of the governments in the region, has contributed to the changing attitude toward the People's Republic of China. The fact that their countries do not hold diplomatic relations with the PRC is harming their interests. The Private Sector Union of Honduras, among others, has publicly expressed its support for extending bonds with China.

On the other hand, China's increased export capacity has had a negative effect on Central America's economy because some products are also important in the region's exports. In particular, China's cheap labour and enormous output in textiles is undercutting the competitiveness of Central America and is causing unemployment. Those in favour of relations with the PRC point out that only by normalising their relations will it be possibly for Central America to compensate for this negative factor with the positive one of better access to China's internal market as well as access to Chinese investments.

Interestingly, there is also an incipient lobby from civil society in favour of the People's Republic of China. A forum called Friends of China in Central America includes civil society groups from Costa Rica, El Salvador, Nicaragua, Panama and Honduras. They promote the establishment of diplomatic relations with the PRC, and want their governments to recognise the PRC as the only legitimate government of the Chinese people. In China, they have a counterpart called the Chinese People's Association for Friendship with Foreign Countries.

The First Rupture

On 1 June 2007, Costa Rica announced the establishment of diplomatic relations with the People's Republic of China, thereby breaking its bonds with Taiwan. The decision was prepared in absolute secrecy; in May, Costa Rica's Vice Minister of Foreign Affairs had still participated as usual in the meeting of the Forum of Central America-Taiwan Cooperation. When Costa Rica's President Oscar Arias announced the decision, he explained it as an expression of the will to move his country ahead in modern times. He stated that the relations with the PRC were part of a strategy for cementing Costa Rica's relations with Asia. Other elements of that strategy were the opening of embassies in Singapore and India, and Costa Rica's aspiration to become a member of the forum for Asia-Pacific Economic Cooperation (APEC). Foreign Minister Bruno Stagno declared that it was important to extend Costa Rican exports to 'an economy in vigorous growth, and simultaneously stimulate Chinese investments in Costa Rica and bilateral cooperation' (Ministerio de Relaciones Exteriores y Culto 2007). As the only country in the region, even prior to this policy move, Costa Rica had been successful in exporting to China, resulting in a small trade surplus: in 2006, Costa Rica's exports to China valued $557 million while its imports valued $551 million (SIECA 2008).

By shifting its relations from Taiwan to the People's Republic of China, Costa Rica obtained immediate benefits. This diplomatic move coincided with Costa Rica's candidacy for becoming an elected member of the Security Council of United Nations (for a two-year term). The support of the PRC helped Costa Rica to become a member. Another immediate effect was President Oscar Arias' announcement, right after his first trip to Beijing, that China would build an oil refinery in Costa Rica (*Prensa Libre* 29 October 2007: 26). And in December 2007, China announced an extraordinary donation of $20 million to Costa Rica for reconstruction after major damage was caused by floods.

The reason for Costa Rica's decision to change relations in the region is that the new Chinese partner better satisfies its national interests, especially in trade and investment. Costa Rica made its decision individually, although it has been said that the Central American countries had confidential regional meetings to discuss the possibility of collectively recognising the PRC. This unilateral decision reflects Costa Rica's attitude toward Central American integration: although it is part of the regional integration process, it continues to give priority to its (immediate) national interests.

Since Costa Rica's shift, Taipei has been looking for means to contain the effects of that decision by offering to strengthen its mechanisms of cooperation and its economic relations. Immediately after the Costa Rican decision was announced, the Vice President of Taiwan, Anette Lu, visited the Latin American countries with which Taiwan has relations, while President Chen Shui-bian travelled to Africa. In the case of Guatemala, Taiwan offered additional cooperation to the amount of $50 million for infrastructure. Additional funds were promised for feasibility studies on the construction of an oil refinery, which is of great interest to Guatemala (Smith 2007). The Taiwanese company Plastic Formosa decided to study the possibility of investing in that megaproject, which may cost $7.2 billion (Larra 2007). To Nicaragua, Taiwan confirmed the shipment of an electrical plant of 30 megawatts to help solve its electric power crisis.

Conclusions

The diplomatic relations that Central American countries maintain with Taiwan is an exception to the recognition by most countries of Latin America and the rest of the world of the People's Republic of China as the representative State of the Chinese nation. Initially, their relations with Taiwan were motivated by anti-communism and Central America's close ties to the United States as well as the benefits of Taiwanese cooperation, in particular military programmes. Since the end of the Cold War, the relations have continued because of Taiwan's extensive cooperation programmes, and the supportive attitude of the Central American political elites toward the programmes.

Currently, however, Central American countries are facing a difficult decision. The diplomatic recognition of the PRC would enable them to establish economic relations with the Asian giant, even though it is not clear what would be the exact benefits. It is expected that it would provide Central America with new export opportunities to China, especially in niches such as coffee and sugar. The Isthmus could also attract Chinese investments and tourists. On the other hand, Beijing does not put much emphasis on cooperation, and its interest in the region is generally smaller than that of Taiwan. Relations with the PRC would imply losing the cooperation of Taiwan, although it can be assumed that the economic relations would continue. The decision is also complex because of the regional framework – ending one's bilateral bonds with Taiwan would affect the Taiwanese regional arrangements as well. So far, the pro-Taiwan lobby in the countries has been strong, which foments resistance among officials, politicians and journalists against starting diplomatic relations with the PRC.

Nevertheless, since Costa Rica recently established relations with the People's Republic of China, it is possible that other states of Central America will follow, depending on their governments' assessment of which relations are more favourable to national (and regional) interests. Private sector organisations in these countries generally stress the advantages of better access to the Chinese market. Nicaragua under the second government of President Daniel Ortega (since 2007) might review its relations with Taiwan, and Panama might do so as well. Finally, although Guatemala, El Salvador and Honduras seem more firm toward maintaining their recognition of Taiwan, a shift in their position cannot be disregarded either.

References

Embassy of the Republic of China (Taiwan) in Guatemala. 2007. 'Brief introduction of the Embassy of China-Taiwan in Guatemala'. Bilateral Trade. http://www.roc-taiwan.org.gt/about.htm (accessed 7 March 2007).

Embassy of the Republic of China (Taiwan) in Nicaragua. 2007. Overview presented at the website of the Foreign Affairs Ministry of Nicaragua. http://www.cancilleria.gob.ni (accessed 7 March 2007).

Figueroa, Luís. 2005. 'Las relaciones entre Guatemala y Taiwán'. *REPRI* (Revista electrónica de la Universidad Francisco Marroquín), August, no. 2. http://epri.ufm.edu/interna.php?isbn=7 (accessed 7 June 2007).

Larra, Myriam. 2007. 'Guatemala es un buen lugar para invertir'. Interview with the Vice President of Taiwan, Annette Lu, *Prensa Libre,* 13 July: 6.

Ministry of Foreign Affairs, Republic of China (Taiwan). 2008. Overview presented at the website http://ww.mofa.gov.tw (accessed 9 January 2008).

Ministerio de Relaciones Exteriores y Culto, República de Costa Rica. 2007. 'Política Exterior'. http://www.rree.go.cr (accessed 8 July 2007).

Misión de Taiwán de servicio a la inversión y al comercio en CentroAmérica. 2007. 'Resumen de Proyectos'. http//www.misiontw.org/comercio/ep_pr.htm (accessed 11 December 2007).

Portillo, Alfonso. 2003. 'Relaciones Económico-Comerciales Centroamérica-China Taiwán'. Discurso durante la IV Reunión de Jefes de Estado y de Gobierno de los países del Istmo centroamericano y la República de China. Taipei, 21 de agosto. http://www.minex.gob.gt/discursos/dispresidenciales/dis.2003 (accessed 4 April 2007).

SIECA (Secretaría de Integración Económica Centroamericana). 2008. 'Central America: 2000–2007 Trade with Third Parties, Trade with China Taiwan'. http://www.sieca.org.gt/site/Enlaces.aspx?ID=007001 (accessed 11 December 2007).

Smith, James. 2007. 'Turn of Costa Rica towards China hits the Isthmus'. *Albeldrío,* year 4, July. http://www.albeldrio.com/ (accessed 8 July 2007).

Wu Rong-I (Viceprimer Ministro, República de China, Taiwán). 2005. 'Inaugurando una era de cooperación entre Taiwán y Centroamérica'. Powerpoint presentation, Managua, Nicaragua, 26 September. http://www.cancilleria.gob.ni/docs/index (accessed 11 March 2007).

Notes

1. While being officially administered as the Taiwan Province of the Republic of China (ROC), the People's Republic of China (mainland China) regards itself as the successor of the ROC and claims that the PRC has sovereignty over all of China, including the island of Taiwan.
2. It is also notable that in Taiwan in 2000, the Kuomintang, which had stayed in power since its transfer from mainland China, lost the elections. As a result, the presidency was taken over by Chen Shui-bian of the Democratic Progressive Party (DPP).

3. The information on the bilateral cooperation was presented by a press officer of the Embassy of the Republic of China (Taiwan) in Guatemala. http://www.roc.taiwan.org/about.htm (accessed 15 November 2007).
4. The website of the General Secretariat of the System of Central American Integration (SGSICA) holds numerous documents of Taiwan's regional meetings and initiatives in Central America, including the meetings of the Commission of Cooperation between the Republic of China (Taiwan) and the Central American Countries (see www.sgsica.org).
5. In 1971, the PRC received support from the United Nations' General Assembly and Security Council to exclude the Republic of China (Taiwan) from the UN.

10 Latin America – from Washington Consensus to Beijing Consensus?

Alex E. Fernández Jilberto and Barbara Hogenboom

In Latin America, the effects of China on their economies and their strategies for insertion into the global economy are heavily debated. There are several important incentives for this debate: China's successes in the global competition among developing countries for foreign direct investment; its transformation into a decisive (f)actor in fixing international prices for commodities; its role as a global point of reference in the productive strategies of large transnational companies; and its rise as an essential component of the world market and international development. Various studies consider China as a threat to Latin American strategies of transforming into an exporter of products of higher technological sophistication and added value. The growing sophistication of Chinese export products together with exports from the rest of Southeast Asia have been crowding out Latin America's production of manufactures for global markets (CEPAL 2004a; Mesquita Moreira 2004; Oliva 2003; Gitli and Arce 2001). Some Latin American contributions claim that this competition for markets and foreign direct investment (FDI) may be tempered by deeper deregulation to improve the 'hospitality' for transnational capital and by the state facilitating linkages between this capital and local companies (cf. Lora 2005). Others have stressed the inevitability of China's prominent position in the global economy and argue that Latin America needs a strategy to improve the international competitiveness of its regional economy (CEPAL 2004b, 2003; González García 2003). This approach emphasises the crucial role of the state to enhance the region's economies in a world of liberalised markets and global competition, using China's success story as a perfect example.

With studies of the nature of the new relations that Brazil, Mexico, Chile, Argentina, Venezuela, Peru, Bolivia and Central America hold with China, this volume contributes to that debate. The valuable analyses of the national experiences in the previous chapters have shown that there is a large variety of 'China effects' on and also within different countries, which may broaden the debate. Simultaneously, looking through a 'political economy lens' at the region's experiences with China's rise enables a critical analysis of the effects on Latin America's recent development, which may deepen the debate. Moreover, by studying the new relations between Latin America and China,

this collection has also produced insight into the changing nature of globalisation, the emergence of new economic and political South-South relations
and the prospects for Latin America's development in this new (emerging)
global environment.

In this final chapter, we link some of the previous chapters' main findings
to Latin America's new political situation, and its international positioning.
First, we look into the new economic and political relations between Latin
American countries and China, and the relevance of these South-South relations for the region's development. Then, we turn to two profound regional
changes: the rise of the Left in Latin America, and the end of the Washington
Consensus. Finally, by considering the relevance of the Beijing Consensus
to Latin America, we aim to provoke a discussion about the direction of
the Sino-Latin American relations, in the process considering the important
shifts that are taking place in the region itself, and its relations with China
and the global context.

Latin America and China: Changing South-South Relations

The intensification of Sino-Latin American relations has recently and rapidly
occurred. Diplomatic relations date back to the nineteenth century, but they
generally remained rather distant. After the People's Republic of China was
established in 1949, it took until the early 1970s before a mutual deide-
ologisation took place that allowed most Latin American countries to start
diplomatic relations with the PRC. Latin America's real interest in China and
the rest of Asia is even more recent. As of the early 1990s, the majority of
countries in the region came to establish regular bilateral contact with China,
but only in part by their initiative. In many cases it was primarily China that
started active policies toward Latin American countries. As we have seen in
chapter one, this new attitude was not only directed to this region; China's
eagerness to become a member of the WTO in order to deepen its insertion
into the global economy was a strong motivation to improve relations with as
many countries as possible. With China's impressively successful globalisation
strategy, its economic relations with Latin America have been extended at an
unparalleled speed since the start of this century. Let us here briefly review
some key findings of the case-studies presented in this volume.

To most Latin American countries, economic relations with China have
rapidly become of great importance. In only a few years, the Chinese market
rose as the second export destiny of Brazil, Argentina, Peru, Costa Rica and
Cuba, and even as Chile's first export market (CEPAL 2008). The mutual resource-based trade interests have been accompanied by Chinese investments

and plans for expanding these investments in the future. When also considering the bigger picture in which China's economy has obtained a central position in Asia's regional production chains, and globally as the 'factory of the world', it is clear that good relations with China have become of utmost interest to Latin American countries. As part of its strategy of Open Regionalism since 1990, Chile was the first country from the region to establish a free trade agreement with China. It aims not only to diversify its exports to China far beyond the huge flows of copper, but also hopes that free trade with China will function as a bridge between the Southern Cone and Asia. Similarly, Peru sees its free trade agreement with China as a cross-Pacific bridge.

The chapters on Bolivia and Central America have shown that there are exceptions to the trend of rapidly intensified relations with China. Japan and South Korea have been more important to the Bolivian economy than China, and, despite the country's mineral riches, there have been almost no Chinese direct investments in Bolivia. Indirectly, however, Bolivia benefited from China's growth through the steep rise of international mineral prices up until 2008. Whereas Bolivia's links with China are likely to intensify in the near future, it is harder to predict what will happen to those of Central America. As long as they stick to their relations with Taiwan, the PRC keeps great distance. In that respect, the many Taiwanese programmes for the Isthmus have been mostly effective, although they consist of aid rather than trade. Still, getting closer to China has become increasingly attractive to Central America despite the fact that its trade with China is far from complementary, and its exports compete with China in US markets. In addition, the PRC's trade-not-aid reward to Costa Rica for being the first Central American country to break the bonds with Taiwan, in 2007, may convince other countries in the Isthmus and the Caribbean to do the same. Next to substantial and immediate support from China, in November 2008, President Hu Jintao visited Costa Rica and announced that the two countries would start negotiating a free trade agreement.

We have also seen that the rise of China produces negative economic effects, both in countries that export manufactures and those that predominantly export raw material. Despite the differences, '(b)oth types of activity have relatively low domestic-value-added content, and neither provides the kind of transformation of the domestic production and export pattern that would allow trade to become an engine of growth' (UNCTAD 2003: 141). From Mexico's recent problems one might easily conclude that a focus on assembly manufacturing and integration into North America is not the road to modernisation, at least not in a liberalised global market in which the large and very competitive Chinese economy continues rising. However, the growth achieved by countries such as Brazil, Chile, Argentina, Venezuela and

Peru based (primarily) on exporting primary products may not provide many jobs and modernisation either, and their industries are also harmed by cheap Chinese imports. In addition, on the bases of these country chapters, we may question whether their trade with China should be labelled 'complementary' or instead 'unbalanced'. Since the era of Latin America's economic wonders (the 1940s to 1960s), the puzzle of how to end dependency and achieve sustainable high growth rates has not been solved. Rather than bringing quick and easy solutions to this puzzle, China's current and ongoing economic wonder is triggering new regional debates on the possibilities for development under global neoliberalism, and on how to reform economic policies, regional integration and the global economic system.

While China's contemporary initiatives toward Latin America are non-ideological and are largely motivated by economic interests, they also serve to modernise and extend its role in international politics, and contribute to a pro-South agenda. It is clear that the end of the Cold War and China's Maoism eased the relations between Latin America, China and other developing countries. In the 1990s, China's numerous foreign policy efforts were strongly related to its highly prioritised aim of entering into the WTO. Since this has been achieved, in 2001, its relations with Latin America have continued on the basis of pragmatism and a mix of economic and political interests. With China's ongoing rise, however, its bilateral relations with Latin American countries are also becoming more asymmetric, as are the regional economic relations between Southeast Asia and Latin America. This asymmetrical interdependence even shows in Brazil's relations with China. Similarly, asymmetries play a role on Global South politics. On the one hand, Brazil and China have an impressive strategic partnership that, next to scientific and technological cooperation, is focused on cooperating in international forums. The joint efforts of Brazil, China, India, South Africa and other countries at the 2003 WTO summit were a remarkable success of South-South cooperation, which has been changing global politics and policies. On the other hand, Henrique Altimani de Oliveira (in chapter two) finds that, so far, this pragmatic cooperation has been more about enhancing reforms that promote the interests of emerging economies than about making structural changes in the international order.

Latin America's Turn to the Left

In the 1980s and 1990s, free markets and a small state were the main elements of international policy prescriptions for low income countries. This neoliberal agenda became known as the Washington Consensus, because it was shared and effectively applied by US government agencies as well as the IMF and the World Bank (all based in Washington, DC). In Latin America, as in most other developing countries and transition economies, the international financial institutions pushed for privatisation, deregulation and other liberalisation policies, in order to transform the private sector into the predominant motor for economic development. Apart from a transfer of economic power from the public sector to the private sector, these policies caused economic concentration in very large and increasingly transnational companies. This restructuring had many victims, but generally failed to produce the sustained growth and modernisation that its proponents had predicted (Fernández Jilberto and Hogenboom 2008).

In contrast, China achieved a miraculous growth based on the apparently paradoxical combination of economic liberalisation and a strong state. This 'headstrong' approach reflects that China's economic restructuring did not have an exogenous origin, as in most of Latin America (see chapter one). In the first years of the twenty-first century, China's rise thus drew the attention of developing countries to a viable alternative to free market policies. Interestingly, this came at a time of economic and political circumstances rendering Latin America open to discussing the hegemonic neoliberal development model for integration in the global economy. By the end of the 1990s, two decades of (debt) crisis, technocratic dominance and the Washington Consensus had virtually ended Latin America's development debate. Despite the negative social effects and weak economic results, in this period the region faced demobilisation and depolitisation. Gradually, however, anti-neoliberal sentiments gave cause to social mobilisation again, culminating in a surprising political shift in Latin America around the turn of the century.

Since the electoral victory of Hugo Chávez in Venezuela in 1998, Latin America has experienced unprecedented electoral successes of the left and centre-left. Citizens elected Ricardo Lagos and Michelle Bachelet in Chile (2000 and 2005, respectively), Luiz Inácio (Lula) da Silva in Brazil (2002 and 2006), Néstor Kirchner and Cristina Fernández de Kirchner in Argentina (2003 and 2007, respectively), Martín Torrijos in Panama (2004), Tabaré Vázquez in Uruguay (2004), Evo Morales in Bolivia (2005), Alan García in Peru (2006), Rafael Correa in Ecuador (2006), Daniel Ortega in Nicaragua (2006), Álvaro Colom in Guatemala (2008) and Fernando Lugo in Paraguay (2008). Two notable exceptions are Colombia's prolonged conservative governments of President Álvaro Uribe (elected in 2002 and 2006), and the dubious defeat with 0.56 per cent of the votes by Andrés López Obrador in the Mexican presidential elections of 2006.

Latin America's turn to the left marked a break with the dominance of neoliberalism. Starting in the 1970s in Chile under dictator Pinochet,[1] neoliberal policies had been pursued by authoritarian as well as democratic regimes, presenting these policies as the only option if their national economy wanted to gain from globalisation. The huge increase of economic inequality and social exclusion generated by neoliberal restructuring was presented as an inevitable cost for achieving economic growth; through this growth, the market's invisible hand would supposedly resolve these social problems (Fernández Jilberto and Mommen 1996). An ideological offensive was used to discredit state intervention in the economy, even for the purpose of diminishing poverty: the only possible way of participating in the modern global economy had to come at the price of rising inequalities.

Following the democratic transitions in the 1980s, Latin America's democratisation was conditioned by this dominance of neoliberalism. Apart from the direct policy influence of the neoliberalised international financial institutions in the context of the debt crisis, all political parties were also affected by the new economic model. Privatisation and transnationalisation eroded the state's protagonist role in the nation and the economy and fundamentally changed the relations between state and society. As economic restructuring caused social fragmentation, political parties faced a far more heterogeneous electorate – a sharp contrast to the traditional homogenous, class-based politics of representation (Garretón 2004). In the period of the popular (or populist) nation-state, the state had been the motor – although permanently incomplete – of development and social integration. Politics had provided regulated access to state resources and was the centre of gravity in the expression of identities and collective action. In the era of neoliberalism, this situation came to an end: the room for ideologised policies shrunk and politics became more abstract and unable to solve social problems and fragmentation.

Most of the old populist parties went through a programmatic and political metamorphosis (such as Peronism in Argentina, the Socialist Party in Chile, the APRA in Peru and the PRI in Mexico), substituting nationalist Keynesianism with neoliberalism. To civil society, this metamorphosis was legitimised by arguing that in the era of globalisation, economic liberalisation was the only possible strategy to reach a democratic order based on 'development with equity', and that economic stability through large-scale privatisation was the basic condition to achieve political stability in the new democracies (Demmers, Fernández Jilberto and Hogenboom 2001). At least from the mid 1980s to the mid 1990s, these views silenced opposition and depoliticised much of the democratic debates and elections.

The government of Hugo Chávez in Venezuela was the first rupture of the loyalty of Latin America's democratic regimes to the Washington Consensus. The region's neoliberal elites as well as the many international commentators immediately considered Chávez and his strategic alliance with Cuba, and later on Bolivia (in Chávez's words 'the axis of the good'), as a resurgence of a statist left that supports excessive public expenses, lacks fiscal discipline and is profoundly anti-US. Several other new political regimes were considered as moderate (social-democratic), with a pragmatic attitude toward globalisation, such as those of Lula da Silva and Néstor Kirchner. Although with greater political moderation, these presidents also challenged the neoliberal orthodoxy that had ruled the continent, and they rejected the US design for a Free Trade Area of the Americas (FTAA), known in Spanish as ALCA (*Área de Libre Comercio de las Américas*). However, such ideas of 'the two lefts' are overly simplistic, as the new Latin American left is profoundly heterogeneous, including candidates and parties that have won national elections as well as social movements and local initiatives (Ramírez Gallego 2006).[2]

In countries such as Venezuela, Argentina, Bolivia and Ecuador, urban and ethnic mobilisation that started in the late 1990s would lead to the fall of democratically elected presidents who had abandoned their electoral promises from their first day in office, in the name of maintaining macro-economic stability and sustained economic growth. These presidents had hoped that urban workers and the unemployed and marginalised would feel some solidarity with a nation conceived of as a corporation; the enterprise-nation required a civil sacrifice and political realism. Instead, social movements rejected the neoliberal model of a strictly formal, low profile state that supported big businesses yet denied its welfare, educational and entrepreneurial responsibilities, while strategic economic decision-making had been displaced to international financial institutions and transnational capital. Meanwhile, dealing with the negative effects of neoliberal development was transferred to micro-businesses, NGOs, micro-credits and families' innumerable subsistence strategies (Salazar 2006).

While internally social movements and the electorate called for policy reforms, external changes have made it easier for Latin America's leftist regimes to implement some new policies. It is well known that the United States has been neglecting the region since the Cold War ended and its geopolitical preoccupation with the Middle East started with the 1991 Gulf war and especially 11 September 2001. But also, China's economic growth has been an influence, as for several years it caused rising demand and higher prices for Latin America's raw materials and more foreign investments. These trends have facilitated leftist governments of resource-rich countries with the space and opportunity to bring about some policy reforms and to increase social spending. In addition to the international economic trends that raised private and public revenues, the implementation of higher royalties and taxes on hydrocarbons and other minerals have brought about a new public-private balance in favour of the first. In the more far-reaching cases, some natural resources were nationalised (certain oil fields in Venezuela, and natural gas in Bolivia) in order to allow for more public control and revenues. A decade earlier such policies were unthinkable.

The End of the Washington Consensus

Latin America's resistance against US plans for the ALCA took several shapes, and although Brazil's rejection under President Lula may have been the most decisive, it was the ALBA, the Bolivarian Alternative for the Americas developed by President Hugo Chávez, which became the most well known. This cooperation and integration mechanism started with Venezuela and Cuba by the end of 2004, and later on Bolivia, Nicaragua, Honduras and Dominica joined in. Meanwhile, the US government under President Bush was using a wide variety of means to discredit Chávez regionally and internationally, to strengthen its bilateral relations with the other Latin American countries and to counter the region's distancing from the United States, but without much success. This showed, for instance, in 2007, when there was insufficient support for the proposal for mutual defence against continental security threats that the United States made to the Organisation of American States (OAS). Many Latin American countries rejected the proposal, which they considered to be directed against the government of Chávez (LeoGrande 2007). In individual countries, however, the influence of the US government and the IMF, the World Bank and the Inter-American Development Bank could still be effective. In 2005, for instance, Ecuador's then Minister of Economy, (current President) Rafael Correa, was replaced after pressure and threats of these institutions, which opposed his plans for more public social spending through limits on foreign debt payments and higher taxes on oil extraction. This reminds us of the long (and ongoing) history in which the Bretton Woods institutions have functioned as instruments of US intervention in Latin America.

A priority of all of the new leftist governments in the region was therefore to end their dependency on Washington-based institutions, in order to be liberated from their structural policy conditions and the less than incidental interventions motivated by US interests. Under President Kirchner, Argentina resisted IMF pressures and opted for an unorthodox policy package to solve the crisis that hit the country in 2001–2002. Helped by the wave of high commodity prices, countries such as Brazil and Argentina paid off their remaining IMF debts before the deadlines. The government of President Chávez turned Venezuela into a new creditor and lender of last resort, using part its large public oil revenues to do so. Among other things, it provided a $2.5 billion credit to Argentina when it paid off its remaining $9.8 billion IMF debt at the end of 2005. Since the start of President Morales' government in 2006, Venezuela has supported Bolivia in various ways, including loans for which the Bolivian government otherwise would have needed to turn to international financial institutions, the United States or European countries. Taken together, while the weakening of the IMF started in the late

1990s in Asia following the financial crisis there, 'it was in Latin America that the IMF was reduced to a shadow of its former self' (Weisbrot 2007: 481).

Latin America's effective estrangement from the paradigm, policies and institutions of the Washington Consensus has contributed to the crisis in the international financial organisations, as well as to their reform. By the end of the 1990s, the World Bank had to start rethinking its pro-market development policies because of poor results, which rendered the Bank more aware of the importance of the state and public institutions (Demmers, Fernández Jilberto and Hogenboom 2004). Moreover, the IMF saw its central role as global lender of last resort crumble after many nations raised their own reserves and developed bilateral and regional alternatives for IMF support. While, in 2003, the IMF granted loans of in total $70 billion, in 2006, this had dropped to $20 billion. Another of its problems was the systematic devaluation of the US dollar, which compared to the euro lost 28 per cent of its value between 2001 and 2005 (Kolko 2006). In 2007 and 2008, major decisions were taken to reform the IMF: slowly but steadily, emerging countries will have more of a say in the institution's board, whereas economic circumstances forced the institution to sell part of its gold reserves and implement spending cuts. And the current crisis is giving way to new reform proposals, including a doubling or trebling of the IMF's lending capacity.

The end of the Washington Consensus implies, next to more sovereignty, an end to the era of market fundamentalism in Latin America. This fundamentalism, or naïve neoliberalism, reflected 'an extreme faith in the efficiency of the traditional private sector and mistrust for the public sector and non-traditional forms of private organization' (Ffrench-Davis 2005: 9). There was also unfounded faith in deregulated, self-adjusting markets. As José Antonio Ocampo notes, the current international crisis shows that markets are inherently instable and lack self-correction (*Tufts Daily* 18 November 2008). Basically, there were four profound problems with the Washington Consensus: 'its narrow view of macroeconomic stability … ; its disregard for the role that policy interventions in the productive sector can play in inducing investment and accelerating growth; its tendency to uphold a hierarchical view of the relation between economic and social policies … ; and, finally, a tendency to forget that it is citizens who should choose what economic and social institutions they prefer' (Ocampo 2005: 294). With this last problem, Ocampo stresses the huge 'democratic deficit' in Latin America's post-transition democracies under the Washington Consensus, a deficit that was caused by market fundamentalism and externally established policy conditions.

The quest for supremacy of the state over the market, and of politics over the economy, is the main coinciding characteristic of the many new democratic 'lefts' in Latin America. This coincidence can in theory form the basis of a minimal Latin American consensus on a new development model. Regional cooperation is crucial if Latin America wants to grow and modernise in an increasingly competitive global context. Without cooperation and integration, there is no way that the region's economies can compete with the integrated East-Asian production chains of manufactures in which China is the pivot. A high level of regional (economic and political) integration will be necessary to initiate a viable new development trajectory. Yet, beyond a consensus, the region requires effective policies and institutions for cooperation and integration. So far, initiatives have focused on regional infrastructure as political differences and asymmetrical relations complicate broader integrative processes. While Latin America has succeeded in putting an end to the Washington Consensus and the ALCA, its governments have not yet started a coordinated process toward creating a regional economy.

Beijing Consensus? China's and Latin America's Converging Development Views

The new ties between Latin America and China indicate that South-South relations have been changing profoundly since the end of the twentieth century. Beyond their direct economic and political relevance for the countries themselves, they are part of the rising 'Global South', including emerging markets as well as underdeveloped countries. This new Global South is increasingly important in the global economy and international politics. Especially, emerging markets have recently surged as the primary source of global economic growth. In 2000, the contribution of emerging markets to global GDP growth was roughly 42 per cent, and equalled that of the US and EU together. In the following years, the share of the first group rose while the latter's share fell. As a result, in 2007, the US and EU only produced 25 per cent of the global growth whereas emerging markets were responsible for 60 per cent! The BRIC (Brazil, Russia, India and China) countries were the motors behind this success: they jointly generated 42 per cent of the total growth (CEPAL 2008: 16).

Simultaneously, Latin America and China, together with the rest of Asia, Africa and the Middle East, have taken a pronounced stance against protectionism of the 'North' since the start of the new century. Joint positioning against the unbalanced situation that resulted after two decades of one-sided open market policies started to bear fruit with the G20 of developing nations in the 2003 WTO summit in Cancún. Since then, international decision-making over economic rules and institutions is increasingly involving emerging economies and large developing countries. In November 2008, the first Leaders Summit of another G20 took place: the presidents and prime ministers of the twenty major economies gathered in Washington, DC to discuss the international crisis. Among others, China's President Hu Jintao was there, and from Latin America Brazil's President Lula da Silva, Argentina's President Cristina Fernández de Kirchner and Mexico's President Felipe Calderón were present.

As a result of the many leftist governments in Latin America, an interesting paradigmatic convergence with China has come about: the state is granted an important role in the economy (again). This neither implies an end to capitalism nor to open market policies. In fact, even under Latin America's more pronounced leftist regimes, many of the neoliberal policies have not been replaced. Still, from the perspective of neoliberalism being hegemonic in the region for about two decades, the 'return of the state' is a remarkable change. From very different backgrounds and through different processes, then, China and Latin America have both been moving in the direction of a development model in which there is a reconciliation of state and market. Chinese state (controlled) companies and public-private partnerships, for instance, are central to China's agenda for international development. As access to foreign resources is vital for China's continued economic growth (and social and political stability), state-controlled Chinese multinationals are entering into many exploration and supply agreements with Latin American and other countries.

The current deep and worldwide crisis that started in the United States illustrates the enormous impact and risks of global neoliberalisation. It is too early to know all of the effects of this crisis on the Latin American economies. Yet, by having amounted high public sector reserves – partly based on extra revenues from the commodity boom – the region is better prepared for this crisis than for the crises of the 1980s and 1990s. Moreover, this crisis seems to stimulate the pro-South globalisation agenda, and pragmatic (non-fundamentalist) models of development. Also, in the North, the state is back in the economy, although there the massive state intervention programmes are primarily directed at saving financial capital. However, also at this point it is too early to tell what will happen now that market fundamentalism has come to an end.

Can we expect a Beijing Consensus to replace the Washington Consensus? So far, China has not produced an alternative international development model, and in light of its tradition to shun international political prominence and to avoid harming its relations with the United States, it seems unlikely that it will do so in the near future. China's foreign policy stresses peaceful coexistence, based on the Four No's (no hegemonism, no power politics, no arms races and no military alliances), and since the beginning of the twenty-first century, its 'trade-not-aid' policy has been further expanded. China has been promoting South-South trade around the world to secure access to the natural resources and commodities that it needs to maintain the dynamism and globalisation of its economy, while offering its internal market as an export destination to developing countries. This principle of 'complementarity' can be seen in China's strategy of establishing economic cooperation and free trade associations. This volume, however, has also pointed out that in practice, there are various instances in which effective complementarity between China and Latin American economies is lacking, including countries with trade deficits with China, and the crowding out of Latin American manufactures. Nevertheless, even though China's model of South-South relations enhances economic globalisation, China does not follow free market policies nor does it intervene in national affairs. With or without a Beijing Consensus, and next to a series of evident economic opportunities and threats, this volume has shown that China's growing global prominence presents interesting possibilities for Latin America.

References

CEPAL. 2003. *La Inversión Extranjera Directa en América Latina y el Caribe 2002.* Santiago: Naciones Unidas.

———. 2004a. *La Inversión Extranjera Directa en América Latina y el Caribe 2003.* Santiago: Naciones Unidas.

———. 2004b. *Panorama de la Inserción Internacional de América Latina y el Caribe 2002–2003.* Santiago: Naciones Unidas.

———. 2008. *Las relaciones económicas y comerciales entre América Latina y Asia-Pacífico. El vínculo con China.* Santiago: Naciones Unidas.

Demmers, Jolle, Alex E. Fernández Jilberto and Barbara Hogenboom, eds. 2001. *Miraculous Metamorphoses. The Neoliberalization of Latin American Populism.* London: Zeds Books.

———. 2004. 'Good governance and democracy in a world of neoliberal regimes'. In *Good Governance in the Era of Neoliberal Globalization. Conflict and Depolitization in Latin America, Eastern Europe, Asia and Africa,* eds. Jolle Demmers, Alex E. Fernández Jilberto and Barbara Hogenboom, 1-37. London: Routledge.

Fernández Jilberto, Alex E. and Barbara Hogenboom. 2008. 'Latin American Conglomerates in the Neoliberal Era: The Politics of Economic Concentration in Chile and Mexico'. In *Big Business and Economic Development: Conglomerates and Economic Groups in Developing Countries and Transition Economies under Globalisation,* eds. Alex E. Fernández Jilberto and Barbara Hogenboom, 135–66. London: Routledge.

Fernández Jilberto Alex E. and André Mommen, eds. 1996. *Liberalization in the Developing World. Institutional and economic changes in Latin America, Africa and Asia.* Routledge: London.

Ffrench-Davis, Ricardo. 2005. *Reforming Latin America's Economies. After Market Fundamentalism.* Basingstoke & New York: Palgrave.

Garretón, Manuel Antonio. 2004. 'La indispensable y problemática relación entre partidos y democracia en América Latina'. In Programa de la Naciones Unidas para el Desarrollo (PNUD) *La Democracia en América Latina. Hacia una Democracia de Ciudadanas y Ciudadanos. Contribuciones para el Debate,* 72–97. Buenos Aires: Aguilar, Altea, Tauros y Alfaguara.

Gitli, Eduardo and Randall Arce. 2001. 'El Ingreso de China a la OMC y su impacto sobre los países de la cuenca del Caribe'. *Revista de la CEPAL* 74: 87–107.

González García, Juan. 2003. *China: Reforma Económica y Apertura Externa. Transformación, efectos y desafíos.* México: El Colegio de México.

Kolko, Gabriel. 2006. 'Inquiétude des Milieux Financiers. Une économie d'apprentis sorciers'. *Le Monde Diplomatique* 631: 14–16.

LeoGrande, William. 2007. 'A poverty of imagination: George W. Bush's policy in Latin America'. *Journal of Latin American Studies* (4): 35–46.

Lora, Eduardo. 2005. 'Debe América Latina Temerle a La China?' Departamento de Investigación, Documento de Trabajo 536. Washington, DC: Banco Interamericano de Desarrollo.

Mesquita Moreira, Mauricio. 2004. 'Fear of China: is there a future for manufacturing in Latin America?'. LAEBA Annual Conference, Beijing.

Ocampo, José Antonio. 2005. 'Beyond the Washington consensus: what do we mean?' *Journal of Post Keynesian Economics* 27(2): 293–314.

Oliva, C. 2003. 'Inversiones en América Latina: La Inserción Regional de los Grupos Económicos Chinos'. Buenos Aires (mimeo).

Ramírez Gallego, Franklin. 2006. 'América Latina en Tiempos de Chávez'. *Nueva Sociedad* 205: 30–44.

Salazar, Gabriel. 2006. 'Ricardo Lagos, 2000–2005: Perfil histórico, transfondo popular'. In Hugo Fazio et al., *Gobierno de Lagos: balance crítico.* Santiago: LOM.

UNCTAD. 2003. *Trade and Development Report 2003.* New York: United Nations.

Weisbrot, Mark. 2007. 'Changes in Latin America: Consequences for Human Development'. *International Journal of Health Services* 37(3): 477–500.

Notes

1. Chile's neoliberal policies started before the debt crisis and the Washington Consensus, and in that sense, Chile represents the proverbial exception that proves the rule of the exogenous origin of neoliberal economic restructuring in Latin America.

2. The cases of Bolivia and Argentina illustrate this heterogeneity. In Bolivia, the protests of 2000–2005 that caused the fall of two presidents showed a combination of indigenous and national-popular battles. Morales' Movimiento Al Socialismo (MAS) has defended representative democracy and has positioned itself in the realm of the reformist left in search of political integration of excluded citizens. In Argentina, Néstor Kirchner's election also followed after a period of protests and innovative social mobilisation, but his government rather represented the triumph of old Peronist populism (Ramírez Gallego 2006).

Contributors

Gabriel Aguilera Peralta studied Law, Political Science and Public Administration and worked as professor at the Rafael Landivar University, Guatemala. Currently, he is ambassador of Guatemala in Peru. In addition, he is Coordinator of the Guatemalan programme for the formation of civil society leaders in defence and security of Interpeace; President of the Foundation for Peace (FUNDAPAZ); and Vice President of the Institute for Studies of Peace and International Relations (IRIPAZ). He has been twice Vice Minister of Foreign Affairs of Guatemala, and has worked in or for many international institutions, including FLACSO, CLACSO, INCEP, CRIES, UNDP and UNESCO. Aguilera Peralta has internationally published books, chapters of books and articles on matters of peace building, conflict resolution, defence and security.

Henrique Altemani de Oliveira received his Ph.D. from the University of Sao Paulo and is currently International Relations Professor and coordinator of the Asia Pacific Research Group at the Pontifical Catholic University of Sao Paulo. His research interests include China, Brazilian Foreign Policy, Asia-Pacific and strategic security. His most recent publications include: *Relações Internacionais do Brasil: temas e agendas* (Saraiva, 2006, two volumes); *Política Internacional Contemporânea: mundo em transformação* (Saraiva, 2006); *Política Externa Brasileira* (Saraiva, 2005); *A Política Externa Brasileira na Visão dos seus Protagonistas* (Lumen Juris Editora, 2005); and, 'China-Brasil: perspectivas de cooperación Sur-Sur' (*Nueva Sociedad* 203: 138–47, 2006).

Rubén Berríos teaches economics at Lock Haven University. He is the author of *Contracting for Development* (Praeger, 2000) and of some thirty journal articles and chapters in books. His articles on relations between Peru and China have appeared in *Actualidad Económica* (1993) and *Agenda Internacional* (2003). He also has a chapter in *Latin America and East Asia: Attempts at Diversification*, edited by J. Faust and M. Mols (LIT Verlag, 2005).

Javier Corrales obtained his Ph.D. in political science from Harvard University and is associate professor and chair of Political Science at Amherst College in Amherst, Massachusetts. His areas of interest include the politics of economic and social policy reform in developing countries. He is the author of *Presidents without Parties: The Politics of Economic Reform in Argentina and Venezuela in the 1990s* (Penn State Press, 2002). His research has also been published in academic journals such as *Comparative Politics, World Development, Political Science Quarterly, International Studies Quarterly, World Policy Journal, Latin American Politics and Society, Journal of Democracy, Latin American Research Review, Studies in Comparative International Studies, Current History* and *Foreign Policy*. Currently he is co-authoring with Michael Penfold a book entitled *Dragon in the Tropics: The Political Economy of Venezuela's Revolution* (Brookings Institution).

Alex E. Fernández Jilberto was senior lecturer in International Relations at the University of Amsterdam. He published various articles and books on the political economy of Latin America and developing countries in general. His recent publications include the co-edited volumes *Big Business and Economic Development—Conglomerates and Economic Groups in Developing Countries and Transition Economies* (Routledge, 2008); *Latin American Conglomerates and Economic Groups under Globalization* (special double issue of the *Journal of Developing Societies* vol. 20, no. 3 & 4, Sage, 2004); *Good Governance in the Era of Global Neoliberalism. Conflict and Depolitisation in Latin America, Eastern Europe, Asia and Africa* (Routledge, 2004); *Labour Relations in Development* (Routledge, 2002); *Miraculous Metamorphoses: The Neoliberalization of Latin American Populism* (Zed Books, 2001); and *Regionalization and Globalization in the Modern World Economy: Perspectives on the Third World and Transitional Economies* (Routledge, 1998).

Barbara Hogenboom is senior lecturer in Political Science at the Centre for Latin American Research and Documentation (CEDLA) in Amsterdam. She writes on transnational politics, globalisation processes, and political and economic development in Mexico and Latin America. Among her publications are various co-edited volumes, including *Big Business and Economic Development—Conglomerates and Economic Groups in Developing Countries and Transition Economies* (Routledge, 2008); *Latin American Conglomerates and Economic Groups under Globalization* (special double issue of the *Journal of Developing Societies* vol. 20, no. 3 & 4, Sage, 2004); *Good Governance in the Era of Global Neoliberalism. Conflict and Depolitisation in Latin America, Eastern Europe, Asia and Africa* (Routledge, 2004); *Miraculous Metamorphoses: The Neoliberalization of Latin American Populism* (Zed Books,

2001); and the monograph *Mexico and the NAFTA Environment Debate: The Transnational Politics of Economic Integration* (International Books, 1998).

Carla V. Oliva studied International Relations, and Integration and International Cooperation at the National University of Rosario (UNR), Argentina. She works as assistant professor of International Politics at the Faculty of Political Science and International Relations, UNR. She is a Ph.D. Scholar of Argentina's National Council of Scientific and Technical Research (CONI-CET) and a research member of the Study Centre for International Relations of Rosario (CERIR). She specialises in relations between China and Argentina, and the effects of the rise of China.

Pablo Poveda is an economy graduate from the Mayor University of San Andrés in La Paz. He works as a researcher for the Centre for Studies of Labour and Agrarian Development (CEDLA) in La Paz, which carries out economic and social studies for the benefit of Bolivian workers. Pablo Poveda has studied a range of themes, including the informal sector's contribution to capitalist accumulation, and the chestnut sector. He has also analysed Bolivian oil and gas politics, and the recomposition of social classes in the Bolivian mining sector and implications for class struggles in the 1985–2007 period.

Index

9 780857 456236